the big book of appetizers

The **Big Book**

of Appetizers

more than 250 recipes for any occasion

by meredith deeds

and carla snyder

CHRONICLE BOOKS

SAN FRANCISCO

Library of Congress Cataloging-
in-Publication Data available.

ISBN-10: 0-8118-4943-0
ISBN-13: 978-0-8118-4943-2

Manufactured in Canada

Designed by Lesley Feldman
Photo styling by Sandra Cook
Photo assistance by Sara Johnson Loehmann

Distributed in Canada by
Raincoast Books
9050 Shaughnessy Street
Vancouver, British Columbia V6P 6E5

10 9 8 7 6 5 4 3 2 1

Chronicle Books LLC
85 Second Street
San Francisco, California
94105

www.chroniclebooks.com

We would like to dedicate this book to our children, Jessica, Justin, and Corey Snyder and Quinn, Connor, and Kyle Deeds, who constantly keep us cooking.

contents

Introduction

Appetizers, hors d'oeuvres, tapas, meze, dim sum, antipasti, and starters are all small plates of food that begin a meal, spur social interaction, and set the stage for an evening's festivity. People instinctively know that spending time with friends and family over a meal is one of the most important aspects of life. Hence the creation of the multicourse meal. Enjoying food over a longer, more convivial space of time helps to bond relationships, create generational ties, and even establish business connections.

Sometimes, serving food in small portions is a matter of practicality. For instance, tapas in Spain are thought to have been created as a complimentary small plate of appetizers served at bars to be used as a "lid" to cover (tapar is Spanish for "to cover") one's glass of sherry and protect it from marauding flies. From this practice evolved the tapas bar, where small plates of food are offered in lieu of larger meal-size portions.

This idea has caught on here in the United States too — so much so that restaurants and bars often create menus that lend themselves to "grazing." Instead of customers committing to only one dish, they can order multiple small plates to be shared by the entire table. This makes for a fun evening of table talk when everybody is sharing the same tastes.

The general idea is that small bites stimulate the appetite without filling the stomach. In modern times, especially in the United States, appetizers are seldom served at family meals. This is a shame, because the expediency with which we consume our meals doesn't allow us the opportunity to share the experiences of the day and truly get to know one another.

Today the home cook often considers appetizers to be party food. The cocktail party is usually centered around an array of hors d'oeuvres. How often do you arrive at someone's house carrying a plate of appetizers and a bottle of wine? This is the way we entertain in the new millennium. Although this type of entertaining may differ from the origins of the appetizer, these small plates are still used to bring people together.

As culinary instructors and former caterers, we have a wealth of knowledge about entertaining. Our classes are often focused on the fine art of cooking for a party, and we know, from the many questions our students ask, where the average host or hostess is likely to have problems. We give you solutions to these problems in the Party Basics chapter, where you'll find tips and professional advice to help you plan and organize your event, whether it's a small dinner party for six or a big bash for sixty.

Because we know how hard it can be to decide what to serve, we've also included a chapter of menus, with lots of ideas for themed parties, such as Finger Food for Forty, New Year's Resolution Party, or Thai One On. You can use these ideas in their entirety or jump-start your own menu with a selection from this chapter. We've also included a Find It Fast index that serves as a tour guide for the book, allowing you to quickly find whatever you're looking for.

We've divided the chapters into categories literally from soup to nuts. Our Nuts, Nibblers, and Cheese chapter will give you ideas for basic party bites. Although you might not think that soup has a place in an appetizer book, we find that one of the most interesting presentations of food at a party can come in a shot glass. Our Soup Shots chapter gives you ideas for soups that can be served in small 2- to 4-ounce glasses that your guests can enjoy on foot while cruising the party.

Among the recipes in this book we've included lots of global flavors. You'll find dishes ranging from Vietnamese-Style Chicken Salad Rolls to Toasted Fontina and Onion Jam Panini. But don't think we've neglected the familiar favorites like Hot and Spicy Buffalo Chicken Wings or Homemade Potato Chips.

Some of the best appetizers are served alongside a cold glass of beer. But lest you think that beer and wine are the only drinks to enjoy with a starter, we've included a Libations chapter that will give you some creative ideas in an often neglected area. If you are having a grilling party, why not serve White Sangría on the deck? Forget the ready-made margarita mix — your Cinco de Mayo fiesta deserves an outstanding Fresh Lime Margarita.

Whatever the occasion or the theme, here you'll find recipes and ideas to make your party or meal a memorable one.

Chapter 1 Party Basics

Party Basics

Before you have a party, you need to make a number of decisions. First you need to find the number of a really good caterer. Just kidding. Entertaining isn't nearly as difficult as most people make it out to be. With a little forethought and organization, you can pull off an event of almost any size with panache.

One of the first issues to be decided is when and where to have the party. You may think that the only place to have it is your home, but thinking outside the box can lead to all kinds of creative locales. If the party is during the time of year when the weather is fine, you can think about a beach party, or a cookout at the park. If it's at a time of year when you can anticipate poor weather, you may be confined to an indoor venue. The location you choose for your event will greatly influence the next question: How many people will be in attendance?

The number of guests will affect the number of different appetizers you'll plan to serve. We've found that for a typical party, on average, each person will consume 8 to 12 individual hors d'oeuvres. The more variety you offer, the more people will eat, simply because people's appetites are stimulated when they have more than a couple of dishes to choose from. If you're serving a meal, one or two appetizers are adequate to get the party started. Remember to keep it light, as no one will want to even look at dessert if your appetizer is too filling.

Does the occasion call for formality, or can you get away with a more casual affair? This decision will also affect your menu. It's just not nice to serve Hot and Spicy Buffalo Chicken Wings to women wearing satin dresses. On the other hand, Grilled Apples with Herbes de Provence and Micro Greens may be off-putting to the tailgating crowd. Determine the kind of mood you want to set, and plan the menu accordingly.

The more variety you offer, the more people will eat.

Now that you know what kind of party you're having and how many guests will attend, let's discuss your menu. Time management plays a key role here. The idea is to make as much ahead as you can and still have time to pull the house together and make a few last-minute appetizers.

We like to begin party preparations as far in advance as possible. Make sure to plan at least a few appetizers that can be frozen a week or more ahead of time. Starters based on phyllo and puff pastry are perfect for making ahead, as they can often be frozen on baking sheets and go right from the freezer to the oven.

Keep in mind the importance of color, texture, and flavor.

When planning your menu, keep in mind the importance of color, texture, and flavor. Guests respond to a colorful array of appetizers. The old adage that people eat with their eyes first is true, so plan accordingly. Grilled Fennel with Truffle Oil and Parmesan Curls is delicious, but it will look bland if its only tablemates are in the same beige color range. The Medley of Grilled Peppers with Capers and Pine Nuts, though, will create a splash of vibrant color that will make the entire table pop.

Texture is also key. The crunch of a crudités tray will contrast beautifully with the soft richness of a crab cake. Again, variety is essential.

Although color and texture are important, flavor is also a critical consideration. Too many spicy or tart dishes will leave your guests bored. And a menu composed entirely of rich, decadent dishes may make them feel ill and certainly less convivial.

Beverages are an often overlooked element of a busy host's or hostess's party, which is a shame because the right drink can set the tone of your event. Cocktails are making a real comeback. Think about the mood you'd like to set for your party and, along with the usual red wine, white wine, and beer, plan on making up a pitcher of mojitos or martinis or sangría that you can pour for your guests as they arrive. And don't forget the garnish for your drinks. Skewer your olives and cut your lime wedges ahead of time for fast service.

Lastly, you need to consider the type of linen, silverware, glassware, and plates you'll need. The advantages of paper and plastic are obvious, as they require no cleanup. They make sense, however, only if you're serving finger food. Managing a fork-and-knife appetizer while walking around with a paper plate can be awkward. A more formal sit-down event definitely calls for china, glass, and silverware. These items are easy to rent, and you don't even have to wash them when the party's over. Just return them and you're done.

Chapter 2 Find It Fast

quick and simple

good and good for you

vegetarian

sit down

(Fork friendly foods that serve well as the beginning of a larger meal)

freezer friendly

Chapter 3 Menus

Tapas Party

Manchego Cheese *and* Quince Paste **32**

45 Warm Rosemary Olives

Spanish Tortilla **148**

129 Picadillo Empanadas

Lemon Marinated Lamb Kebabs *with* Cilantro Yogurt Sauce **150**

214 Steamed Mussels *with* Wine and Garlic Butter

Medley of Grilled Peppers *with* Capers *and* Pine Nuts **180**

328, 329 Red *and* White Sangría

Cinco *de* Mayo Fiesta

Pico *de* Gallo **264**

265 Guacamole

Shrimp Salsa **239**

Tortilla chips

Monterey Jack *and* Roasted Poblano Chile Quesadillas **79**

78 Chicken *and* Black Bean Quesadillas

Smoke *and* Fire Beef Kebabs *with* Sour Cream,
Lime, *and* Cilantro Dipping Sauce **156**

316 Fresh Lime Margaritas *and* cold Mexican beer

Spring Fling

The Ultimate Crudités Tray *with* Yogurt Green Onion Dip **42, 260**

55 Herbed Shrimp *with* Snow Peas

Asparagus Quiche *with* Bacon *and* Feta Cheese **86**

183 New Potatoes *with* Crème Fraîche *and* Caviar

Smoked Trout *and* Cucumber Sandwiches *with* Dilled Mayonnaise **241**

157 Chicken Kebabs *with* Green Herb Sauce

Chilled Carrot *and* Cauliflower Soup *with* Dill **282**

313 Mint Juleps

Holiday Cocktail Party

The Ultimate Cheese Tray **28**

42 The Ultimate Crudités Tray *with* Feta Cheese, Roasted Red Pepper, *and* Pine Nut Dip **261**

Curried Mixed Nuts **34**

82 Grape Leaves *with* Rice *and* Pine Nut Filling

Pear, Gorgonzola, *and* Hazelnut Bundles **83**

112 Wild Mushroom Turnovers

White Pizza *with* Prosciutto, Arugula, *and* Parmesan **103**

140 Chicken Skewers *with* Cranberry Dipping Sauce

Chicken Liver Pâté **164**

210 Miniature Crab Cakes *with* Tomato Ginger Jam

Smoked Salmon *and* Goat Cheese Pinwheels **217**

292 Beef Loin *with* Horseradish Aïoli

Dirty Martinis **309**

310 Holiday Spiced Cider

Beer, wine, *and* champagne

Thai One On

Spicy Red Curry Beef Summer Rolls **64**

72 Spicy Pork Dumplings *with* Spicy Thai Dipping Sauce

Thai-Style Chicken Salad *in* Baby Pitas **153**

70 Lettuce Wrap *with* Thai-Style Ground Pork Salad (Larb)

Chicken Satay *with* Thai Peanut Sauce **159**

215 Grilled Spicy Thai Shrimp

The Ultimate Crudités Tray *with* Spicy Thai Dipping Sauce **42, 271**

311 Mango Daiquiris and cold Thai beer

Après Ski

Spicy Kettle Popcorn **41**

110 Pizza Margherita

Porcini Fonduta with Truffle Oil *and* Polenta Cubes **270**

142 Basil Crusted Chicken Fingers *with* Red Bell Pepper Aïoli

Italian Sausage Stuffed Mushrooms **197**

285 Potato *and* Leek Soup *with* Lemon Thyme (Soupe Bonne Femme)

Orange Mulled Wine **315**

Outdoor Concert Picnic

Spicy Marinated Feta Cubes **30**

67 Vietnamese-Style Chicken Salad Rolls

122 Roasted Tomato *and* Mozzarella Tart

Green Apple Slices *with* Tapenade **175**

198 Edamame

Hummus *and* Pita Wedges **275, 96**

307 Basil Lemonade

Beer *and* wine

Super Bowl Party

36 Taco Popcorn

Crispy Reuben Roll-Ups **77**

110 Pizza Margherita

Macho Nachos **165**

169 Hot and Spicy Buffalo Chicken Wings

Not Your Mama's Onion Dip *and* Chips **256**

100 Sausage *in* Pastry *with* Mustard Dipping Sauce

Beer

Campfire *at the* Beach

Lavash Pinwheels *with* Curried Cream Cheese, Ham, *and* Spinach **68**

118 Focaccia *with* Roasted Red Peppers *and* Kalamata Olives

Southwest Frittata **162**

192 Cherry Tomatoes Stuffed *with* Feta, Green Onion, *and* Bacon

Oven-Fried Chicken Lollipops *with* Buttermilk Ranch Dipping Sauce **168, 278**

258 Sun-Dried Tomato Spread *with* baguette slices

Beer *and* wine

Bastille Day

The Ultimate Cheese Tray **28**

44 Marinated Olives

Wild Mushroom Palmiers **104**

186 Terrine of Carrot, Leek, *and* Asparagus

Veal and Ham Pâté **154**

173 Endive *with* Herbed Cheese *and* Sprouts

Salmon Mousse **236**

289 Zucchini Vichyssoise *with* Tarragon Pesto

Wine *and* champagne

Wine Harvest Party

The Ultimate Cheese Tray **28**

45 Warm Rosemary Olives

Baby Bellas *with* Prosciutto *and* Pine Nuts **172**

116 Walnut Focaccia *with* Red Grapes

Figs *with* Saga Blue *and* Prosciutto **196**

287 Chilled Roasted Tomato Soup *with* Pesto

Lamb Patties *with* Eggplant Relish **146**

232 Potted Shrimp *with* Red Bell Peppers *and* Shallots

Beaujolais

Summer Deck Party

42, 251 The Ultimate Crudités Tray *with* Cucumber *and* Cilantro Yogurt Dip

Tomato, Basil, *and* Fresh Mozzarella Bruschetta **125**

98 Prosciutto-Wrapped Breadsticks

Grilled Fennel *with* Truffle Oil *and* Parmesan Curls **179**

156 Smoke *and* Fire Beef Kebabs *with* Sour Cream, Lime, *and* Cilantro Dipping Sauce

Chicken Kebabs *with* Green Herb Sauce **157**

233 Halibut Skewers *with* Moroccan Herb Sauce

Sea Breezes **325**

329 White Sangría

East Meets West

34 Curried Mixed Nuts

Cucumber, Carrot, *and* Wasabi Mayo Rolls **76**

74 California Roll

The Ultimate Crudités Tray *with* Spicy Thai Dipping Sauce **42, 271**

60 Pan-Fried Salmon Shiu Mai *with* Mango Relish

Tamarind Glazed Lamb Kebabs **152**

153 Thai-Style Chicken Salad *in* Baby Pitas

Black Pepper Seared Tuna Skewers *with* Wasabi Aïoli **225**

Asian and domestic beers

Evening *in* Italy

Italian red *and* white wines

Finger Food *for* Forty

Beer *and* wine

New Year's Resolution Party

Edamame **198**

42, 251 The Ultimate Crudités Tray *with* Cucumber *and* Cilantro Yogurt Dip

Vietnamese-Style Chicken Salad Rolls *with* Spicy Thai Dipping Sauce **67, 271**

133 Pita Nachos with Hummus *and* Greek Salsa

Jerked Chicken *and* Melon Bites **145**

188 Roasted Vegetable Skewers *and* Yogurt Lemon Sauce

Chilled Shrimp *with* Bloody Mary Cocktail Sauce **226**

Club soda *with* lime wedges

Summer Soups *and* Sandwiches

Chilled Carrot *and* Cauliflower Soup *with* Dill **282**

286 Yellow Tomato Gazpacho *with* Avocado Relish

Roasted Red Pepper Soup *with* Basil Crème Fraîche **288**

102 Toasted Fontina *and* Onion Jam Panini

Bacon, Tomato, *and* Avocado Wrap-Ups **50**

123 Kalamata Olive, Goat Cheese, *and* Roasted Red Pepper Bruschetta

Bruschetta *with* Roasted Tomato, Pesto, *and* Mascarpone **126**

323 Peach Ginger Iced Tea

Mojitos **327**

Nibblers, *and* Cheese

The Ultimate Cheese Tray

No party is complete without the obligatory cheese tray. It's the easiest thing possible to set on an appetizer table, and guests invariably eat it up. The problem is that most cheese trays are thrown together without imagination. Cubes of cheddar, Swiss, and Monterey Jack are usually tossed on a platter with a large cluster of grapes and set on the table, which is a shame because beautiful, interesting, aromatic artisanal cheeses are being produced all over the world. Many of these cheeses are available at your local grocer and, with just a little effort, can transform an ordinary cheese tray into something quite memorable.

When constructing a cheese tray, try to keep in mind that variety is important. Don't serve all soft, or semisoft, or hard cheese. A tray consisting only of Parmigiano-Reggiano, aged Asiago, and Pecorino Romano—all wonderful hard cheeses—is too close in texture and flavor to be an interesting offering to your guests.

Our standard cheese tray has at least three different cheeses and typically consists of a blue cheese, a soft goat cheese, and an aged cheddar. This combination stays within most people's comfort level, as well as catering to different tastes. To expand the offering, we might add a chunk of Parmigiano-Reggiano and a wedge of Camembert or Brie. And we always allow the cheese to sit at room temperature for 1 hour before serving. This brings out the true character of the cheese.

The best way to select good cheese is to find a cheese shop whose staff is well educated on the subject and will allow you to taste before you buy. There are so many choices on the market today that a trip to the cheese store can be a real adventure. So go ahead and be daring. Try something new, and when you find a cheese you love you can expand your guests' cheese horizons as well.

The cheese selection is only the first step in constructing a wonderful cheese tray. You also must think about the accompaniments to the cheese. Wonderfully dense walnut bread, thinly sliced, and seeded crackers are lovely on a platter. And yes, grapes do have their place, but so do fresh figs and dried fruits such as apricots and golden raisins. Meredith spent one unforgettable evening on the patio of a Tuscan hilltop restaurant, where the chef delivered an incredible array of cheeses, each drizzled with a different type of honey. The combination of the strong cheeses with the deeply flavorful honey was indescribable. The view was pretty good too.

The point is to think outside the box when it comes to your cheese platter, and you will turn a mediocre plate of cheese that your guests nosh on without much thought into a special presentation that will inspire oohs and ahhs from the crowd.

serves six

Spicy Marinated Feta Cubes

ingredients

10 ounces feta cheese, cut into ½-inch cubes

½ cup extra-virgin olive oil

3 tablespoons fresh lemon juice

2 cloves garlic, thinly sliced

½ teaspoon dried oregano

¼ teaspoon crushed red pepper flakes

Pita bread, cut into wedges, for serving

Offer this appetizer with an assortment of olives and lots of fresh pita bread. Icy cold ouzo, the licorice-flavored liqueur from Greece, makes a wonderful accompaniment to this effortless first course.

Mix the cheese cubes, oil, lemon juice, garlic, oregano, and red pepper flakes in a resealable plastic bag. Chill for at least 2 hours or overnight. Place the feta cubes in a serving bowl, and serve with pita wedges.

Make-ahead: *This can be made up to 1 week ahead and kept, covered, in the refrigerator.*

makes one 12-inch log

Cheddar Cheese Pecan Log

ingredients

Two 8-ounce packages cream cheese, at room temperature

1 tablespoon milk

¼ teaspoon cayenne pepper

2 teaspoons Worcestershire sauce

1 teaspoon finely minced garlic

2 cups grated sharp cheddar cheese

1 cup chopped toasted pecans

½ cup minced fresh chives

¼ cup finely minced fresh Italian parsley

Crackers, for serving

Although cheese balls are an easy and popular addition to any party, they often lack a certain sophistication. A swirl of fresh herbs and toasted pecans gives this log a pinwheel effect, making it an updated version of an old classic.

Place the cream cheese in a large bowl and, using an electric mixer, beat until soft and creamy. Add the milk, cayenne, Worcestershire, garlic, and cheddar cheese, and continue to beat just until the ingredients are combined.

Line an 8-by-12-inch pan with parchment or wax paper, making sure there is a 3-inch overhang at each of the long ends. Sprinkle the pecans evenly over the paper. Drop spoonfuls of the cheese mixture onto the pecans. Using a flexible rubber spatula or an offset spatula, spread the cheese into the pan, making sure you reach into the corners. Sprinkle the chives and parsley evenly over the cheese. Using the ends of the parchment, gently lift the cheese out of the pan. Starting at a long end, begin rolling the cheese into a log, as if you were rolling up a jelly roll.

Using the parchment paper, wrap the log, twisting both ends tightly. Refrigerate for at least 3 hours or overnight before serving. Serve with crackers.

Make-ahead: *This can be made 3 days ahead and kept, tightly wrapped in plastic wrap, in the refrigerator.*

serves eight to ten

Manchego Cheese and Quince Paste

ingredients

1 1/4 pounds manchego cheese

One 14-ounce package quince paste (membrillo)

There was a time, not too long ago, when trying to find a Spanish cheese in your local grocery store was mission impossible. Now, with the recent interest in Spanish cuisine in general and tapas in particular, manchego cheese can be found in the cheese section of many groceries. Quince is a relative of the apple and, when cooked down with sugar to a paste, makes a wonderfully sweet foil to the sharpness of the cheese.

Cut the cheese into 1/4-inch-thick wedges, discarding the rind. Cut the quince paste into 1/8-inch-thick rectangles. Top the cheese wedges with the quince paste and arrange on a platter. Serve at room temperature.

Make-ahead: *The cheese and quince paste can be assembled up to 8 hours ahead, covered in plastic wrap, and kept in the refrigerator. Allow 30 minutes for the cheese to come to room temperature before serving.*

Tip: *Although you can find quince preserves, for this use it's much better to buy it in paste form, because it can be sliced. This makes it more manageable both for you to work with and for your guests to eat.*

makes about two cups

Spiced Pecans

ingredients

2 cups pecan halves

2 tablespoons unsalted butter, melted

1 teaspoon ground cinnamon

1/4 teaspoon cayenne pepper

2 tablespoons sugar

3/4 teaspoon salt

Serve these sweet, spicy pecans warm in a bowl or, better yet, use them to embellish a cheese platter for a simple but memorable meal starter.

Preheat the oven to 325°F. Place the pecans in a medium bowl. Add the butter, cinnamon, cayenne, sugar, and salt and stir to coat. Transfer to a baking pan. Bake until the nuts are toasted, stirring occasionally, about 20 minutes. Serve warm or at room temperature.

Make-ahead: *The pecans can be prepared up to 5 days ahead and stored in an airtight container.*

Tip: *It's always fun to add height to an appetizer table. With this in mind, our friend Marsha Russell likes to serve spiced nuts in oversized martini glasses.*

makes 2½ cups

Curried Mixed Nuts

ingredients

- *2½ cups mixed whole almonds, raw cashews, pecans, and/or raw peanuts*
- *2 tablespoons vegetable oil*
- *2 teaspoons curry powder, or to taste*
- *¼ teaspoon cayenne pepper, or to taste*
- *2 tablespoons sugar*
- *1 teaspoon salt*

Curry powder is a blend of spices that often includes black pepper, cinnamon, cardamom, cumin, ginger, and turmeric. Here we've highlighted the earthy, complex flavors of curry with a bit of sugar and salt, making these nuts absolutely addictive.

Preheat the oven to 350°F. Place the mixed nuts in a large bowl. Heat the vegetable oil in a small, heavy saucepan over medium heat. Add the curry powder and cayenne pepper to taste and stir until aromatic, about 15 seconds. Pour over the mixed nuts. Add the sugar and salt and stir to blend. Transfer to a baking pan. Bake until the nuts are toasted, stirring occasionally, about 15 minutes. Serve warm or at room temperature.

Make-ahead: *The nuts can be made 5 days ahead, placed in an airtight container, and stored at room temperature.*

Tip: *Because ground spices begin to lose their flavor quickly after being ground, if you choose to buy curry powder in a jar, make sure you purchase it from a store that has a lot of turnover. Otherwise you could be getting a jar that has sat on the shelf for a year and will likely have very little flavor.*

makes two cups

Honeyed Almonds

ingredients

2 cups raw almonds with skins

¼ cup plus 2 tablespoons sugar, divided

2 tablespoons honey

2 tablespoons unsalted butter

¾ teaspoon salt

Okay, these addictive salty, sweet treats could easily step over the line into the dessert category, but we found them too tempting to leave out of this book. They are great to set out in a bowl for everyone to nibble on before dinner. They're also an interesting addition to a salad, perhaps with crumbled blue cheese.

Preheat the oven to 400°F. Place the almonds in an even layer on a baking sheet. Roast for 10 to 12 minutes. Remove from the baking sheet and place in a large bowl.

In a small saucepan, combine ¼ cup sugar with the honey and butter. Bring to a boil over medium heat, stirring occasionally. Once boiling, do not stir. Boil for 3 minutes. It should darken slightly as it cooks, but if it begins to go past the golden brown stage, remove it from the heat immediately to avoid burning.

Pour the hot syrup over the nuts. Stir well. Sprinkle with the remaining 2 tablespoons sugar and the salt and toss to coat. Transfer the nuts to a greased baking sheet and separate with a fork. Let cool completely. Store in an airtight container at room temperature for up to 1 week.

Make-ahead: *The almonds can be prepared up to 7 days ahead and stored in an airtight container.*

makes about eight cups

Taco Popcorn

ingredients

½ teaspoon salt

2 teaspoons chili powder

¼ teaspoon garlic powder

¼ teaspoon ground cumin

⅛ teaspoon cayenne pepper

2 tablespoons vegetable oil

⅓ cup unpopped popcorn kernels

2 tablespoons unsalted butter, melted

We were going to give this a more sophisticated name, like "Chilied Popcorn," but when Meredith served this to her sons, they said, "Cool, Mom, this popcorn tastes like tacos," which really is the case here. It contains all the familiar taco flavors, with the added punch of a little extra cayenne.

In a small bowl, combine the salt, chili powder, garlic powder, cumin, and cayenne. Set aside.

Heat the oil with 3 popcorn kernels in a 3-quart heavy saucepan over moderate heat, covered, until 1 or 2 kernels pop. Quickly add the remaining popcorn and cook, covered, shaking the pan frequently, until the popping stops, about 3 minutes.

Drizzle the butter over the hot popcorn in a large bowl, and toss to coat. Then toss with the spice mixture. Serve warm or at room temperature.

Make-ahead: *Popcorn is really best fresh, but this can be made up to an hour ahead and kept, uncovered, at room temperature.*

makes about eight cups

Parmesan Popcorn

ingredients

- *2 tablespoons vegetable oil*
- *1/3 cup unpopped popcorn kernels*
- *2 tablespoons extra-virgin olive oil*
- *1/2 cup finely grated Parmigiano-Reggiano cheese*
- *1/4 teaspoon freshly ground black pepper*
- *1/4 teaspoon salt*

It's amazing how the simple addition of Parmesan cheese and black pepper can transform plain popcorn into something really special. This is an easy dish to make up and have in bowls around the house for a party or to surprise the family at your next movie night.

Heat the vegetable oil with 3 popcorn kernels in a 3-quart heavy saucepan over moderate heat, covered, until 1 or 2 kernels pop. Quickly add the remaining popcorn and cook, covered, shaking the pan frequently, until the popping stops, about 3 minutes.

Drizzle the olive oil over the hot popcorn in a large bowl and toss to coat, then toss with the cheese, pepper, and salt.

Make-ahead: *Popcorn is really best fresh, but this can be made up to an hour ahead and kept, uncovered, at room temperature.*

serves ten to twelve

Homemade Potato Chips with Blue Cheese

ingredients

- *2 to 3 baking potatoes, about 2 pounds*
- *Peanut oil, for frying*
- *Kosher salt to taste*
- *8 ounces blue cheese, finely crumbled*

Homemade potato chips are a treat so rarely experienced that your guests will surely be impressed. Here we've added layers of blue cheese to the chips and warmed them in the oven, making them a gooey, absolutely wonderful treat. It's important to serve these warm, so think about these chips for your next poker party, when everyone is already seated around the table. Don't forget the napkins, or you'll have blue cheese all over the queen of spades.

Peel the potatoes and slice them into thin ⅛-inch slices, using a mandoline or sharp knife. Soak the potatoes in water for 5 minutes. Drain them and thoroughly pat them dry.

Pour enough oil into a large, heavy-bottomed saucepan to reach halfway up the sides (don't go any higher up the sides than that, because the oil will bubble up considerably as you put in the potatoes). Heat the oil until a deep-frying thermometer registers 375°F. Carefully slip about 15 potato slices into the oil and fry, moving the slices with tongs or a slotted spoon, until golden, 1 to 2 minutes. Transfer the chips to paper towels to drain, and season immediately with salt. Don't overseason, as the blue cheese will be very salty as well. Repeat until all the potato slices are fried.

Preheat the oven to 450°F. Place a layer of chips in a baking dish and sprinkle with some of the blue cheese. Place another layer of chips on top and add some more cheese. Continue until you have used up all the chips and cheese. Put into the oven and bake until the cheese has melted, about 5 minutes. Serve warm.

Make-ahead: *The potatoes can be sliced and soaked in the water up to 1 hour ahead of time.*

Tip: *Although there is nothing better than hot-out-of-the-oil potato chips, there is a shortcut that is almost as good. Buy kettle-type potato chips and proceed with the recipe, layering them with the cheese and then baking them in the hot oven. They will come out hot and cheesy and close to the real deal.*

makes five cups

Cumin Roasted Almonds

ingredients

- *2 tablespoons whole cumin seed*
- *2 tablespoons sugar*
- *1 teaspoon cayenne pepper*
- *1½ teaspoons salt, divided*
- *4 tablespoons unsalted butter*
- *1 tablespoon Worcestershire sauce*
- *1 tablespoon soy sauce*
- *6 cups raw almonds with skins*

Nut snacks are popular munchies to employ close to where the drinks are made or distributed. No matter how much you pay for them, store-bought nut mixes are never as good as homemade. The cumin and cayenne in this nut mix add spice, but we think the butter and salty Worcestershire really make these almonds stand out.

Preheat the oven to 250°F.

Add the cumin seed to a heavy-bottomed skillet and heat over medium heat until fragrant. Grind the seeds in a spice mill, or crush them with a mortar and pestle.

Add the cumin, sugar, cayenne, 1 teaspoon of the salt, butter, Worcestershire, and soy sauce to a medium saucepan and heat over medium heat until the butter is melted and the mixture is hot.

Place the almonds in a large bowl and pour the butter mixture over them, tossing with large spoons to coat the nuts with the seasonings. Transfer the nuts to a large baking sheet lined with parchment and bake until dry and crispy, about 1½ hours. Remove the nuts from the oven and sprinkle with the remaining ½ teaspoon salt. Let cool.

Make-ahead: *The nuts keep for up to 1 month in a tightly covered container.*

makes about sixteen bites

Herbed Goat Cheese Bites

ingredients

- 8 ounces goat cheese (two 4-ounce packages)
- 2 tablespoons thinly sliced fresh basil
- 2 tablespoons minced fresh Italian parsley
- 2 tablespoons finely chopped oil-packed sun-dried tomato
- 1 teaspoon minced fresh thyme
- 1 teaspoon minced fresh marjoram or oregano
- 1/2 teaspoon salt
- 1/8 teaspoon freshly ground black pepper
- About 1 cup extra-virgin olive oil

Small bites of goat cheese infused with fresh herbs and olive oil are an easy-to-make dish with strong appeal. Try your own mix of fresh herbs, using whatever you have growing in your garden. We found that these bites are even better a couple of days after they're made (if any leftovers remain). Just be sure to keep them submerged in the olive oil.

Combine the goat cheese, basil, parsley, sun-dried tomato, thyme, marjoram, salt, and pepper in a medium bowl. Chill for about 1 hour and then, using a 1-tablespoon scoop, shape the herbed goat cheese into balls, rolling them lightly between your hands to make smooth balls. Place the goat cheese balls in a medium bowl, add enough olive oil to cover them, and let them sit in the refrigerator for about 24 hours to let the flavors develop. To serve, arrange the balls on a tray with toothpicks, or serve them as part of a cheese plate with assorted cheeses, fruit, and nuts.

Make-ahead: *The bites can be kept, refrigerated and covered with oil, for up to 1 week.*

Tips: *Save the olive oil and use it for salad dressings, or drizzle it over bread, toast it under a broiler, and spread with the goat cheese for an easy side to a salad supper.*

To thinly slice basil, roll up the leaves into a cigarlike roll and make thin crosswise cuts. Cutting basil in this way prevents the leaves from becoming overchopped and slimy.

makes about eight cups

Spicy Kettle Popcorn

ingredients

6 cups freshly popped popcorn (start with 1/3 cup unpopped popcorn kernels)

1 cup slivered almonds

1 cup coarsely chopped walnuts

1 1/2 cups firmly packed brown sugar

1/2 cup (1 stick) unsalted butter

1/3 cup light corn syrup

1 teaspoon salt

1/2 teaspoon baking soda

1/4 teaspoon cayenne pepper, or to taste

Sweet caramel, salt, and spicy cayenne pepper add flavor to crunchy popcorn and nuts. When we tested this recipe it disappeared so fast that we had to make another batch. Guests are guaranteed to keep coming back for more of this addictive munchie.

Preheat the oven to 250°F.

Line a baking sheet with parchment paper and spread the popcorn and nuts over it. Place the sheet in the oven while you make the syrup. (Heating the popcorn and nuts helps the caramel to spread more evenly later on.)

Place the brown sugar, butter, and corn syrup in a medium saucepan. Stir over medium heat until the butter melts, then increase the heat to high and boil the mixture without stirring for 4 to 5 minutes. Drop a tiny bit of the syrup into a cup of cool water. When the drop of syrup hardens in the water, it is ready. If you have a candy thermometer, cook the mixture until the temperature reaches 250°F. Remove the pan from the heat and stir in the salt, baking soda, and cayenne. The mixture will bubble up. Drizzle the syrup over the warm popcorn-nut mixture, stirring gently with a fork to coat. Bake the mixture in the oven, stirring 2 or 3 times, for about 45 minutes. Remove from the oven and let cool in the pan. It will firm up as it cools. Break it up into smaller pieces.

Make-ahead: *Store in an airtight container at room temperature for up to 1 week.*

serves eight

The Ultimate Crudités Tray

ingredients

- *2 tablespoons salt*
- *8 ounces green beans, trimmed*
- *3 stalks broccoli, cut into florets*
- *½ head cauliflower, cut into florets*
- *16 baby zucchini, washed*
- *16 baby pattypan squash, washed*
- *3 stalks celery, thick white ends trimmed and cut into 4-inch sticks*
- *5 carrots, peeled and cut into 4-inch sticks*
- *1 pint cherry tomatoes, rinsed and dried*
- *½ head fennel, cored, trimmed, and cut into 4-inch sticks*
- *1 red bell pepper, rinsed, dried, and cut into 4-inch sticks*
- *1 head of red cabbage to use as a reservoir for dip (optional)*
- *Yogurt Green Onion Dip (page 260), Buttermilk Ranch Dipping Sauce (page 278), Blue Cheese and Toasted Walnut Spread (page 249), or Not Your Mama's Onion Dip (page 256)*
- *Flowering kale or chard, as a garnish*

Think of the crudités tray as a floral arrangement that you can eat. It should look striking. Buy the freshest vegetables available. It will really make a difference. And lastly, the secret to avoiding the dreaded double dip lies in cutting the vegetables so they can easily be eaten in one bite.

Bring a large pot filled with 4 quarts of water to a boil over high heat. Add the salt to the water, and then add the green beans. When the water returns to a boil, turn the heat to medium and cook the beans for 3 minutes. Remove the beans from the water with a slotted spoon and transfer to a bowl of ice water to stop the cooking and set the color. After the beans have chilled in the water, remove them to a kitchen towel and roll them up in it to dry them off. Store in the refrigerator.

Bring 1 cup of water to a boil in a steamer. Add the broccoli florets and steam for 3 minutes. Remove the broccoli and immerse in ice water to stop the cooking. Add the cauliflower to the steamer and steam for 3 minutes. Remove and immerse in ice water to stop the cooking.

Add the zucchini to the steamer and steam for 5 minutes. Remove and immerse in ice water to stop the cooking. Add the pattypan squash to the steamer and steam for 5 minutes. Remove and immerse in ice water to stop the cooking. Remove the vegetables from the ice bath and roll them up in kitchen towels. Store the vegetables in the refrigerator until you're ready to assemble the tray. Prepare and store the celery, carrots, cherry tomatoes, fennel, and red pepper, covered, in the refrigerator also.

If you want to serve the dip in a cabbage "bowl," slice the top fourth of the cabbage head off, and slice the stem end so that it stands firmly. Hollow out the cabbage, leaving a thin wall along the outside edge. Fill with the dip of your choice.

On the largest tray that you have, arrange a layer of flowering kale or chard leaves. Set the dip-filled cabbage on the tray and arrange the chilled vegetables in groups around it. Keep the tray covered and chilled until ready to serve, or arrange it at the last minute.

Make-ahead: *This can be assembled up to 8 hours ahead and kept, covered, in the refrigerator.*

makes about six cups

Wasabi Sesame Mix

ingredients

2 cups wasabi peas

2 cups sesame sticks

2 cups salted cashews

Nothing is easier to put together than this nibbler. Wasabi peas are available in grocery stores everywhere. Crunchy and spicy hot, they go well with the rich, nutty sesame sticks and luscious, salty cashews.

Combine the peas, sesame sticks, and cashews in a bowl and mix well.

Make-ahead: *Store the mix in a tightly covered container for up to 1 month.*

makes about three cups

Marinated Olives

ingredients

1 cup extra-virgin olive oil

2 tablespoons minced garlic

2 tablespoons minced red onion

2 teaspoons fennel seed

1/4 teaspoon crushed red pepper flakes

2 sprigs rosemary, each 5 inches long

1 red bell pepper, cut into matchsticks

1 cup kalamata olives, drained

1 cup niçoise olives, drained

1 cup picholine olives, drained

1/4 cup fresh lemon juice

2 tablespoons thinly sliced fresh basil

2 tablespoons minced fresh Italian parsley

Marinated olives are quick and easy to pull together, and bathing them in this Provençal marinade raises their appeal from a 5 to a 10. Try to buy a variety of colors and shapes of olives from the selection at the grocery store, and don't worry about the pits. The olives will be more presentable and will keep their shape if they are left whole. Pair these with nuts like the Cumin Roasted Almonds (page 39) or Spiced Pecans (page 33).

Heat the olive oil in a large saucepan over medium heat. When the oil is hot, add the garlic, onion, fennel seed, red pepper flakes, rosemary, and red bell pepper. Cook for 1 minute and add the olives to the pan. Simmer the olives for 3 minutes and remove the pan from the heat. Let the mixture stand at room temperature for about 1 hour. Cover and refrigerate for at least 2 hours or up to 3 days.

Just before serving, remove the rosemary and add the lemon juice, basil, and parsley. Toss to mix and serve in a decorative bowl.

Make-ahead: *The olives can be made up to 3 days ahead of time and kept, covered, in the refrigerator.*

Tip: *It is considerate to leave a plate beside the bowl with an olive pit on it so that guests can see where to dispose of them.*

makes about two cups

Warm Rosemary Olives

ingredients

- *12 ounces kalamata olives*
- *Zest of 1 lemon, grated or cut into fine slivers*
- *Zest of 1 orange, grated or cut into fine slivers*
- *Several sprigs of fresh rosemary, bruised*
- *½ cup extra-virgin olive oil*
- *¼ teaspoon crushed red pepper flakes*
- *1 teaspoon fennel seed*
- *Several sprigs of fresh rosemary, cut into small sections, for garnish*

For a bit of Spanish pizzazz, serve these olives with Marcona almonds and a medium-bodied dry sherry.

Place the olives, lemon and orange zest, rosemary sprigs, olive oil, red pepper flakes, and fennel seed in a saucepan and heat until the herbs sizzle. Remove from the heat and let sit at room temperature for about 5 hours. Before serving, remove the browned herbs and replenish with fresh herbs. Serve garnished with rosemary sprigs.

Make-ahead: *These olives will keep for 2 weeks in your refrigerator. Let them come to room temperature before serving.*

Chapter

0 Bacon, Tomato, *and* Avocado Wrap-Ups
lollandaise **52** Grape Leaves *with* Lamb *and* Dill
5 Herbed Shrimp *with* Snow Peas
eta, Sun-Dried Tomatoes, Olives, *and* Radish Sprouts
0 Pan-Fried Salmon Shiu Mai *with* Mango Relish
ream Sauce **64** Spicy Red Curry Beef Summer Rolls

5 Wrap It Up

7 Vietnamese-Style Chicken Salad Rolls
am, *and* Spinach
Brown Butter, Sage, *and* Pecan Sauce
alad (Larb) **71** Oven-Baked Chipotle Chicken Flautas
3 Gyoza
5 Spicy Tuna Rolls
7 Crispy Reuben Roll-Ups
ack *and* Roasted Poblano Chile Quesadillas
oasted Vegetables *and* Herbed Goat Cheese Sauce
3 Pear, Gorgonzola, *and* Hazelnut Bundles

makes about thirty-six balls

Arancini

ingredients

- *3 cups chilled Mushroom Risotto (facing page) or leftover risotto*
- *36 cubes (½ inch each) mozzarella cheese (about 3 ounces)*
- *½ cup all-purpose flour*
- *3 large eggs, beaten*
- *1½ cups fine dry breadcrumbs*
- *4 cups vegetable oil, for frying*

We like to make a double recipe of risotto for dinner one night and save what's left over for these delicious, crispy on the outside, gooey on the inside morsels. Make them small so that they are pop-in-your-mouth, one-bite snacks that will disappear as fast as you can make them. We've given you a wonderful risotto recipe, but any leftover risotto will work.

Wet your hands with water and roll the chilled risotto into balls about 1 inch in diameter. Poke a small hole in the center of each and push in a cube of the mozzarella, covering it with the rice and re-forming it into a ball.

Arrange the flour, eggs, and breadcrumbs in 3 separate large bowls. Dredge the balls in the flour, shaking off the excess. Dip the balls in the egg and then dredge them in the breadcrumbs. Transfer the balls to a parchment-lined baking pan.

Heat the oil in a large, heavy pot until a deep-fat thermometer registers 360°F. Working in batches of 6 or 7, lower the rice balls into the hot fat with a slotted spoon or spatula and fry, turning occasionally, until the balls are golden brown, about 3 minutes. Remove the balls from the fat with the slotted spoon or spatula and drain them on paper towels to absorb the excess fat. When the heat returns to 360°F, cook another batch until all the balls are fried.

Make-ahead: *Once the rice balls are breaded, they can be kept, covered, in the refrigerator for 4 hours. The fried arancini can be kept in a warm (200°F) oven for 30 minutes.*

serves six

Mushroom Risotto

ingredients

6 tablespoons unsalted butter, divided

1 medium onion, chopped

Two 1/4-ounce packages dried porcini mushrooms, soaked in hot water to cover for 30 minutes

8 ounces cremini or other fresh mushrooms, wiped clean and sliced

2 cups homemade or canned chicken broth

3 cups water

1 1/2 cups raw Arborio rice

1/2 cup dry white wine

1/4 cup chopped fresh Italian parsley

1/2 cup grated Parmesan cheese

1/4 cup heavy cream

Salt and freshly ground black pepper to taste

Heat 3 tablespoons of the butter in a heavy-bottomed 4-quart pot over medium-high heat. Add the onion and sauté until translucent, about 3 minutes.

Remove the mushrooms from the soaking liquid, reserving the liquid. Chop the mushrooms and add them to the onions, stirring until they are fragrant, about 2 minutes. Add the sliced fresh mushrooms and sauté until they soften and give off their juices, about 3 minutes. Reduce the heat to medium. Meanwhile, strain the mushroom soaking liquid through a coffee filter to remove the grit from the mushrooms. Heat the broth, water, and mushroom liquid to a simmer in a medium saucepan.

Add the rice to the onions and mushrooms and stir until the rice begins to look opaque, 3 or 4 minutes. Reduce the heat to medium-low or low. Add the wine to the pan and cook, stirring, until the wine has evaporated, about 3 minutes. Ladle about 1/2 cup of the hot broth mixture into the rice and stir for about 2 minutes. When the liquid is absorbed and the rice is beginning to look pasty, add another 1/2 cup of broth, stirring for a few minutes until the liquid is again absorbed. Repeat this process, adding the broth 1/2 cup at a time until the rice is tender, about 20 minutes.

Taste the rice for doneness. It should be cooked through, with no trace of chalkiness, but the center of the rice shouldn't be mushy.

When the rice is done, add the remaining 3 tablespoons butter, parsley, cheese, heavy cream, and then salt and pepper to taste.

makes thirty-six pieces

Bacon, Tomato, and Avocado Wrap-Ups

ingredients

- *2 teaspoons curry powder*
- *½ cup mayonnaise*
- *3 teaspoons fresh lemon juice, divided*
- *1 ripe avocado, halved, pitted, and sliced lengthwise*
- *2 lavash wraps, tomato or spinach or a combination, cut in half crosswise to make four 12-inch squares*
- *8 slices bacon, cooked until crisp, drained on paper towels*
- *1 ripe tomato, seeded and thinly sliced*
- *2 cups thinly sliced romaine lettuce*
- *½ cup fresh cilantro leaves*

Lavash is a type of flatbread that resembles a flour tortilla in texture. It comes in flavors such as tomato and spinach in bright colors. Using a variety of different-colored lavash will make a colorful platter of hors d'oeuvres.

Heat the curry powder in a small skillet over medium heat until fragrant. Transfer to a small bowl and mix with the mayonnaise and 2 teaspoons of the lemon juice.

In a separate small bowl, toss the avocado with the remaining teaspoon of lemon juice.

Place 1 lavash square on a work surface. Spread the lavash with 2 tablespoons of the curried mayonnaise. Place 2 slices of bacon in the center. Top the bacon with 2 slices of tomato, 2 slices of avocado, ½ cup of lettuce, and 2 tablespoons of cilantro.

Starting with one of the short ends, roll the lavash up jelly-roll style. Repeat with the remaining lavash. Wrap each roll up tightly in plastic wrap and place in the refrigerator for at least 30 minutes.

To serve, slice each roll crosswise into 9 pieces. Transfer the pinwheels to a serving platter. Serve cold or at room temperature.

Make-ahead: *The rolls can be kept, unsliced and wrapped in plastic, in the refrigerator overnight.*

serves four

Crêpes with Roasted Asparagus and Easy Hollandaise

roasted asparagus

1 bunch asparagus (about 12 spears)

2 tablespoons olive oil

1/4 teaspoon salt

Dash of freshly ground black pepper

easy hollandaise sauce

1/2 cup (1 stick) unsalted butter

2 large egg yolks

2 teaspoons tarragon vinegar

2 teaspoons heavy cream

1 teaspoon fresh lemon juice

1/4 teaspoon salt

Dash of cayenne pepper

Dash of freshly ground black pepper

Basic Crêpes (page 333)

2 tablespoons minced fresh chives, for garnish (optional)

2 tablespoons finely diced red bell pepper, for garnish (optional)

Roasting results in the best asparagus you have ever tasted. And the hollandaise is so easy you will be tempted to make it every Sunday to pour over your poached eggs with bacon and toast.

To roast the asparagus: Preheat the oven to 400°F. Snap the tough ends from the asparagus and arrange the spears on a baking sheet. Drizzle them with oil, along with the salt and pepper. Roast the asparagus in the oven for about 10 minutes. Remove the asparagus from the oven and keep warm.

To make the hollandaise: Heat the butter to a simmer in a medium saucepan over medium-high heat. While it is heating, add the egg yolks, vinegar, cream, lemon juice, salt, cayenne, and pepper to the jar of a blender. Place the lid over the top and blend for 3 seconds. Remove the middle insert from the lid so that you can pour the hot butter into the blender while it is running. Turn the blender to blend and pour the hot butter through the hole in a slow, steady stream. It should take about 15 seconds to get it all in. Taste the hollandaise for seasoning and adjust if necessary with salt, pepper, or lemon juice.

To serve: Arrange a crêpe on a plate and place 3 spears of asparagus in the middle. Fold the sides up over the asparagus to cover it. Pour a few tablespoons of the hollandaise over the top. Garnish with chives and red bell pepper, if desired. Serve warm.

Make-ahead: *The hollandaise will keep in a metal bowl over just warm water (about 120°F) for up to 1 hour. Be careful not to let it get too warm or it will break and become greasy. On the other hand, don't let it sit out for too long or it becomes a breeding ground for bacteria. It is easiest to make it right before using it.*

makes about eighty stuffed grape leaves

Grape Leaves with Lamb and Dill

ingredients

- *Two 1-pound jars brine-packed grape leaves, drained*
- *2 cups water*
- *1 teaspoon salt, divided, plus more to taste*
- *1 cup raw jasmine rice*
- *4 tablespoons olive oil, divided*
- *1 cup minced red onion*
- *2 cloves garlic, minced*
- *1 pound finely ground lamb*
- *½ teaspoon freshly ground black pepper, plus more to taste*
- *¼ cup toasted pine nuts*
- *¼ cup chopped fresh dill*
- *¼ cup chopped fresh Italian parsley*
- *½ cup currants*
- *Grated zest and juice of 2 large lemons (½ cup juice)*
- *1 tablespoon whole coriander seeds, ground in a mortar or spice mill*
- *⅛ teaspoon cayenne pepper*
- *2 cups chicken stock*

The Gross family of Pittsburgh, Pennsylvania, first introduced Carla to the magic of disappearing grape leaves. When they ran out of grape leaves, the children were sent out to the wild grapevines that grew along the property to gather more. They blanched them in salted water for about 5 minutes and voilà—more grape leaves to fill. This is a great activity for 6 or 8 friends to work on together while talking, laughing, and sharing a few beers, preferably from Iron City Brewery, a Pittsburgh institution.

Soak the grape leaves in a large bowl filled with cold water for about 30 minutes. Remove the leaves and separate them, laying them out on towels to dry. Some of the leaves will be ripped or torn and unsuitable for rolling. Use them to line the bottom of the large, heavy-bottomed pot in which you will cook the stuffed grape leaves.

Bring the water and ½ teaspoon of the salt to a boil over medium-high heat. Add the rice, cover, and turn the heat to low. Cook until the water is absorbed, 17 to 20 minutes. Remove the rice from the heat and let sit, covered, for 2 minutes. Transfer the cooked rice to a large bowl.

In a medium skillet, heat 2 tablespoons of the olive oil. When it is hot, add the onion and garlic and cook until the onion is translucent, about 3 minutes. Add the lamb, ½ teaspoon salt, and pepper and cook until the meat is no longer pink. Add the lamb-onion mixture to the rice along with the pine nuts, dill, parsley, currants, lemon zest, ¼ cup of the lemon juice, coriander, and cayenne. Toss to combine, and season with salt and freshly ground black pepper to taste.

To roll the grape leaves, place 1 grape leaf, smooth side down, on a work surface. Trim the stem if there is one. Spoon 1 tablespoon of the filling onto the leaf near the stem end, and tightly roll the leaf, folding in the sides about halfway and squeezing to pack the filling tightly. (Loosely rolled grape leaves will become soggy and fall apart during cooking.) The size of the rolls may vary according to the size of the leaves. Make more rolls in the same manner. Arrange the rolls in the pot that you have lined with the ripped leaves. Drizzle with the remaining 2 tablespoons olive oil and add the chicken stock and remaining lemon juice to the pot so that the liquid comes up to the top layer of grape leaves. Cover with an inverted heatproof plate and bring the stock to a boil. Cover with a lid and turn the heat to low so that the leaves cook at a bare simmer for about 30 minutes. Remove from the heat and transfer the rolls with tongs to a large platter to cool. Serve at room temperature, or cover with plastic wrap and chill in the refrigerator overnight. Remove from the refrigerator an hour before you plan to serve them.

Make-ahead: *The filling can be made 24 hours in advance. The rolled grape leaves keep, covered and chilled, for up to 3 days.*

makes about sixty rolls

Grilled Vegetable and Herbed Cheese Pinwheels

ingredients

- 2 medium zucchini, about 10 inches long and 3 inches thick
- 2 small Japanese eggplants, about 10 inches long and 3 inches thick
- 2 large carrots, about 10 inches long and 2 inches thick
- 2 tablespoons olive oil
- Sea salt and freshly ground black pepper to taste
- 2 cups Boursin cheese (two 5-ounce packages), at room temperature

A mandoline or Japanese slicer makes it easy to slice the vegetables for this dish (see the tips at the end of the recipe). It is essential that the slices be very thin, so that when lightly cooked they are pliable enough to form into little sushi-like rolls. These rolls have great color and a good bit of zip from the Boursin cheese. The orange carrot, green-tinged zucchini, and purple eggplant look terrific on the serving plate. We've found that using vegetables of the sizes called for in the recipe makes for a uniform pinwheel that is pretty in presentation.

Prepare a grill or preheat the oven to 400°F.

Using a mandoline, a Japanese slicer, or a very sharp knife, slice the zucchini, eggplant, and carrots lengthwise into long, thin strips about 1/8 inch thick. Brush them lightly with oil and sprinkle with salt and pepper.

Grill the vegetables over a hot fire, 1 minute per side, or arrange them on a parchment-lined baking sheet and roast them in the preheated oven for 5 minutes. Remove the vegetables from the heat and let cool. They should be pliable.

Spread 1 teaspoon of the cheese down the length of each vegetable slice and roll them up tightly, starting at the narrow end. Arrange the rolls on a platter and serve at room temperature.

Make-ahead: *The rolls can be made up to 4 hours ahead and kept covered and refrigerated. Bring back to room temperature before serving.*

Tips: *Boursin is a triple-cream cheese, made from cow's milk. It has a rich, nutty flavor and is often flavored with pepper, herbs, or garlic.*

A mandoline is a manually operated slicer with adjustable blades. It is used to obtain uniform thin slices, matchsticks, or waffle cuts.

makes about thirty-three shrimp

Herbed Shrimp with Snow Peas

ingredients

2 teaspoons salt, divided

1 lime, cut in half

1 pound medium shrimp (31 to 35 per pound)

Grated zest of 1 lemon

1/4 cup fresh lemon juice

2 large cloves garlic, minced

1/4 cup minced fresh dill

2 tablespoons Dijon mustard

1/4 cup olive oil

1/4 teaspoon freshly ground black pepper

4 ounces snow peas, trimmed

Martha Stewart's Shrimp Vinaigrette Wrapped in Snow Peas was the inspiration for this dressed-up version of marinated shrimp. The snow pea wrapper adds color and crunch to what would otherwise be a bland-looking pile of shrimp. This light, addictive recipe is a nice alternative to the usual shrimp with cocktail sauce.

Bring 6 cups water to a boil in a large saucepan over medium-high heat. Add 1 teaspoon of the salt, and squeeze the lime into the water. Add the shrimp, cover the pot, and remove from the heat. Let the pan sit for about 3 minutes. Remove the shrimp from the water with a slotted spoon and immerse them in an ice bath to stop the cooking. Peel the shrimp, removing the tail.

In a large bowl, combine the lemon zest and juice, 1/2 teaspoon of the salt, garlic, dill, and mustard. Stir to combine, and let the mixture sit for 3 minutes to give the salt a chance to dissolve. Whisk in the olive oil and black pepper. Add the shrimp to the marinade and toss to coat. Cover the bowl and refrigerate for at least 3 hours and up to 24 hours.

Bring a pot with 4 cups of water to a boil. Add the remaining 1/2 teaspoon salt to the water, along with the snow peas. Cook for 3 minutes. Remove the snow peas from the hot water with a slotted spoon and immerse them in an ice bath to stop the cooking. Remove from the ice bath and lay them out on a towel to dry.

Wrap a snow pea around the circumference of each shrimp. Secure it in place with a toothpick. Arrange the shrimp on a decorative platter and keep refrigerated until ready to serve.

Make-ahead: *The shrimp can be made and assembled up to 5 hours ahead and kept, covered, in the refrigerator.*

Tip: *For a unique presentation, arrange the shrimp on a head of cabbage. Trim the bottom of a red or green cabbage so that it is stable. Cover the cabbage with the shrimp by sticking the toothpicks through the shrimp and into the cabbage.*

makes twelve filled crêpes, serving six

Mu Shu Duck Crêpes with Hoisin Sauce

crepes

Basic Crêpes (page 333)

filling

- *3 duck breast halves, boned and skinned*
- *4 tablespoons dry sherry or dry white wine, divided*
- *4 tablespoons light soy sauce, divided*
- *8 tablespoons vegetable oil, divided*
- *2 cloves garlic, minced*
- *2 large eggs, beaten*
- *Dash plus 1 teaspoon salt, divided*
- *Freshly ground black pepper, plus more to taste*
- *4 cups thinly sliced napa cabbage*
- *1 cup stemmed and thinly sliced shiitake mushrooms*

Mu shu is generally made with pork or chicken, but duck is an indulgence. This hearty appetizer can be made in stages; the crêpes and filling can be made a day ahead and reheated. These are a lot of fun to assemble and eat, though a bit messy. Put out lots of napkins. Your guests will have a ball.

Wrap the crêpes in aluminum foil and keep warm in an oven at the lowest setting for up to 30 minutes.

To make the filling: Slice the duck on the diagonal into the thinnest possible slices. Combine the duck, 2 tablespoons of the sherry, 2 tablespoons of the soy sauce, 2 tablespoons of the vegetable oil, and the garlic in a small bowl, toss together, and refrigerate while assembling the remaining ingredients.

Heat 2 tablespoons vegetable oil in a wok or sauté pan over medium heat. When the oil is hot, add the eggs and a dash each of salt and pepper, and stir-fry them until they become firm, about 1 minute. Remove the eggs from the pan and set them aside in a large bowl.

Add another 2 tablespoons oil to the wok or sauté pan and heat over medium heat. When the oil is hot, add the cabbage, mushrooms, and green onions. Sauté the vegetables until they begin to soften, about 3 minutes. Add the garlic, ginger, and 1/2 teaspoon salt and continue to cook until the garlic and ginger are fragrant, about 1 minute more. Transfer the cabbage mixture to the bowl containing the eggs.

Reheat the wok or sauté pan and add the remaining 2 tablespoons oil to the pan over medium heat. When the oil is hot, add the duck mixture and stir-fry until the duck is almost cooked, about 2 minutes. Return the cabbage and eggs to the wok or sauté pan along with the chicken stock, remaining 2 tablespoons sherry, remaining 2 tablespoons soy sauce, sesame oil, brown sugar, chili sauce, remaining 1/2 teaspoon salt,

4 green onions, thinly sliced

2 cloves garlic, minced

1 tablespoon minced fresh ginger

1/4 cup chicken stock

1 tablespoon Asian (dark) sesame oil

1 teaspoon brown sugar

1/2 teaspoon Chinese chili sauce

Freshly ground black pepper to taste

1 tablespoon cornstarch mixed with 2 tablespoons water

1/2 cup hoisin sauce, for serving

and pepper to taste. When the sauce boils, add the cornstarch mixture and cook until the sauce thickens, another minute or so longer. Remove the duck mixture from the pan and transfer it to a heated platter.

Arrange the platter of filling, crêpes, and hoisin sauce on the table or kitchen counter and let your guests make their own mu shu.

Make-ahead: *You can freeze the crêpes for up to 1 month or hold them in the refrigerator for up to 2 days. Separate them with layers of parchment or wax paper to make peeling them apart easier, cover with plastic wrap, and, if freezing, cover with a layer of aluminum foil.*

makes thirty-six pieces

Lavash with Feta, Sun-Dried Tomatoes, Olives, and Radish Sprouts

ingredients

- *2/3 cup crumbled feta cheese*
- *1/3 cup chopped oil-packed sun-dried tomatoes*
- *1/4 cup pine nuts*
- *3 tablespoons oil from the tomatoes*
- *10 kalamata olives, chopped*
- *1/8 teaspoon freshly ground black pepper*
- *2 lavash wraps, tomato or spinach or a combination, cut in half crosswise to make four 12-by-12-inch squares*
- *1 cup radish sprouts, divided*

All kinds of sprouts can now be found in most grocery stores. Radish sprouts have a peppery bite that complements the bold Mediterranean flavors in this wrap. The feta cheese filling is also good as a spread on crackers.

In a medium bowl, combine the feta cheese, sun-dried tomatoes, pine nuts, oil from the tomatoes, olives, and pepper. Mash the ingredients together to make a paste.

Place 1 lavash square on a work surface. Spread the lavash with about 1/4 cup of the cheese mixture. Top with 1/4 cup of the sprouts.

Starting with one of the short ends, roll the lavash up jelly-roll style. Repeat with the remaining lavash. Wrap each roll tightly in plastic wrap and place in the refrigerator for at least 30 minutes.

To serve, slice each roll crosswise into 9 pieces. Transfer the pinwheels to a serving platter. Serve cold or at room temperature.

Make-ahead: *The rolls can be kept, unsliced and wrapped in plastic, in the refrigerator overnight.*

makes thirty pieces

Brie and Pear Quesadillas

ingredients

3 pears, peeled, halved, and cored

1 large yellow onion, halved and cut into thin slices

4 tablespoons unsalted butter

4 tablespoons oil

10 flour tortillas

3 poblano chiles, roasted, peeled, and sliced into thin strips

8 ounces Brie, thinly sliced

Salt and freshly ground black pepper to taste

When you team up pears and chiles with rich, buttery Brie, you've created an untraditional, savory, but slightly sweet take on a south of the border classic. Roasting poblano chiles gives them a totally different flavor—not so green, but smoky and deep—while roasting the pears gives them a concentrated sweetness.

Preheat the oven to 400°F.

Arrange the pears, cut side down, on a baking sheet lined with parchment. Roast the pears in the oven until they soften and dry on the outside, about 20 minutes. Remove from the oven and let cool. Slice thinly.

Meanwhile, bring 3 cups water to a boil in a medium skillet. Add the onions, cover, and remove from the heat. Let stand until the onions wilt, about 12 minutes. Drain completely and pat dry on paper towels.

Heat a nonstick or well-seasoned skillet over medium heat and add 1 teaspoon butter and 1 teaspoon oil to the pan. Place 1 of the tortillas in the pan and quickly top with some of the onion, chile, Brie, pear, and then more Brie on top. Be careful not to overfill, or it will be impossible to turn the quesadilla in the pan. Sprinkle with salt and pepper, and then top with another tortilla. Turn the heat down to low and cook the quesadilla until it is lightly browned on the bottom. Using a wide spatula and your hand, turn the quesadilla to brown the other side. (Once turned, the cheese will begin to melt and act like glue to make the quesadilla stick together.)

Repeat with the remaining tortillas and fillings. Cut each quesadilla into 6 wedges. Serve warm.

Make-ahead: *The uncooked quesadillas can be assembled 8 hours ahead of time and kept, covered, in the refrigerator. Once the quesadillas are cooked, they can be kept in a 200°F oven for 1 hour. Slice right before serving.*

makes about forty-five small dumplings

Pan-Fried Salmon Shiu Mai with Mango Relish

shiu mai

1 medium carrot, peeled and trimmed

One 1-inch piece fresh ginger, peeled

1 clove garlic, peeled

1 pound salmon, boned and skinned

2 tablespoons chopped fresh chives

1 egg white, beaten

2 tablespoons oyster sauce

2 teaspoons dry sherry

2 teaspoons Asian (dark) sesame oil

1 teaspoon soy sauce

½ teaspoon salt

⅛ teaspoon ground Szechwan pepper or freshly ground black pepper

45 wonton wrappers, trimmed into circles using a 3- to 4-inch round cutter

Of all the Chinese dumplings, these are by far the easiest to make. The filling can be made in the food processor a day ahead, and the wrapper needs no special sealing, pleating, or folding. We think the best plan is to have all the ingredients ready to go and to involve your guests in the production of these tasty bundles. A quick pan-fry is all it needs, and you will be rewarded with a substantial appetizer that goes well with soups or other lighter main-course offerings.

Grate the carrot, ginger, and garlic in a food processor or using a box grater. Add the salmon to the bowl of the food processor and chop roughly. Avoid mincing the salmon so finely that it turns to paste. If you don't have a food processor, chop the salmon finely with a knife and combine with the grated carrot mixture. Place the salmon mixture in a medium bowl and combine with the chives, egg white, oyster sauce, sherry, sesame oil, soy sauce, salt, and pepper. Mix to combine the ingredients thoroughly. The filling can be used immediately or refrigerated for up to 3 hours.

To make the shiu mai: Place 1 tablespoon of the filling in the center of each wonton wrapper. Bring the edges of the wrapper up around the sides of the filling. Hold the dumpling in one hand and wrap your thumb and index finger around the sides, squeezing gently. Tamp down the top to compress the filling lightly, then press the bottom of the dumpling on a work surface to flatten it and make the shiu mai stand up. It should look like a round cylinder with an open flat top and bottom. Place the filled dumplings on a parchment-lined baking sheet.

To make the relish: Combine the mango, vinegar, wine, sugar, salt, and chili sauce in a small bowl. Stir to combine.

mango relish

1 mango, peeled, pitted, and finely diced

1/4 cup rice vinegar

1/4 cup dry white wine

2 tablespoons sugar

1/4 teaspoon salt

1/4 to 1/2 teaspoon Chinese chili sauce, or to taste

2 tablespoons vegetable oil, or enough to cover the surface of your skillet

To fry the shiu mai: Heat a large, nonstick frying pan over medium-high heat and add the vegetable oil. When it is hot, add the dumplings to the pan, bottoms down, and fry them until the bottoms are brown, about 2 minutes. Add the mango relish and quickly cover the pan. Cook the dumplings until they are firm, another 2 minutes. Remove the lid and continue to cook the dumplings until the relish is thick and the bottoms of the shiu mai are dark, about 1 minute. Carefully remove the shiu mai to serving plates and serve hot.

Make-ahead: *The uncooked dumplings can be arranged on a parchment-lined baking sheet and refrigerated, uncovered, for up to 2 hours.*

Tip: *Sometimes the shiu mai filling will pop out of its skin. Try not to agitate them too much when cooking. These are best eaten with chopsticks, right off the serving dish.*

serves six

Wonton Ravioli with Butternut Squash and Sage Cream Sauce

ingredients

- *1 butternut squash, halved and seeded*
- *1 tablespoon olive oil*
- *1 tablespoon plus 3/4 teaspoon salt, divided, plus more for seasoning*
- *1/8 teaspoon freshly ground black pepper, plus more for seasoning*
- *3 tablespoons unsalted butter*
- *1 medium onion, cut into small dice*
- *2 cloves garlic, minced*
- *1 tablespoon minced fresh sage*
- *1/4 teaspoon ground nutmeg, divided*
- *48 wonton wrappers*
- *1 egg white, beaten*
- *4 tablespoons unsalted butter*
- *18 fresh sage leaves, stemmed*
- *1 cup heavy cream*
- *1/2 teaspoon cider vinegar*

Don't think of these tender ravioli filled with butternut squash and sage as only a fall first course, since butternut squash can be purchased year round. Wonton wrappers make these rich ravioli a cinch to assemble, which is a good thing because your family and friends will clamor for them again and again. Even those who aren't fans of sage will like these ravioli fried in butter, and the cream sauce is as easy as 1, 2, 3.

Preheat the oven to 375°F.

Rub the cut side of the squash with the olive oil, and sprinkle it with a little salt and pepper. Lay the squash on a parchment-lined baking pan, cut side down, and bake until tender when pierced with a knife, about 40 minutes. Remove the squash from the oven and let it rest in the pan until it is cool enough to handle. Scoop out the flesh from the shell. Reserve.

Heat a large skillet over medium heat and add the butter. When the butter is melted and hot, add the onion to the pan and sauté until it is translucent, about 2 minutes. Add the garlic and continue to cook until the onion is soft, about 2 minutes. Add the sage and 1/2 teaspoon of the salt and continue to cook over medium-low heat for about 2 minutes longer. Add the cooked squash along with 1/8 teaspoon of the nutmeg and 1/8 teaspoon black pepper, and mix to combine well. Cook over medium-low heat until some of the water has cooked out of the squash and it is thickened slightly, about 10 minutes. Taste for seasoning and adjust with salt and pepper.

Lay a wonton wrapper on a work surface (keeping the rest covered so they don't dry out) and place a heaping teaspoon of the squash mixture in the middle. Brush the edges with the egg white to create a seal, and top the squash with another wonton wrapper. Seal the edges, working from the inside edge of the filling out to the edge of the wonton wrapper to rid it of air pockets, which will swell when heated and cause your ravioli to burst. Continue to make ravioli with the remaining wonton wrappers and filling. (You may have some leftover filling.) The wontons will keep, lightly covered on a parchment-lined baking pan in the refrigerator, for up to 4 hours.

Bring a large pot of water (1 gallon) to a boil.

Heat a large skillet over medium heat, and add the butter. When the butter is melted and hot, add the sage leaves and fry them in the butter until they are crisp, about 2 minutes. Transfer the sage leaves to a paper towel–lined plate, and add the heavy cream to the sage butter in the skillet. Boil the cream until it has reduced and becomes thick, about 3 minutes. Add the vinegar, remaining 1/8 teaspoon nutmeg, 1/4 teaspoon salt, and pepper to taste. If making the sauce ahead, turn off the heat and let it sit for up to 30 minutes. (You may need to add a tablespoon or so of water to thin the sauce, as it will thicken as it sits.) Reheat before adding the cooked wontons.

Add 1 tablespoon salt to the boiling water, and add the ravioli. Cook until they float to the surface, about 2 minutes. Carefully drain the ravioli and add them to the cream sauce. Toss to coat with the sauce, and transfer to heated serving plates. Garnish with the fried sage leaves, and serve hot.

Make-ahead: *The uncooked wontons can be frozen in a single layer on a parchment-lined baking pan. When frozen firm, they can be stored in freezer bags in the freezer for up to 2 months. They can be cooked directly from the freezer, adding a minute to the cooking time.*

makes ten rolls

Spicy Red Curry Beef Summer Rolls

marinade

- 2 tablespoons Asian fish sauce
- 6 tablespoons rice vinegar
- 3 tablespoons sugar
- 2 tablespoons vegetable oil
- 2 tablespoons Thai red curry paste

- 1 to 1¼ pounds skirt steak or flank steak

rolls

- 3 ounces rice-stick vermicelli noodles
- Ten 8-inch rice-paper rounds, plus additional in case some tear
- 60 fresh cilantro leaves (from about 1 bunch)
- 60 fresh mint leaves (from about 1 bunch)
- 1 medium seedless cucumber, peeled, cored, and cut into ⅛-inch matchsticks
- 3 green onions, cut into 3-inch julienne strips

- Spicy Thai Dipping Sauce (page 271), for serving

Summer rolls are a light and fresh alternative to the fried spring roll. They're made with rice paper rounds, which are found in Asian markets. When you take them out of the package, these rounds feel like disks of hard plastic, but after being soaked briefly in warm water, they become pliable and are easy to roll up around a filling. The result is a soft, slightly transparent roll filled with tender noodles, crisp vegetables, and, in this case, flavorful grilled flank steak. The contrast in flavors and textures makes for an exciting kickoff to any Asian meal.

To make the marinade: In a medium bowl, whisk together the fish sauce, rice vinegar, sugar, and vegetable oil. Remove ¼ cup of this mixture and set aside. Add the red curry paste and continue to whisk until smooth.

In a large, resealable plastic bag, combine the marinade and steak and seal the bag, pressing out the excess air. Marinate in the refrigerator, turning once or twice, for at least 4 hours or overnight.

When you are ready to make the rolls, in a large bowl soak the rice-stick vermicelli in hot water to cover until softened and pliable, about 15 minutes.

Prepare a grill or preheat the broiler.

Discard the marinade and grill the steak on an oiled rack set 5 to 6 inches over glowing coals, about 5 minutes on each side for medium-rare. (Alternatively, broil the steak on the rack of a broiler pan about 3 inches from the heat for about the same amount of time.) Transfer to a cutting board and let rest for 10 minutes.

Drain the noodles in a colander, then rinse under cold running water and drain well again. Place the noodles in a medium bowl, add the ¼ cup reserved marinade, and toss to coat.

Thinly slice the steak on the diagonal.

Put a double thickness of paper towel on a work surface, and fill a shallow baking pan with warm water. Check the rice-paper rounds and use only those that have no holes. Soak 1 round in warm water until pliable, 30 seconds to 1 minute. Carefully transfer to the paper towels.

Arrange 3 cilantro leaves and 3 mint leaves across the bottom third (the part nearest you) of the soaked rice paper. Top with 1 slice of steak. Spread 1/4 cup noodles on top of the steak and arrange 8 cucumber matchsticks and 6 green onion strips on top of the noodles. Fold the bottom of the rice paper over the filling and begin rolling it up tightly, stopping at the halfway point. Arrange 3 more mint leaves and 3 more cilantro leaves along the crease, then fold in the ends and continue rolling. Transfer the summer roll, seam side down, to a plate and cover with dampened paper towels. Make 9 more rolls in the same manner and serve, whole or halved diagonally, with the dipping sauce.

Make-ahead: *The summer rolls can be made 4 hours ahead and chilled, covered with lightly dampened paper towels and then with plastic wrap. Let them sit at room temperature for 30 minutes before serving.*

makes sixty mini rolls or eight large rolls

Shrimp Egg Rolls with Chili Sauce

chili sauce

- 1 cup Asian sweet chili sauce (brands vary, so make adjustments to taste)
- 1 tablespoon Asian fish sauce
- 1 tablespoon rice vinegar
- 1 tablespoon chopped fresh cilantro
- 1 clove garlic, minced
- 1 teaspoon grated fresh ginger
- 1 teaspoon minced seeded serrano chile

egg rolls

- 1½ pounds shrimp, peeled and deveined
- ½ cup coarsely chopped fresh cilantro
- ½ teaspoon salt
- 15 spring roll wrappers, quartered if making mini rolls, or 8 spring roll wrappers if making large rolls
- 1 tablespoon water, in a small cup
- About 1 cup vegetable oil

The flavors of Asian sweet chili sauce and fresh shrimp really dominate this finger-friendly appetizer. Your guests will be eternally grateful for the ease with which they can be grabbed, dunked in the sauce, and gobbled up.

To make the chili sauce: Combine the chili sauce, fish sauce, rice vinegar, cilantro, garlic, ginger, and chile in a bowl and stir to combine. Cover and refrigerate until needed.

To make the egg rolls: Combine the shrimp, cilantro, and salt in the bowl of a food processor. Pulse the mixture until it is chopped to ½-inch pieces, about 8 pulses.

Place a spring roll wrapper on a work surface with a point facing you. Keep the remaining wrappers covered with plastic wrap while you are working, to keep them from drying out. Arrange a teaspoon of the shrimp mixture across the wrapper (if making large rolls, use 2 tablespoons filling), fold up the point end to cover, and fold in the pointed sides to enclose the shrimp. Roll up as tightly as possible. Dip a finger into the water and run it along the open pointed end. Continue to roll tightly, and seal. Transfer the egg roll, seam side down, to a parchment-lined baking sheet. Make more egg rolls in the same manner.

Heat 2 inches of oil in a heavy skillet over medium-high heat until hot but not smoking. Fry 4 or 5 small egg rolls (or 2 large ones) until golden, about 1 minute, and turn to fry the other side, about 1 minute. Transfer to paper towels to drain. Fry the remaining egg rolls in the same manner. Serve hot with the chili sauce.

Make-ahead: *The uncooked egg rolls can be assembled and kept in a single layer on a baking sheet, covered and refrigerated, for up to 8 hours. The cooked rolls can be kept hot in a 200°F oven for up to 1 hour. Chile sauce can be made 2 days ahead.*

makes ten rolls

Vietnamese-Style Chicken Salad Rolls

ingredients

3 ounces rice-stick vermicelli noodles

3 tablespoons rice vinegar

1 tablespoon Asian fish sauce

1 tablespoon sugar

2 cups shredded cooked chicken

2 cups peeled and coarsely shredded carrots

2 cups shredded napa cabbage

1/4 cup (loosely packed) coarsely chopped fresh basil (preferably Thai)

1/4 cup (loosely packed) coarsely chopped fresh mint

1/4 cup (loosely packed) coarsely chopped fresh cilantro

Ten 8-inch rice-paper rounds, plus additional in case some tear

Thai Peanut Dip or Sauce (page 272), for serving

Because these rolls are so fresh and light, they are the perfect foil for the richness of the peanut sauce. If you're planning a low-cal affair, feel free to substitute Spicy Thai Dipping Sauce for the peanut sauce. It will still give you lots of flavor, but with less fat.

In a large bowl, soak the rice-stick vermicelli in hot water to cover until softened and pliable, about 15 minutes. Drain in a colander, rinse under cold running water, and drain well again.

In a small bowl, whisk together the rice vinegar, fish sauce, and sugar until the sugar is dissolved.

Place the vermicelli in a nonreactive salad bowl with the chicken, carrots, cabbage, basil, mint, cilantro, and rice vinegar mixture. Toss to combine.

Put a double thickness of paper towel on a work surface, and fill a shallow baking pan with warm water. Check the rice-paper rounds and use only those that have no holes. Soak 1 round in warm water until pliable, 30 seconds to 1 minute. Carefully transfer to the paper towels.

Place 1/2 cup filling across the bottom third (the part nearest you) of the soaked rice paper. Fold the bottom of the rice paper over the filling and begin rolling it up tightly, stopping at the halfway point. Fold in the ends and continue rolling. Transfer the salad roll, seam side down, to a plate and cover with dampened paper towels. Make 9 more rolls in same manner.

To serve, cut the rolls in half crosswise; stand the pieces upright. Serve with the peanut sauce.

Make-ahead: *The salad rolls can be made 4 hours ahead and chilled, covered with lightly dampened paper towels and then with plastic wrap. Let them sit at room temperature for 30 minutes before serving.*

makes thirty-six pieces

Lavash Pinwheels with Curried Cream Cheese, Ham, and Spinach

ingredients

- *8 ounces cream cheese, at room temperature*
- *1 teaspoon curry powder*
- *1 tablespoon fresh lemon juice*
- *1/2 cup chopped roasted cashews*
- *1/3 cup golden raisins*
- *Four 10-by-9-inch sheets Middle Eastern–style soft flatbread such as lavash, or four 8- to 9-inch flour tortillas*
- *8 thin slices cooked ham*
- *32 baby spinach leaves*

Meredith's favorite meal as a child was her grandmother's decidedly unauthentic version of Indian chicken curry. The meat and sauce were ladled over rice and served with a dizzying array of garnishes, which, frankly, was the best thing about the dish. Those garnishes always included golden raisins and roasted cashews, which gave the dish flavor and texture and were the inspiration for these pinwheels.

In a medium bowl, mix together the cream cheese, curry powder, and lemon juice. Stir in the cashews and raisins.

Lay the lavash out on a work surface. Place 1/3 cup of the cream cheese mixture on each piece of lavash, spreading it out in a thin layer that covers the lavash completely.

Place 2 slices of ham crosswise down the middle of each lavash, and then lay 8 spinach leaves down the middle of the ham.

Starting with one of the short ends, roll the lavash up jelly-roll style. Repeat with the remaining lavash. Wrap each roll tightly in plastic wrap and place in the refrigerator for at least 30 minutes or up to 8 hours.

To serve, slice each roll crosswise into 9 pieces. Transfer the pinwheels to a serving platter. Serve cold or at room temperature.

Make-ahead: *The rolls can be kept, unsliced and wrapped in plastic, in the refrigerator overnight.*

serves six

Sweet Potato and Goat Cheese Wonton Ravioli with a Brown Butter, Sage, and Pecan Sauce

ravioli

- 1 sweet potato, about 1 pound
- 1 tablespoon light brown sugar
- 2 tablespoons unsalted butter, at room temperature
- ¼ teaspoon salt
- Pinch of freshly grated nutmeg
- One 12-ounce package wonton wrappers
- 4 ounces goat cheese, softened
- 1 egg white, beaten until frothy

sauce

- 6 tablespoons unsalted butter
- 1 tablespoon fresh lemon juice
- 8 large fresh sage leaves, thinly sliced
- Salt and freshly ground black pepper to taste
- ¼ cup chopped toasted pecans
- 2 tablespoons salt

Fresh sage leaves, for garnish

This dish is impressive anytime, but the combination of sweet potatoes and pecans offers a fun alternative as a starter for the traditional Thanksgiving table.

To make the ravioli: Preheat the oven to 425°F. Oil a rimmed baking sheet. Cut the sweet potato in half and lay it, cut side down, on the baking sheet. Roast until a sharp knife easily slides in and out of the potato, about 40 minutes.

When the potato is just cool enough to handle, scoop the pulp into a food processor. Add the brown sugar, butter, salt, and nutmeg and pulse until the sweet potato is a smooth purée. This step can be done a day ahead, and the filling covered and chilled in the refrigerator.

Lay a wonton wrapper on a work surface, and place 1 teaspoon of the sweet potato filling and ½ teaspoon of the goat cheese in the center of the wonton. Brush the edges with the egg white to create a seal, and top with a second wonton wrapper. Seal the edges, working from the inside edge of the filling out to the edge to rid it of air pockets, which will swell when heated and cause your ravioli to burst. Continue to make ravioli with the remaining wonton wrappers and filling. The ravioli will keep, lightly covered, on a parchment-lined baking pan in the refrigerator for up to 4 hours.

Bring a large pot of water (1 gallon) to a boil.

To make the sauce: Melt the butter in a large skillet over medium heat, and continue to cook until it begins to turn light brown. Add the lemon juice and sage. Season the sauce with salt and pepper. Remove from the heat. Add the pecans and taste to correct the seasoning. (Be careful: The sauce will be tongue-searing hot.)

Add the salt to the boiling water and add the ravioli. Cook until they float to the surface, about 2 minutes. Carefully remove the ravioli with a large slotted spoon or small strainer, and add them to the sauce. When all the ravioli are cooked and in the pan, gently turn them in the sauce to coat. Serve immediately. Garnish with fresh sage leaves.

Make-ahead: *The uncooked ravioli can be frozen in a single layer on a parchment-lined baking pan. When frozen firm, store them in freezer bags in the freezer for up to 2 months. Cook directly from the freezer, adding a minute to the cooking time.*

makes twelve wraps

Lettuce Wrap with Thai-Style Ground Pork Salad (Larb)

Thai cuisine is filled with big, bold flavors, and this meat salad is a perfect example. Cooked ground pork and fragrant lemongrass are tossed with a simple but intensely flavorful dressing and wrapped up taco-style in a lettuce leaf. The toasted rice powder is a traditional Thai and Vietnamese garnish for salads.

toasted rice powder

3 tablespoons raw rice

dressing

1/3 cup fresh lime juice

3 tablespoons Asian fish sauce

1 tablespoon light brown sugar

3/4 teaspoon cayenne pepper

salad

1 pound ground pork

1/2 cup thinly sliced green onions

1/4 cup very thinly sliced tender inner stalk of fresh lemongrass

1/2 cup coarsely chopped peanuts

1/4 cup chopped fresh mint

1/4 cup chopped fresh cilantro

12 leaves Boston lettuce, washed

To make the toasted rice powder: Sauté the rice for 3 minutes in a small skillet over medium-high heat, shaking the pan so the rice colors evenly to a toasty light brown. Let the rice cool, and then grind it in a spice grinder to a sandy powder.

To make the dressing: Mix the lime juice, fish sauce, brown sugar, and cayenne in a medium bowl, stirring until the sugar is dissolved.

To make the salad: In a saucepan, cover the pork with water. Simmer about 10 minutes until all the pink is gone, stirring to break up any lumps. Remove and drain. Mix the pork with the dressing. Add the toasted rice powder, green onions, lemongrass, peanuts, mint, and cilantro.

To assemble: Spoon the salad onto the lettuce leaves, and serve. The wraps are eaten in taco fashion. Lots of napkins may be necessary.

Make-ahead: *The salad can be made, without the rice powder, up to 4 hours ahead and kept, covered, in the refrigerator. Add the rice powder and spoon into the lettuce leaves just before serving.*

Tip: *When working with fresh lemongrass, it's important to use the tender part of the inner stalk. At the root end of each stalk is a woody center that is too chewy to eat. The tender, more palatable part of the lemongrass is above this solid core. When you trim the root end, you should be able to see rings. If you still see a woody center, you're not far enough up the stalk. Once you trim the root end, you should have about 6 inches of tender stalk before the stalk becomes too tough again.*

makes forty pieces

Oven-Baked Chipotle Chicken Flautas

ingredients

3 pounds bone-in chicken breasts

2 teaspoons salt, divided

2 tablespoons vegetable oil, plus more for brushing

3/4 cup finely chopped onion

2 cloves garlic, chopped

2 canned chipotle chiles in adobo sauce, chopped

1 cup tomato sauce

20 small flour tortillas

Guacamole (page 265), for serving

It's not necessary to deep-fry these smoky, spicy, Southwestern taquito-like rolls to bring out their crunch. A light brushing of oil and some time in a hot oven will do the trick and eliminate a great deal of mess too!

In a large pot, cover the chicken breasts with water and bring to a simmer. Add 1 teaspoon of the salt and poach the chicken until firm to the touch, about 20 minutes. Remove the pan from the heat, uncover, and let the chicken cool in the liquid for 30 minutes. Remove the chicken from the pot and cool. Pull the chicken meat apart into small shredded pieces.

Preheat the oven to 450°F. In a large skillet, heat 2 tablespoons oil over medium heat. Add the onion and sauté until it begins to brown, about 5 minutes. Add the garlic and continue to cook for another 2 minutes. Add the chipotle and tomato sauce and continue to cook for 1 minute. Add the chicken and stir to coat. Stir in the remaining teaspoon of salt. Remove from the heat.

Place 1/3 cup of the chicken filling along the middle of a tortilla. Roll the tortilla up and put a toothpick through the middle of the flauta to hold it in place. Once rolled, place the flauta on a large baking sheet. Repeat with the remaining tortillas. Lightly brush the flautas with vegetable oil. Bake until golden brown, about 12 minutes. Allow to cool for 5 minutes. Remove the toothpicks and slice each flauta in half on the diagonal. Transfer to a serving platter and serve with guacamole for dipping.

Make-ahead: *The filling can be made 2 days ahead and kept, covered, in the refrigerator. The flautas can be formed, placed on a baking sheet, and kept, covered, in the refrigerator for up to 8 hours.*

makes about sixty dumplings

Spicy Pork Dumplings with Spicy Thai Dipping Sauce

ingredients

1 pound ground pork

¼ cup minced green onions

One 5-ounce can water chestnuts, drained and minced

1 tablespoon minced fresh ginger

2 cloves garlic, minced

½ teaspoon crushed red pepper flakes

1½ tablespoons soy sauce

2 teaspoons sugar

2 tablespoons chopped fresh cilantro

60 wonton wrappers, thawed if frozen

1 egg, lightly beaten

3 tablespoons vegetable oil, divided

Spicy Thai Dipping Sauce (page 271), for serving

The technique for making these little packages does not take intricate handwork. Anyone can do it, which makes them perfect for a party when guests like to get in on the action. Make your filling ahead of time, clear a large workspace, hand your friends a glass of wine, and set them to work. Before you know it, you will have dumplings for everyone, with very little effort on your part.

In a large bowl, use your hands to combine the pork, green onions, water chestnuts, ginger, garlic, red pepper flakes, soy sauce, sugar, and cilantro.

Place the bowl of filling, the wonton wrappers, a saucer with the beaten egg, and a pastry brush on a clean work surface. Have a lightly oiled cookie sheet nearby to hold the dumplings.

Place a scant tablespoon of the filling in the center of each wonton. Brush the beaten egg around the edges of the wrapper. Gather up the corners of the wrapper and pinch them together around the top to form a little square package. Make sure all the edges are sealed. Continue to make dumplings until the filling is used up. Space them on a large cookie sheet, making sure they don't touch.

In a large sauté pan with a lid, heat 1 tablespoon of the oil over medium-high heat. Place one-third of the dumplings in the pan so they aren't touching, and sauté until they are nicely browned on the bottom. Add ½ cup water to the pan and steam the dumplings, covered, until the pork is cooked through, about 3 minutes. Repeat the process with the remaining oil and dumplings.

Place the cooked dumplings on a warm platter and serve with the sauce.

Make-ahead: *The filling can be made 8 hours ahead and kept, covered, in the refrigerator. The dumplings can be made up to 1 month ahead. Freeze them in a single layer on a baking sheet, and then transfer to a freezer bag. Cook directly from the freezer, adding a few minutes to the cooking time.*

makes about sixty dumplings

Gyoza

ingredients

- *1 pound ground pork*
- *1 cup finely chopped cabbage*
- *1 clove garlic, minced*
- *½ cup finely chopped green onion*
- *2 teaspoons Asian (dark) sesame oil*
- *1 tablespoon dry sherry*
- *2 tablespoons soy sauce*
- *1 tablespoon finely minced fresh ginger*
- *60 gyoza or wonton wrappers*
- *3 tablespoons vegetable oil, divided*

Sesame-Soy Dipping Sauce (page 273), for serving

These ginger-infused dumplings make a great start to any Asian meal. They can be made well in advance and brought right from the freezer to the pan for a seemingly effortless first course.

Combine the pork, cabbage, garlic, green onion, sesame oil, sherry, soy sauce, and ginger in a bowl. Mix all ingredients well, using your hands.

Place 1 rounded teaspoon of filling in the center of each gyoza wrapper; moisten the edges with water, and bring the sides of the wrapper up like a taco. Slightly pleat the outside ends of the dumpling in and together. To close the dumpling, make 3 additional pleats across the top. Place on a baking sheet and repeat the process with the remaining filling and wrappers. Space them on a large cookie sheet, making sure they don't touch.

In a large sauté pan with a lid, heat 1 tablespoon of the oil over medium-high heat. Place one-third of the dumplings in the pan so they aren't touching, and sauté until they are nicely browned on the bottom. Add ½ cup water to the pan and steam the dumplings, covered, until the pork is cooked through, about 3 minutes. Repeat the process with the remaining oil and dumplings.

Place the cooked dumplings on a warm platter and serve with the sauce.

Make-ahead: *The filling can be made 8 hours ahead and kept, covered, in the refrigerator. The dumplings can be made up to 1 month ahead. Freeze them in a single layer on a baking sheet, and then transfer to a freezer bag. Cook directly from the freezer, adding a few minutes to the cooking time.*

Tip: *Gyoza wrappers are traditionally round. If using wonton wrappers, you can cut them with a 3-inch round cookie or biscuit cutter before filling, or you can form them as described in the Spicy Pork Dumplings recipe (page 72).*

makes thirty-six pieces

California Roll

ingredients

- *1 avocado, halved lengthwise, pitted, peeled, and cut lengthwise into ½-inch-thick slices*
- *1 tablespoon fresh lemon juice*
- *Six 8-by-7-inch sheets nori (toasted dried seaweed)*
- *4½ cups Basic Sushi Rice (page 336)*
- *2 tablespoons wasabi paste*
- *2 frozen Alaska king crab legs, thawed, shelled, and thick sections halved lengthwise, or 12 ounces frozen Alaska king crabmeat, thawed and drained*
- *½ cucumber, peeled and cut into matchsticks*

- *Soy sauce, for serving*
- *Wasabi paste, for serving*
- *Sliced pickled ginger, for serving*

Sushi chefs really are artists. It's beautiful to watch a skilled sushi chef wield a knife as he or she delicately cuts paper-thin slices of tuna. But not all sushi requires the mastery of a sushi chef. California roll, although an American sushi bar favorite, can be accomplished easily by the home chef.

In a small bowl, toss the avocado gently with the lemon juice.

Lay a bamboo mat (used for rolling sushi and other foods) on a work surface so that the slats run horizontally. Put a piece of the nori on the mat with a long side facing you, and with dampened hands spread ¾ cup sushi rice onto it, leaving a 1½-inch border along the top edge. Spread 1 teaspoon of the wasabi paste horizontally across the center of the rice. Arrange 3 avocado slices, overlapping slightly, in a horizontal line over the wasabi paste, and top them with one sixth of the crab meat, and one sixth of the cucumber. Grasp the edge of the nori closest to you. Lift the nori and the mat slightly, and roll the nori evenly and tightly away from you, pressing down slightly with each quarter turn. Seal the roll with a drop of water on the far edge of the nori, press the seam closed, and transfer the roll to a cutting board. Repeat with the remaining ingredients.

With a serrated knife dipped in hot water, trim the ends of the rolls, and cut each roll crosswise into six 1-inch sections.

Arrange the rolls, cut side up, decoratively on a platter, and serve them with soy sauce, wasabi paste, and pickled ginger on the side.

makes twenty-four pieces

Spicy Tuna Rolls

ingredients

3 tablespoons mayonnaise

1½ tablespoons Asian chili paste

½ teaspoon Asian chili oil

½ teaspoon Asian (dark) sesame oil

8 ounces sushi-quality fresh tuna, diced

Four 8-by-7-inch sheets nori (toasted dried seaweed)

3 cups Basic Sushi Rice (page 336)

Soy sauce, for serving

Wasabi paste, for serving

Sliced pickled ginger, for serving

Just because you don't see sushi-grade tuna on display at your local fish market doesn't mean it's not there. Most good fish markets will sell sushi- or sashimi-grade tuna that has been flash frozen almost immediately after being caught, and they'll keep it frozen until purchased. As always with fish, it's important to know your fish market, so do a little investigating to make sure you're buying the best-quality fish available.

In a small bowl, mix together the mayonnaise, chili paste, chili oil, and sesame oil. Add the tuna and toss to coat.

Lay a bamboo mat (used for rolling sushi and other foods) on a work surface so that the slats run horizontally. Put a piece of the nori on the mat with a long side facing you, and with dampened hands spread ¾ cup sushi rice onto it, leaving a 1-inch border along the top edge. Lay one fourth of the spicy tuna in a row, horizontally across the center of the rice. Grasp the edge of the nori closest to you. Lift the nori and the mat slightly, and roll the nori evenly and tightly away from you, pressing down slightly with each quarter turn. Seal the roll with a drop of water on the far edge of the nori, press the seam closed, and transfer the roll to a cutting board. Repeat with the remaining ingredients.

With a serrated knife dipped in hot water, trim the ends of the rolls and cut each roll crosswise into six 1-inch sections.

Arrange the rolls, cut side up, decoratively on a platter and serve them with the soy sauce, wasabi paste, and pickled ginger on the side.

makes twenty-four pieces

Cucumber, Carrot, and Wasabi Mayo Rolls

ingredients

1/4 cup mayonnaise

1 tablespoon wasabi paste

Four 8-by-7-inch sheets nori (toasted dried seaweed)

3 cups Basic Sushi Rice (page 336)

1/2 medium cucumber, peeled, seeded, and cut into matchsticks

1 medium carrot, peeled and cut into matchsticks

Soy sauce, for serving

Wasabi paste, for serving

Sliced pickled ginger, for serving

Vegetarian sushi rolls are always a welcome addition to any sushi party. They can make an easily accessible entry into sushi, even for your meat-loving friends. Here we've used cucumber and carrot, but feel free to use your imagination where fillings are concerned. Try a mango roll or a guacamole roll. They may turn out to be your favorites.

In a small bowl, mix together the mayonnaise and wasabi paste.

Lay a bamboo mat (used for rolling sushi and other foods) on a work surface so that the slats run horizontally. Put a piece of the nori on the mat with a long side facing you, and with dampened hands spread 3/4 cup sushi rice onto it, leaving a 1-inch border along the top edge. Spread 1 tablespoon of the wasabi mayonnaise horizontally across the center of the rice. Arrange one fourth of the cucumber and one fourth of the carrot in a horizontal line on top of the wasabi paste. Grasp the edge of the nori closest to you. Lift the nori and the mat slightly, and roll the nori evenly and tightly away from you, pressing down slightly with each quarter turn. Seal the roll with a drop of water on the far edge of the nori, press the seam closed, and transfer the roll to a cutting board. Repeat with the remaining ingredients.

With a serrated knife dipped in hot water, trim the ends of the rolls and cut each roll crosswise into six 1-inch sections.

Arrange the rolls, cut side up, decoratively on a platter and serve them with the soy sauce, wasabi paste, and pickled ginger on the side.

makes thirty-six pieces

Crispy Reuben Roll-Ups

russian dressing

½ cup mayonnaise

⅓ cup ketchup

¼ cup minced green onions

2 tablespoons chopped drained capers

reuben

1 medium onion, diced

1 tablespoon vegetable oil, plus extra for brushing tortillas

8 ounces (1 cup) rinsed and drained sauerkraut

6 large flour tortillas

1½ cups grated Swiss cheese

12 ounces pastrami, thinly sliced

We confess that when we came up with the idea for this recipe to round out one of our appetizer classes, we rolled our eyes just a little bit. We were concerned that our students would find this recipe too easy and perhaps a bit unsophisticated. Much to our surprise, it was the hit of the class. They loved the simplicity and the familiar flavors wrapped up in a brand new package.

To make the Russian dressing: In a small bowl, combine the mayonnaise, ketchup, green onions, and capers. Chill until needed.

Preheat the oven to 400°F.

In sauté pan, sauté the onion in 1 tablespoon oil until lightly browned, about 5 minutes. Add the drained sauerkraut and cook for another 2 minutes. Lay the tortillas out on a large work surface. Spread each tortilla with ¼ cup of the cheese. Lay a few slices of the pastrami down the center, and spread about ¼ cup of the sauerkraut mixture over the pastrami.

Starting at an end that is crosswise to the pastrami strip, roll the tortillas up jelly-roll style, so that the pastrami and sauerkraut run down the length of the middle. Lightly brush the rolls with vegetable oil. Place on a large baking sheet and bake until lightly browned on the outside and melted on the inside, about 10 minutes. Cut each roll on the diagonal into 6 pieces. Serve with the Russian dressing for dipping.

serves six to eight

Chicken and Black Bean Quesadillas

ingredients

- *1 tablespoon vegetable oil, plus more for frying quesadillas*
- *1 large onion, chopped*
- *2 large cloves garlic, minced*
- *3½ cups shredded cooked chicken*
- *8 ounces jalapeño Monterey Jack cheese, grated (about 2 cups)*
- *Salt and freshly ground black pepper to taste*
- *One 15-ounce can black beans, rinsed and drained*
- *1¼ cups Easy Tomato and Chipotle Salsa (page 266), divided*
- *8 large flour tortillas*

It's great to have a party without feeling stressed, and there's no better theme for your stress-free event than a Quesadilla Fiesta. Whether you make them ahead of time or have your guests make their own when they arrive, it's easy and fast, leaving you with lots of time to socialize. Round out the menu with chips, salsa, and margaritas, and all you'll have left to do is sit back and relax.

In a large, nonstick skillet, heat 1 tablespoon oil over medium heat. Add the onion and cook, stirring occasionally, until golden, about 6 minutes. Add the garlic and cook, stirring, until fragrant, about 1 minute. Transfer to a large bowl. Add the chicken to the onion mixture, along with the cheese. Season to taste with salt and pepper.

In a food processor, combine the black beans with ¼ cup of the salsa and pulse a few times. The mixture shouldn't be totally smooth. Taste the mixture and season with salt if necessary. Set aside.

To assemble: Spread the black beans onto 4 of the tortillas. Top with the chicken and cheese mixture and then with the remaining tortillas. Heat a large frying pan over medium heat. Lightly oil the pan. Carefully place one of the quesadillas in the frying pan. Cook on each side until lightly browned, 2 to 3 minutes. Transfer to a cutting board and cut the quesadilla into 8 wedges. Repeat with the remaining quesadillas.

Serve warm with the remaining salsa.

Make-ahead: *The uncooked quesadillas can be assembled 8 hours ahead of time and kept, covered, in the refrigerator. Once the quesadillas are cooked, they can be kept in a 200°F oven for 1 hour. Slice right before serving.*

serves six to eight

Monterey Jack and Roasted Poblano Chile Quesadillas

ingredients

- *4 poblano chiles*
- *1 tablespoon vegetable oil, plus more for frying quesadillas*
- *1 medium white onion, chopped*
- *1 clove garlic*
- *8 ounces Monterey Jack cheese, grated (about 2 cups)*
- *8 large flour tortillas*

Much like pizza, quesadillas can be made with a variety of ingredients. All you really need are tortillas and cheese; the rest is up to you. Here we've added rajas (roasted chile strips) to the filling. We're using poblano chiles, which are a mild but flavorful option. If you like your quesadillas spicy, you could chop up a couple of jalapeños and sauté them with your onions and chile strips.

Roast the chiles over a gas flame or on a tray under the broiler. Keep turning so the skin is evenly charred, without burning and drying out the flesh. Enclose in a paper bag, and let stand for 10 minutes. Peel the charred skin from the chiles, remove the stem and seeds, and slice the roasted chiles into $^1/_4$-inch strips.

Heat 1 tablespoon oil in a large skillet over medium heat. Add the onion and sauté until golden brown, about 5 minutes. Stir in the garlic and chiles. Sauté for 5 minutes more. Set aside.

To assemble: Lay 4 of the tortillas out on a work surface. Divide the chile-onion mixture among these tortillas, spreading it out to the edges. Top with the cheese and the remaining tortillas. Heat a large frying pan over medium heat. Lightly oil the pan. Carefully place one of the quesadillas in the frying pan. Cook on each side until lightly browned, 2 to 3 minutes. Transfer to a cutting board and cut the quesadilla into 8 wedges. Repeat for the remaining quesadillas.

Make-ahead: *The uncooked quesadillas can be assembled 8 hours ahead of time and kept, covered, in the refrigerator. Once the quesadillas are cooked, they can be kept in a 200°F oven for 1 hour. Slice right before serving.*

serves six

Crêpes with Roasted Vegetables and Herbed Goat Cheese Sauce

Roasted vegetables have a rich, caramelized flavor that pairs beautifully with tangy goat cheese sauce. Make this recipe your own by using parsnips, turnips, cauliflower, asparagus, or mushrooms instead of the suggested vegetables. The three parts of this recipe can all be made ahead, assembled, and reheated right before serving.

vegetable filling

- *½ small eggplant, cut into ½-inch dice*
- *1 carrot, peeled, trimmed, and cut into ¼-inch dice*
- *1 parsnip, peeled, trimmed, and cut into ¼-inch dice*
- *1 zucchini, trimmed and cut into ½-inch dice*
- *1 small red onion, peeled, trimmed, and thinly sliced*
- *1 red bell pepper, trimmed, seeded, and cut into ½-inch dice*
- *½ small fennel bulb, trimmed, cored, and thinly sliced*
- *4 plum tomatoes, cut into quarters and seeded*
- *2 cloves garlic, minced*
- *3 tablespoons extra-virgin olive oil*

To make the filling: Preheat the oven to 400°F.

Spread the cut vegetables onto 2 baking sheets. Drizzle the olive oil over the vegetables and sprinkle the salt, pepper, thyme, and parsley over the top. With your hands, toss the vegetables so that they are evenly coated with the oil and seasonings. Roast until they are soft and beginning to brown around the edges, about 25 minutes. Remove the vegetables from the oven and cover with foil.

To make the sauce: Place the chicken stock in a medium saucepan and bring to a simmer over medium heat. Remove from the heat and let sit for about 5 minutes.

Add the goat cheese to the stock and whisk until the cheese is melted. Add the chives, parsley, and lemon juice. Season to taste with salt and pepper. The sauce can be reheated over medium heat just before serving.

1/2 teaspoon salt

Freshly ground black pepper to taste

2 tablespoons minced fresh thyme

2 tablespoons minced Italian parsley

sauce

1/2 cup chicken stock

6 ounces goat cheese or mascarpone

1 tablespoon minced chives

1 tablespoon minced Italian parsley

1 teaspoon fresh lemon juice

Salt and freshly ground black pepper to taste

Basic Crêpes (page 333)

Chopped fresh chives and parsley, for garnish

To assemble the crêpes and vegetables: Reheat the vegetables in the hot oven for a few minutes if necessary. Lay the crêpes on a work surface and spoon some of the vegetables in the center of each crêpe. Fold the crêpe over to make a half circle, and then fold it again into a quarter circle. Place the rolled crêpes on a baking sheet and heat in the preheated oven until heated through, about 5 minutes. Serve the crêpes on warm plates with the heated goat cheese sauce. Garnish with chopped chives and parsley.

makes about four dozen stuffed grape leaves

Grape Leaves with Rice and Pine Nut Filling

ingredients

One 1-pound jar brine-packed grape leaves

1/4 cup extra-virgin olive oil

1 cup minced onion

1/2 cup pine nuts

1 cup raw jasmine rice

1/2 cup chopped currants or raisins

1/4 cup minced fresh Italian parsley

2 tablespoons chopped fresh chives

2 tablespoons chopped fresh tarragon

2 tablespoons chopped fresh fennel greens

1/2 teaspoon grated lemon zest

1/2 teaspoon salt

1/4 teaspoon ground cardamom

1/8 teaspoon ground cinnamon

2 3/4 cups chicken stock, divided

1/4 cup fresh lemon juice

1/4 cup olive oil

1 lemon, cut in half lengthwise and thinly sliced, for garnish

Among the many variations of stuffed grape leaves or dolmas, this Greek version is a party favorite. The crunch of the pine nuts and sweetness of the currants combine to make these dolmas irresistible.

Separate the grape leaves, and rinse them under cold running water. Soak the leaves in cold water while the rice cooks and cools.

Heat a medium saucepan over medium heat and add the 1/4 cup extra-virgin olive oil. When the oil is hot, add the onion and sauté until it is soft. Add the pine nuts, rice, and currants and cook, stirring, for 2 or 3 minutes. Add the parsley, chives, tarragon, fennel greens, lemon zest, salt, cardamom, cinnamon, and 2 cups of the chicken stock and bring to a simmer. Do not stir. Cover, turn down the heat, and let the rice cook until it is tender and the liquid has been absorbed, about 20 minutes. Remove the rice from the heat, fluff it with a fork, and transfer it to a large bowl to cool.

Drain the grape leaves and lay them out on a towel to dry. Working with one leaf at a time, place a rounded teaspoonful (don't overstuff) of the rice filling at the base of the leaf where it connects to the stem. Cover the filling with the tail end of the leaf and roll it. Fold the sides of the leaf to the center to enclose the filling, and roll up the package. Finish with the seam on the bottom. Repeat to roll the remaining grape leaves. Line the bottom of a 3-quart saucepan with grape leaves that have ripped or torn. Place a layer of rolls in the pan, drizzle a little of the lemon juice on top, and lay a few grape leaves over them to cover. Continue to layer the rolls in the pan. Top with more ripped or torn grape leaves to cover.

Pour the olive oil, remaining 3/4 cup chicken stock, and remaining lemon juice into the pan, cover, and place the pan over medium heat. Braise for about 45 minutes at a bare simmer. Remove the pan from the heat and let cool until the rolls are easily handled. Arrange the grape leaves on a tray and garnish with sliced lemon. Serve warm or room temperature.

Make-ahead: *The stuffed grape leaves can be kept, covered and refrigerated, for 3 days.*

makes about fifty-four pieces

Pear, Gorgonzola, and Hazelnut Bundles

ingredients

8 ounces Gorgonzola cheese, at room temperature, crumbled

4 tablespoons unsalted butter, at room temperature

½ cup toasted, skinned, chopped hazelnuts

3 medium Bartlett pears, halved and cored

1 tablespoon fresh lemon juice

20 thin slices prosciutto

3 ounces fresh baby arugula (about 3 cups), washed and dried

Pears and Gorgonzola are a classic cheese plate combination. Here we've paired them with crunchy toasted hazelnuts and peppery arugula, wrapped up together in salty prosciutto for an elegant and easy to eat package.

Mash together the Gorgonzola and butter in a medium bowl with a fork until well combined. Stir in the hazelnuts. Set aside.

Slice each pear half lengthwise into 9 slices. Place the pear slices in a medium bowl with the lemon juice and cover with water to prevent browning. Set aside.

Working with 1 slice at a time, cut the prosciutto lengthwise into 1-inch-wide strips (you should have about 3 strips per prosciutto slice). Space the strips 2 inches apart on a work surface. Remove a slice of pear from the water, pat gently with a paper towel to dry, and spread a scant teaspoon of the cheese mixture on the pear slice. Lay the pear slice crosswise at one end of a prosciutto strip. Arrange 3 arugula leaves atop each pear slice. Roll up the prosciutto around the pear tightly, so that the prosciutto is holding the pear and arugula securely. The arugula should peek out on either side of the prosciutto. Transfer to a platter.

Make-ahead: *The bundles can be made 1 hour ahead. Cover the rolls tightly and refrigerate.*

Tip: *Two or three of these bundles are terrific as a garnish on a salad plate.*

Chapter

6 Bread *and* Pastry

serves eight

Asparagus Quiche with Bacon and Feta Cheese

ingredients

Flaky Pastry (page 335), fitted into a 9-inch tart pan with a removable rim and chilled

8 slices bacon, diced

1 cup minced onion

1 bunch asparagus, trimmed

2 tablespoons extra-virgin olive oil

3/4 teaspoon salt, divided

1/8 teaspoon freshly ground black pepper, plus more to taste

Grated zest of 1 lemon

3 large eggs

1/2 cup heavy cream

Dash of cayenne pepper

Dash of ground nutmeg

1/2 cup crumbled feta cheese

Salty feta cheese works and plays well with the smoky bacon and roasted asparagus in this quiche. It is a nice spin on the traditional quiche Lorraine and opens the door to many variations. If asparagus is not in season, try roasting broccoli or cauliflower. This dish can also serve as a luncheon entrée (or as a dinner with a salad, bread, and wine).

Preheat the oven to 375°F.

Line the chilled tart shell with parchment and fill it with pie weights (or raw rice or dried beans). Bake the shell for 20 minutes. Carefully remove the parchment and the weights to a heatproof plate and return the shell to the oven to bake for another 15 minutes. Remove from the oven and let cool on a rack.

Meanwhile, heat a large skillet over medium heat and add the bacon to the pan. Cook until the bacon has rendered its fat and is crispy. Transfer to a paper towel-lined plate. Drain off all but 1 tablespoon of the bacon fat and add the onion to the pan. Cook until the onion is soft and lightly brown, about 3 minutes. Remove the pan from the heat and let cool.

Preheat the oven to 400°F.

Lay the asparagus out on a baking sheet and drizzle with the olive oil, 1/4 teaspoon of the salt, and pepper to taste. Toss to mix, and roast the asparagus until tender, 8 to 10 minutes. Remove the pan from the oven and let cool.

In a medium bowl, beat the zest and eggs together. Beat in the cream, remaining 1/2 teaspoon salt, 1/8 teaspoon pepper, cayenne, and nutmeg. Set aside.

Remove the onion from the skillet with a slotted spoon and arrange it with the asparagus and bacon over the bottom of the tart shell. Pour the custard mixture over the top and then sprinkle the cheese over all. Bake the quiche on a baking pan positioned in the lower third of the oven until the filling is set and the top is lightly browned, about 25 minutes. Transfer to a rack to cool for at least 10 minutes. This will allow the filling to set up so the quiche will cut more neatly. Serve warm or at room temperature.

Make-ahead: *To make 1 day ahead, bake the quiche and let it cool. Refrigerate, and when ready to serve let it come to room temperature for 30 minutes, then crisp it up in a 350°F oven for about 20 minutes.*

serves eight

Mediterranean Roasted Vegetable Tart

ingredients

- *1 cup sliced zucchini (cut the zucchini in half lengthwise and then into 1/4-inch slices)*
- *1/2 cup thinly sliced red onion*
- *1 red bell pepper, cut into 1/4-inch slices*
- *1 cup diced eggplant (1/2-inch dice)*
- *2 tablespoons olive oil*
- *1 teaspoon harissa (see Tip)*
- *3/4 teaspoon salt, divided*
- *1/4 teaspoon plus 1/8 teaspoon freshly ground black pepper, divided*
- *1/2 cup goat cheese*
- *1/2 cup grated mozzarella cheese*

Roasting vegetables concentrates their flavor, and the caramelization that occurs gives them a complex, sweet taste. Tossing the vegetables with harissa adds a spicy North African flair. If you can't find harissa, sprinkle the vegetables lightly with red pepper flakes, cumin, coriander, and garlic. Here we've teamed the browned vegetables with rich cheese in flaky, buttery phyllo pastry for a great starter or luncheon entrée.

Preheat the oven to 375°F.

Arrange the zucchini, red onion, red bell pepper, and eggplant on a baking sheet and drizzle with the olive oil, harissa, 1/2 teaspoon of the salt, and 1/4 teaspoon of the pepper. Toss the vegetables to coat them with the oil, and roast them until they have softened and begun to brown around the edges, about 20 minutes. Remove from the oven and let cool on the baking sheet.

In a bowl, mix together the goat cheese, mozzarella, ricotta salata, yogurt, and egg. Mix well and season with the remaining 1/4 teaspoon salt and 1/8 teaspoon pepper.

Remove the phyllo from the package, unroll it onto a work surface, and immediately cover it with a large sheet of plastic wrap. Cover the plastic wrap with a damp towel to weigh it down and keep the pastry from drying out. Working with 5 sheets of phyllo at a time, cut the phyllo into ten 12-inch squares, returning it under the plastic wrap quickly.

Working quickly so that the phyllo doesn't dry out, arrange 1 sheet of phyllo on a parchment-lined baking pan. Brush the phyllo with the melted butter and quickly place another sheet of phyllo on top of the buttered sheet, offsetting it so that you have 8 points. Butter the phyllo and top with another sheet, offsetting it slightly so that after a few more sheets are laid down a circle begins to appear. Continue with the remaining

1/3 cup grated ricotta salata cheese

1/4 cup yogurt

1 large egg

10 sheets phyllo pastry, thawed in the refrigerator for 12 hours if frozen

4 tablespoons unsalted butter, melted

phyllo sheets, brushing each with butter. Spread half of the cheese mixture evenly over the bottom of the tart shell. Top the cheese with the roasted vegetables, and dot the top of the vegetables with the remaining cheese filling. Fold the sides up over the filling, pleating the edges until the edge of the filling is covered and an open circle of vegetables (about 7 inches round) and cheese remains in the center. Butter the top of the phyllo generously.

Bake the tart in the lower third of the oven until golden brown around the edges and crisp on the bottom, 25 to 30 minutes. Let cool for 5 minutes, then slide the tart off the pan and onto a serving plate. Slice and serve hot, warm, or at room temperature.

Make-ahead: *The tart can be assembled and frozen, wrapped in plastic wrap, for up to 2 weeks. No need to thaw—just bake it frozen, adding a few minutes to the baking time.*

Tip: *Harissa is a fiery North African chile paste generally containing oil, chiles, garlic, cumin, coriander, caraway, and sometimes a bit of dried mint. It usually comes in a can that must be opened with a can opener. Keep it in the refrigerator after opening, or freeze tablespoon-sized drops on a parchment-lined pan and then transfer the frozen drops to a freezer bag to use whenever. It is traditionally used to flavor couscous, soups, meats, and vegetables.*

makes eight purses, serving four

Phyllo Purses with Brie, Pistachios, and Apricots

ingredients

- 1 cup apricot nectar
- 1/4 cup white rum
- 1/2 cup chopped natural (green) pistachios
- 1/2 cup (1 stick) plus 2 tablespoons unsalted butter, melted, divided
- 1/4 teaspoon salt
- About 8 sheets phyllo pastry, thawed in the refrigerator for 12 hours if frozen
- 4 ounces Brie, cut into 8 square pieces
- 1/3 cup dried apricots, snipped into quarters with kitchen shears
- 4 teaspoons apricot preserves

Working with phyllo is really easy once you get the hang of it. The bonus of phyllo appetizers is that they freeze well and can be baked while still frozen. This works out well for the organized party giver who likes to begin preparations a week or so before the party. We think of this dish as a sit-down appetizer with the sauce, or as a stand-up appetizer without it.

Cook the apricot nectar and rum in a medium saucepan over medium heat until the mixture has reduced to 1/4 cup. Remove from the heat and reserve.

Preheat the oven to 350°F.

Toss the pistachios with 2 tablespoons of the melted butter and the salt. Transfer the nuts to a baking sheet and lightly brown in the oven for about 5 minutes. Remove from the oven and let cool.

Increase the oven temperature to 425°F.

Remove the phyllo from the package, unroll it onto a work surface, and immediately cover it with a large sheet of plastic wrap. Cover the plastic wrap with a damp towel to weigh it down and keep the pastry from drying out. Cut 4 or 5 sheets of the pastry at a time into 5-inch squares, returning it under the plastic wrap quickly. You will need 32 of these squares.

Working quickly so that the phyllo doesn't dry out, lay out 8 squares of phyllo separately. Brush each with melted butter and place another sheet of phyllo on top of each, offsetting them so that each piece has 8 points. Repeat with the rest of the phyllo so that each piece has 4 buttered layers. Transfer the phyllo to 2 parchment-lined baking sheets.

Add a piece of Brie to the center of each phyllo stack. Top with a few pieces of dried apricot and a light scattering of the toasted pistachios, reserving about half for garnish. Add about ½ teaspoon of apricot preserves to the top of each. Gather the sides of the phyllo up to enclose the cheese mixture, and twist so that the package stays closed. Brush the outside of each package with butter and bake until browned and the cheese inside has melted, 15 to 20 minutes.

Reheat the reduced apricot nectar and drizzle it over 4 heated plates. Place 2 Brie packages on top of the sauce and garnish with a scattering of the remaining pistachios. Serve hot.

Variations: *Substitute Gorgonzola for the Brie, dried figs for the apricots, toasted walnuts for the pistachios, and cider for the apricot nectar.*

Make-ahead: *The unbaked Brie bundles can be frozen, arranged on a parchment-lined baking sheet and wrapped in plastic, for 2 weeks. They can be baked without thawing; just give them 5 more minutes in the oven.*

makes thirty-six mini gougères

Cheddar Herbed Gougères (Pâte à Choux)

ingredients

- 1 cup water
- 6 tablespoons unsalted butter, cut into pieces
- 3/4 cup unbleached all-purpose flour
- 1/2 teaspoon crumbled dried rosemary
- 1/4 teaspoon salt
- 1/8 teaspoon cayenne pepper
- 1/8 teaspoon grated nutmeg
- 3 large eggs
- 1 large egg yolk
- 1/2 cup grated cheddar cheese

Pâte à choux is the French term for cream puff pastry. This savory version includes cheddar cheese and rosemary and is made into little puffs known as gougères. They are a fantastic appetizer staple that can be filled with anything from egg salad to smoked trout.

Heat the water and butter in a heavy saucepan over medium-high heat. Bring the mixture to a boil. While the water is heating, combine the flour, rosemary, salt, cayenne, and nutmeg in a small bowl.

Reduce the heat to medium and add the flour mixture all at once. Beat the paste vigorously with a wooden spoon. It will come together and form a ball, pulling away from the sides of the pan. Cook the paste until a film forms on the bottom of the pan, about 2 minutes. Remove the pan from the heat and continue to stir vigorously for 2 minutes to cool the dough before adding the eggs.

Add the eggs and yolk, one at a time, beating with the wooden spoon until each egg is incorporated before adding the next. The batter should be stiff enough to hold a soft peak. Stir in the cheese and mix to blend.

Preheat the oven to 425°F.

Transfer the mixture to a pastry bag with a plain 1/4-inch tip. Line 2 baking sheets with parchment paper and pipe small rounds 2 inches in diameter onto the sheets, leaving 2 inches between them. They will rise and puff in the oven. Bake until they are golden brown and firm on the sides, about 18 minutes. Remove the puffs from the oven and poke each one with the tip of a sharp knife to allow the hot air inside to escape. Return the puffs to the oven to dry out for about 5 more minutes. Remove from the oven and let cool on racks on the baking sheet.

Serve plain, or cut in half and filled with your choice of fillings.

Make-ahead: *The gougères can be stored overnight in a loosely covered container.*

Tip: *You can omit the rosemary or substitute thyme, basil, sage, or any herb that complements your filling of choice.*

makes about seventy-two pieces

Phyllo Triangles with Chicken and Pecans

There is no end to the kinds of fillings you can stuff into phyllo pastry. This chicken and pecan stuffing is a nice change of pace from the usual Mediterranean vegetarian fillings. Since this appetizer freezes so well, it is a great way to use your Thanksgiving leftovers. Just replace the chicken with turkey, freeze, and at least one holiday hors d'oeuvre is already in the bag.

filling

- *2 tablespoons olive oil*
- *½ cup minced onion*
- *2 cloves garlic, minced*
- *1 cup thinly sliced napa cabbage*
- *¼ teaspoon salt*
- *⅛ teaspoon freshly ground black pepper*
- *⅛ teaspoon freshly grated nutmeg*
- *Dash of cayenne pepper*
- *⅓ cup heavy cream*
- *¼ cup crumbled goat cheese*
- *1½ cups finely diced cooked chicken*
- *½ cup toasted and chopped pecans*
- *1 tablespoon chopped fresh Italian parsley*
- *2 teaspoons chopped fresh tarragon*

- *24 sheets phyllo pastry, thawed in the refrigerator for 12 hours if frozen*
- *1 cup (2 sticks) unsalted butter, melted*

To make the filling: Heat a large sauté pan over medium heat and add the olive oil. When the oil is hot, add the onion and cook until it is soft, about 2 minutes. Add the garlic and cabbage and cook until the cabbage begins to soften, about 2 minutes more. Add the salt, pepper, nutmeg, cayenne, and heavy cream and cook the mixture until the cream has reduced and thickened, about 4 minutes. Stir in the goat cheese, chicken, pecans, parsley, and tarragon. Stir and taste the mixture for seasoning, adding more salt and pepper if desired. Remove the pan from the heat and let cool.

Preheat the oven to 400°F.

To assemble: Remove the phyllo from the package, unroll it onto a work surface, and immediately cover it with a large sheet of plastic wrap and a damp towel to keep the pastry from drying out.

Working as quickly as possible, carefully remove one sheet of phyllo dough and lay it out on the work surface. Brush with melted butter and lay a second phyllo sheet on top of the first. Brush again with melted butter. With a pizza cutter or sharp knife, cut the phyllo crosswise into 6 strips. Place about 1 teaspoon of the cooled filling on the short end of each strip. Fold the phyllo over the filling to form a triangle, as you would fold a flag, and continue to fold, leaving a seam on the bottom of the triangle. Brush the triangle with melted butter and place it on a parchment-lined baking sheet. Repeat with the remaining phyllo and filling, leaving about ½ inch between triangles.

Bake the triangles until golden, 12 to 15 minutes. Serve hot or at room temperature.

Make-ahead: *The unbaked triangles can be frozen, arranged on a parchment-lined baking sheet and wrapped in plastic, for 2 weeks. They can be baked without thawing; just add 5 minutes to the baking time.*

makes about seventy-two pieces

Phyllo Triangles with Spinach and Feta

ingredients

- 2 tablespoons olive oil
- 4 green onions, trimmed and thinly sliced, white and green parts
- 2 packages frozen chopped spinach, thawed and squeezed dry
- 2 cloves garlic, minced
- ¼ cup chopped fresh Italian parsley
- ¼ cup chopped fresh mint
- 1 cup crumbled feta cheese
- Salt to taste (optional)
- ¼ teaspoon freshly ground black pepper
- ⅛ teaspoon freshly grated nutmeg
- ⅓ cup pine nuts, toasted
- 24 sheets phyllo pastry, thawed in the refrigerator for 12 hours if frozen
- 1 cup (2 sticks) unsalted butter, melted

Feta and spinach are a favorite Mediterranean combination often found sandwiched between buttery layers of phyllo. This recipe makes a great deal of pastries, but trust us, they will disappear fast.

Heat a large sauté pan over medium heat and add the olive oil to the pan. When the oil is hot, add the green onions and the spinach and sauté until the spinach breaks up and the onions are soft, about 4 minutes. Add the garlic, parsley, and mint and cook until the mixture is fragrant, another minute or so. Remove the pan from the heat and stir in the feta cheese. Taste the mixture to see if it needs more salt. (Sometimes feta is very salty and no more salt is needed.) Add the salt if you need it, along with the pepper, nutmeg, and pine nuts. Stir to combine and allow the mixture to cool.

Preheat the oven to 400°F.

Remove the phyllo from the package, unroll it onto a work surface, and immediately cover it with a large sheet of plastic wrap. Cover the plastic wrap with a damp towel to weigh it down and keep the pastry from drying out.

Working as quickly as possible, carefully remove one sheet of phyllo and lay it out on a work surface. Brush the sheet with melted butter and lay a second sheet on top of the first. Brush again with melted butter. With a pizza cutter or sharp knife, cut the phyllo crosswise into 6 strips. Place about 1 teaspoon of the cooled filling on the short end of each strip. Fold the phyllo over the filling to form a triangle, as you would fold a flag, and continue to fold, leaving a seam on the bottom of the triangle. Brush the triangle with melted butter and place it on a parchment-lined baking sheet. Repeat with the remaining phyllo and filling, leaving about ¼ inch between triangles.

Bake the triangles until golden, 12 to 15 minutes. Serve hot or at room temperature.

Make-ahead: *The unbaked triangles can be frozen, arranged on a parchment-lined baking sheet and wrapped in plastic, for 2 weeks. They can be baked without thawing; just add 5 minutes to the baking time.*

Tip: *Phyllo (filo) pastry is readily available in your grocer's freezer case. It consists of very thin sheets of pastry made of water and flour. The layers must be built up and each one brushed with melted butter or oil. Phyllo appetizers are always a welcome addition to the party table. Since they are as good hot as they are at room temperature, they are also easy on the hostess.*

makes seventy-two wedges

Pita Wedges

ingredients

Eight 6-inch or small pita rounds, cut into sixths and separated into 2 pieces each

1/3 cup olive oil or unsalted butter, melted

Kosher salt to taste

Pita wedges or chips are tasty homemade crispy breads that can be used to carry dips to your mouth. They are worth the time it takes to make them because they taste so much better than anything you can buy ready-made.

Preheat the oven to 400°F.

Brush the inside of each pita wedge with olive oil and arrange them on a baking sheet. Sprinkle the sheet with salt and bake until the wedges are crisp, about 8 minutes. Let cool on the pan.

Make-ahead: *Pita wedges can be made 1 day ahead and kept in an airtight container at room temperature.*

makes two 16-inch pizzas

Pizza with Figs, Goat Cheese, and Walnuts

ingredients

Basic Pizza Dough (page 108)

4 tablespoons extra-virgin olive oil

1 cup dried figs, stems removed, soaked in 1 cup hot water for 15 minutes

4 ounces prosciutto, cut into thin strips

5 ounces goat cheese, crumbled

½ cup chopped walnuts

¼ cup chopped fresh rosemary

3 tablespoons honey

Pizza is one of the most fun and creative appetizer bases to work with. Believe it or not, this version came about when taping a cooking segment hosted by teenagers. We needed an out-of-the-ordinary pizza that teenagers would like. The sweet figs and honey, salty prosciutto, rich goat cheese, piney rosemary, and tannic walnuts create a symphony in your mouth. The kids loved it, and so will you.

Shape and prebake the pizza crusts as directed in the dough recipe. Remove from the oven, leaving the oven set at 450°F.

Drizzle each partially baked crust with 2 tablespoons of the olive oil. Scatter the figs and prosciutto over the pizzas. Sprinkle evenly with the goat cheese, walnuts, and rosemary.

Drizzle the honey over the top of the pizzas and bake directly on a pizza stone or tiles for about 10 minutes.

Remove the pizzas from the oven and allow to cool for 3 or 4 minutes before cutting. Each pizza cuts into 8 ample slices.

Make-ahead: *Pizza is best eaten directly from the oven, but if you have to make it earlier in the day, it can be reheated in a 375°F oven for 10 minutes.*

makes about twenty-two breadsticks

Prosciutto-Wrapped Breadsticks

ingredients

Cornmeal Grissini with Fennel (page 115) or one 5-ounce box grissini (about 22 sticks)

22 thin slices prosciutto, cut lengthwise into 44 long strips

Grissini are very dramatic long, thin Italian (Piedmontese) breadsticks. Wrapped in salty prosciutto, they make an easy starter or an elegant accomplice to soups, salads, and antipasti. Look for grissini at specialty Italian grocers or, in more urban areas, in the Italian section of your local grocery store.

Wrap 2 strips of prosciutto tightly around each breadstick. Arrange the grissini upright in a decorative jar or vase, much like a bouquet of flowers, and serve.

Make-ahead: Wrap the grissini in the prosciutto just before serving.

makes twenty-four wedges

Rosemary Socca

ingredients

- 1⅔ cups water
- ⅓ cup plus 2 tablespoons extra-virgin olive oil, divided
- 1 tablespoon chopped fresh rosemary
- ¾ teaspoon salt
- 2 cups chickpea flour
- 2 tablespoons olive oil
- Coarse sea salt or kosher salt to taste
- Freshly ground black pepper to taste

Socca are delicate pancakes made with chickpea flour and olive oil. They are commonly sold as street food in southern France on the Côte d'Azur, and their roots go back to North Africa's Arabic cuisines. Cut into wedges and drizzled with extra-virgin olive oil, socca are delicious alone or paired with a topping such as Caponata (page 250).

Place the water, ⅓ cup of the extra-virgin olive oil, rosemary, and salt in a large bowl. Whisk in the chickpea flour until completely incorporated. Let the batter stand at room temperature for 1 hour.

Preheat the oven to 425°F.

Oil four 8-inch round cake pans or small pizza pans with 2 tablespoons olive oil, and pour in the batter evenly so that it coats the bottoms of the pans. The batter should be about ¼ inch thick. Bake the socca until they are golden brown and set, about 20 minutes.

Remove the socca from the pans and cut them into wedges. Drizzle the pancakes with the remaining 2 tablespoons extra-virgin olive oil, and sprinkle with coarse salt and freshly ground pepper. Serve warm.

Make-ahead: *The socca can be made up to 8 hours ahead and kept, covered, at room temperature. Reheat in a 400°F oven for 5 minutes before serving.*

makes about thirty-two pieces

Sausage in Pastry with Mustard Dipping Sauce

mustard sauce

½ cup Dijon mustard

1 teaspoon minced fresh thyme

1 teaspoon minced fresh oregano

½ teaspoon fennel seed, ground with a mortar and pestle

¼ teaspoon freshly ground black pepper

About 2 tablespoons dry white wine

sausage in pastry

1 pound chorizo, kielbasa, or other spicy smoked sausage

½ recipe Quick Puff Pastry (page 332), or 1 sheet of frozen puff pastry, thawed in the refrigerator

Egg wash made with 1 egg yolk beaten with 2 teaspoons water

Nothing is easier than putting together this juicy, rich, man-pleasing appetizer. Use any kind of precooked sausage that appeals to you, from spicy chorizo to everyday kielbasa.

To make the mustard sauce: Whisk the mustard, thyme, oregano, fennel seed, and black pepper in a bowl to blend. Thin to a dipping sauce consistency with the white wine. Let the sauce sit at room temperature for 1 hour to allow the flavors to mix. Serve at room temperature. Leftover sauce can be refrigerated for up to 1 week.

Remove the sausages from their package, and dry with a paper towel. Set aside.

If using homemade puff pastry, roll it out to a thickness of ¼ inch, making it as long as one of the sausages and wide enough to roll around the sausage with a ½-inch overlap. If using store-bought pastry, just trim the pastry to fit the sausage in the same way. Lay a sausage on top of the pastry, and brush one long side with the egg wash. Roll the sausage up in the pastry, beginning at the dry side and ending at the egg-washed end of the pastry. Lightly press the pastry into itself along the seam to get it to adhere and form a seal. Place the sausage on a parchment-lined baking sheet, seam side down. Refrigerate for at least 30 minutes to firm up the pastry. Repeat with the remaining sausages and pastry.

Preheat the oven to 425°F. Remove the sausages from the refrigerator and brush with the egg glaze. Make cuts in the pastry (not into the sausage) along the length of it in 1-inch intervals with a sharp knife to delineate where you will be slicing the sausage into serving pieces. This will make for neater cuts and less pastry cracking after it has baked and puffed.

Bake the pastry-wrapped sausage until the pastry is puffed and golden brown, 20 to 25 minutes. Remove from the oven and let cool for 5 minutes before cutting it into serving portions. Serve warm or at room temperature with the mustard sauce.

Make-ahead: *Can be frozen uncooked for up to 2 weeks. Bake directly from the freezer adding 5 minutes to cooking time.*

makes sixteen 12-inch-long crackers

Sesame Crackers

ingredients

- 2½ cups unbleached all-purpose flour
- ½ cup rye flour
- 1¾ teaspoons salt, divided
- 1 teaspoon baking powder
- 1 teaspoon baking soda
- ¼ teaspoon freshly ground black pepper
- ½ cup (1 stick) unsalted butter, cut into pieces
- 1 cup sour cream
- 1 large egg yolk
- 1 cup toasted sesame seeds, divided
- 1 egg, beaten
- 1 tablespoon sugar
- 1 tablespoon soy sauce
- Kosher salt for sprinkling (optional)

Homemade crackers are one of life's little luxuries. Rye flour gives this flatbread a bit more bite than the usual store-bought varieties. Snap them into smaller pieces and serve these crackers with good cheese and ripe seasonal fruit for a memorable cheese plate.

In a food processor or the bowl of a stand mixer, place the flours, 1½ teaspoons of the salt, baking powder, baking soda, and black pepper. Pulse or stir with the paddle attachment. Add the butter and pulse or stir until the mixture resembles coarse meal. Add the sour cream, egg yolk, and ¾ cup of the sesame seeds and process or stir just until the mixture comes together. Remove the dough from the bowl and knead it on a work surface until well mixed. Divide the dough into 16 pieces and form each piece into a log. Wrap in plastic and refrigerate for 30 minutes.

Preheat the oven to 375°F.

On a lightly floured surface, roll out each log into a 12-inch strip about 1/16 inch thick (it is important that you roll the cracker dough thinly in order for them to bake up crisply). Transfer the crackers to parchment-lined baking sheets and poke them multiple times with a fork.

In a small bowl, beat the egg, sugar, soy sauce, and remaining ¼ teaspoon salt. Brush generously over the crackers and sprinkle with the remaining ¼ cup sesame seeds and with kosher salt if desired.

Bake the crackers until golden brown and crisp, 15 to 20 minutes. Transfer to racks to cool.

Make-ahead: *Sesame crackers will keep for 1 week in an airtight container.*

makes about twenty-eight, depending on the length of your baguettes

Toasted Fontina and Onion Jam Panini

Savory, buttery little rounds made with cheese and melted onions are a year-round favorite. Men seem to love these hearty little sandwiches, but we've seen women gobble them up just as fast. Have your bakery slice the baguette for you. It will save you time and the slices will be neater.

ingredients

- *4 tablespoons unsalted butter*
- *2 pounds red onions, thinly sliced*
- *1 teaspoon sugar*
- *1 teaspoon salt*
- *1 teaspoon minced fresh thyme*
- *1/4 teaspoon freshly ground black pepper*
- *1/4 cup balsamic vinegar*
- *1 1/2 baguettes, sliced into about 56 slices*
- *1/2 cup (1 stick) butter, at room temperature*
- *Salt and freshly ground black pepper to taste (optional)*
- *2 cups grated fontina cheese*

Heat a large skillet over medium-high heat and add the 4 tablespoons butter. When it has melted, add the onions, sugar, salt, thyme, and black pepper. Sauté for 5 minutes, stirring the onions until they become soft, then turn the heat to low and cook the onions slowly, stirring occasionally, until they are very soft and browned, about 30 minutes. Add the balsamic vinegar and turn the heat back to medium-high. Cook the onions until the vinegar has evaporated, about 1 minute. Remove the pan from the heat and set aside.

Butter the baguette slices and lay them, buttered side down, on a work surface. Spread some of the onion jam on the unbuttered side of half the baguettes, and season with salt and pepper if desired. Top the onion jam with about 1 tablespoon of the grated cheese. Top the cheese with a baguette slice, buttered side up.

Heat a panini maker or a large, nonstick skillet over medium heat. Arrange 4 or 5 of the panini on the hot surface. Close the lid of the panini maker or, if using a skillet, weigh the panini down with a smaller heavy skillet that fits inside the one you are cooking in. It should take about 2 minutes to cook the panini until brown in a panini maker. If using a skillet, cook 2 minutes on the first side, 1 or 2 minutes on the second side.

Arrange the cooked panini on a platter. Serve hot or at room temperature.

Make-ahead: *The panini can be assembled and cooked a few hours in advance. To serve, arrange on a baking sheet and reheat in a 350°F oven for 5 minutes.*

makes two 16-inch pizzas

White Pizza with Prosciutto, Arugula, and Parmesan

ingredients

- *2 heads garlic*
- *2 tablespoons plus 2 teaspoons olive oil, divided*
- *Salt and freshly ground black pepper to taste*
- *Basic Pizza Dough (page 108)*
- *2 small bunches arugula (3 cups lightly packed)*
- *10 thin slices prosciutto, cut into thin strips*
- *3/4 cup grated Parmesan cheese*

The sauce base of this white pizza is a paste made of creamy roasted garlic. Don't worry about too much garlic here. Roasting makes it sweet and smooth, nothing like its raw state. The arugula lends peppery spice and the prosciutto and Parmesan a nice salty tang.

Preheat the oven to 350°F.

Cut off the top 1/2 inch of the garlic heads and drizzle each with 1 teaspoon of the olive oil. Salt and pepper the garlic, wrap in foil, and bake until the garlic is soft, about 40 minutes. Allow to cool.

Reset the oven to 475°F, with a pizza stone or tiles in the lower section of the oven.

Shape and prebake the pizza crusts as directed in the dough recipe. Remove from the oven and drizzle each pizza with 1 tablespoon of olive oil.

Gently squeeze each cooled garlic bulb upside down over the pizzas. The smooth garlic paste will ooze out of the bulb. Some of the cloves may still be solid — just smash them with the back of a spoon. Spread the paste over the pizza crusts.

Arrange the arugula over the pizzas and top with the prosciutto and Parmesan cheese. Slide the pizzas into the oven directly on the heated pizza stone or tiles and bake until crispy on the bottom, about 12 minutes. Cut into wedges and serve hot or at room temperature.

Make-ahead: *Pizza is best eaten directly from the oven, but if you have to make it earlier in the day, it can be reheated in a 375°F oven for 10 minutes.*

makes forty to fifty palmiers

Wild Mushroom Palmiers

ingredients

1/4 cup olive oil

2 tablespoons unsalted butter

3 shallots, finely diced

2 cloves garlic, minced

2 pounds assorted wild or cultivated mushrooms, such as shiitake, cremini, or oyster, wiped clean and coarsely chopped

1/2 ounce dried porcini mushrooms, rehydrated and squeezed dry (see Tips)

1/3 cup white wine

1/4 cup soy sauce

1/3 cup heavy cream

1/4 cup chopped fresh Italian parsley

1/2 teaspoon dried thyme

Salt and freshly ground black pepper to taste

The palmier is an elegant shape, sometimes called an elephant ear. This appetizer is a party favorite, good hot or at room temperature, and they freeze beautifully. In other words, they are a great asset to a busy hostess. The mushrooms, with their meaty flavor, please carnivores and vegetarians alike.

Heat a large sauté pan over medium heat. When hot, add the olive oil and butter. Add the shallot and garlic and cook for 1 minute. Add the fresh and rehydrated mushrooms and cook until the liquid has released and then cooked off, about 15 minutes. Add the white wine and soy sauce and cook until almost dry, about 10 minutes. Add the heavy cream and reduce until the mixture is thick, about 5 minutes. Add the parsley and thyme, and season with salt and pepper.

Transfer the mixture from the pan to a food processor. Pulse on and off to chop the mixture coarsely. Do not purée. Let it cool. (If making ahead, cool to room temperature and refrigerate, covered, overnight.)

Roll half of the pastry out into a rectangle, 14 by 10 inches, and brush one side with the beaten egg. Sprinkle with half of the mustard seeds and some cornmeal. Turn the pastry over and spread with half of the mushroom mixture. Working on the long side, fold the edge of the pastry over and roll it halfway to the other long side. Roll the other side to meet in the middle. You now have two rolls touching in the center. Repeat with the remaining pastry and filling.

Place the mushroom logs on parchment-lined baking sheets and freeze until firm but not frozen hard, about 1 hour.

Preheat the oven to 375°F.

Quick Puff Pastry (page 332), or one 17½-ounce package frozen puff pastry, thawed in the refrigerator

1 egg, beaten

¼ cup mustard seeds

Coarse cornmeal, for sprinkling

Remove from the freezer and, using a sharp knife, cut each palmier into ¼-inch slices. Arrange on parchment-lined baking pans, leaving 1 inch between them, and bake until golden brown, 20 to 25 minutes.

Make-ahead: *Freeze the slices completely on a baking sheet. When frozen, place the palmiers in a freezer bag and return to the freezer until needed. To bake them without thawing, add a few minutes to the baking time.*

Tips: *Choose mushrooms that are firm, with no discoloration or sliminess. To hydrate dried mushrooms, cover them with boiling water and let them sit for about 10 minutes. Remove the mushrooms from the water and gently squeeze them dry. The mushroom liquid can be used in soups or stews. Pour it into a container, leaving the grit at the bottom of the bowl to be thrown away.*

If you run out of time and cannot complete the recipe, simply pack the mushroom mixture into an attractive ramekin and voilà—you have mushroom pâté to serve with toasted baguette slices or crackers.

serves eight

Zucchini and Carrot Quiche with Lemon Sauce

quiche

Flaky Pastry (page 335), fitted into a 9-inch tart pan with a removable rim and chilled

2 carrots, peeled, trimmed, and cut into matchsticks

2 medium zucchini, trimmed and cut into matchsticks

2 tablespoons unsalted butter

½ cup diced onion

⅓ cup diced celery

½ teaspoon salt, plus a dash for seasoning vegetables

⅛ teaspoon freshly ground black pepper, plus a dash for seasoning vegetables

Grated zest of 1 lemon

3 large eggs

½ cup heavy cream

Dash of cayenne pepper

Dash of ground nutmeg

¾ cup grated Gruyère cheese

Quiches and tarts were all the rage in the eighties. Remember "real men don't eat quiche"? Well, they do eat quiche, and they like it a lot. This elegant starter includes sweet vegetables baked in rich custard served with a citrusy butter sauce. It is heaven on a plate.

Preheat the oven to 375°F.

Line the chilled tart shell with parchment and fill with pie weights (or rice or dried beans). Bake the shell for 20 minutes. Carefully remove the parchment and the weights to a heatproof plate and return the shell to the oven to bake for another 15 minutes. Remove the shell from the oven and let cool on a rack.

Fill a large bowl with ice and water and set aside.

Bring 4 cups of salted water to a boil over high heat. Add the carrot and cook for 1 minute. Add the zucchini and cook for 1 minute longer. Drain the vegetables, using a large strainer, and transfer the strainer to the bowl filled with ice and water so that the vegetables are immersed in the cold water to stop the cooking and set the color. Remove the strainer from the water after a few minutes and lay the vegetables out on a towel to dry.

Heat a medium skillet over medium heat and add the butter. When the butter melts, add the onion and cook until soft, about 2 minutes. Add the celery and a dash of salt and pepper and cook for about 2 minutes longer. Turn the heat to low and let the vegetables cook until they are soft and sweet, about 10 minutes more.

In a medium bowl, beat the grated zest and eggs together. Beat in the cream, ½ teaspoon salt, ⅛ teaspoon pepper, cayenne, and nutmeg. Set aside.

Arrange the blanched and sautéed vegetables in the partially baked tart shell, and pour the egg mixture over them. Top with the cheese and bake the quiche on a baking

lemon sauce

3 tablespoons fresh lemon juice

3 tablespoons water

½ cup (1 stick) cold unsalted butter, cut into tablespoon-size pieces

¼ teaspoon salt

Lemon zest cut into curly strips with a zester, for garnish

sheet in the lower third of the oven until the filling is set and the cheese is lightly browned, about 25 minutes. Transfer the quiche to a rack to cool for at least 10 minutes. This will allow the filling to set up, and the quiche will cut more neatly.

To make the lemon sauce: Heat a medium, nonreactive skillet over high heat and add the lemon juice and water. Cook until only a tablespoon of liquid remains. Remove the pan from the heat and add 1 tablespoon of the cold butter to the pan, whisking. Add another tablespoon of butter to the pan before the first one melts completely, and continue to add butter to the pan until you have a nice sauce. It is important that the butter doesn't break or become watery, so be careful to cool the pan down by placing it on a cool work surface if the butter melts too fast.

Drizzle some of the sauce on each plate and top with a slice of warm quiche. Serve warm, garnished with the lemon curls.

Make-ahead: *The quiche can be made up to 4 hours ahead and kept, covered, at room temperature. Reheat in a 375°F oven for 10 minutes.*

makes two 16-inch pizza crusts

Basic Pizza Dough

ingredients

- 1 tablespoon sugar
- 1 package active dry yeast (2 1/4 teaspoons)
- 1 1/3 cups lukewarm water (105 to 115°F) water
- 1 tablespoon olive oil
- 3 1/3 cups unbleached all-purpose flour
- 1 tablespoon salt
- Cornmeal, for dusting

With a little practice, you can make better pizza at home in the same time it takes for pizza delivery on a busy Friday night. Once you get used to making your own great pizza exactly the way you want it, you will be able to lose the pizza guy's delivery number with no regrets.

We like to partially cook the pizza dough before topping it. This allows us to put lots of toppings on the pizza and still easily and safely return it to the oven. Pizza baked directly on a pizza stone or unglazed tiles will have a crisper crust. If you don't have tiles or a stone, you can bake pizza directly on an inverted cookie sheet that has been placed in the hot oven for 10 minutes.

Place a pizza stone or unglazed tiles on a rack in oven. Preheat the oven to 450°F.

In a measuring cup with a pouring spout, add the sugar and yeast to the warm water and stir. Allow the water-yeast mixture to sit for 3 or 4 minutes and, when foamy on top, add the olive oil. Stir.

Place the flour and salt in the bowl of a food processor and pulse a few times to blend the salt evenly into the flour.

Turn on the processor and quickly pour the yeast mixture through the feed tube. Process until the dough forms a ball, about 30 seconds. Let the dough rest in the processor for about 10 minutes. (The dough can also be made with a stand mixer. Begin to mix the dough with the paddle attachment, and once it has come together switch to the dough hook. Knead the dough for 3 or 4 minutes, then let it rest for 10 minutes, covered loosely with plastic wrap.)

Remove the dough from the processor and cut it in half. With a rolling pin, roll the dough out on a floured surface to the desired shape and thickness.

Sprinkle cornmeal over the surface of a rimless cookie sheet or a pizza peel. Place the rolled-out dough on top of the cornmeal. Pierce the dough a few times with a fork (to keep it from puffing up in the oven), and place it in the hot oven, sliding the dough off the sheet and onto the hot stone or tiles.

Bake for about 5 minutes and remove from the oven by sliding the crust back onto the cookie sheet. Top your pizza as desired. Repeat with the second piece of dough.

Make-ahead: *The pizza shells can be partially baked 1 hour before serving and then topped and baked.*

Tip: *A peel is what bakers use to place bread in the oven and retrieve it when loaves are baked directly on the oven floor. It has a handle and a flat wooden or metal surface, resembling a flat shovel.*

makes two 16-inch pizzas

Pizza Margherita

ingredients

- *Basic Pizza Dough (page 108)*
- *1/2 recipe (1/2 cup) Pesto (page 337)*
- *4 large tomatoes, thinly sliced*
- *Salt and freshly ground black pepper to taste*
- *1/2 cup grated Asiago cheese*
- *1/2 cup grated mozzarella cheese*
- *1/2 cup grated Parmesan cheese*

Margherita is the Italian name for the daisy, a common flower, but beautiful in its clean, fresh simplicity. This pizza, our version of a Naples classic, lives up to its namesake. It has no business being as good as it is—it's topped with nothing but pesto, tomatoes, and cheese—but sometimes simple really is best.

Shape and partially bake the pizza crusts as directed in the dough recipe. Remove from the oven, leaving it set at 450°F.

Spread pesto over each partially baked crust and top with a single layer of tomatoes. Season with salt and pepper, and top with the cheeses.

Place the pizzas in the oven, directly on top of the pizza stone or tiles. Bake until hot and the cheese browns, 6 to 8 minutes.

Make-ahead: *Pizza is best eaten directly from the oven, but if you have to make it earlier in the day, it can be reheated in a 375°F oven for 10 minutes.*

Tip: *The key to this simple pizza is in the slicing of the tomatoes. Thinly sliced tomatoes will become more concentrated in flavor as they bake in the oven. Thick slices will make for a wet, heavy pizza that the crust may not be able to support and will cause the topping to slide off.*

makes two 10-by-12-inch tarts

Pissaladière

ingredients

- 3 tablespoons olive oil
- 3 medium onions, peeled and thinly sliced
- ½ teaspoon salt
- ⅛ teaspoon freshly ground black pepper
- Quick Puff Pastry (page 332), or one 17½-ounce package frozen puff pastry, thawed in the refrigerator
- 2 tomatoes, thinly sliced
- ¼ teaspoon salt
- ⅛ teaspoon freshly ground black pepper
- ½ cup pitted and coarsely chopped kalamata olives
- ¼ cup thinly sliced fresh basil
- 2 tablespoons chopped fresh Italian parsley

A French version of a pizza, the puff pastry—based pissaladière is rich and flaky. Briny olives and caramelized onions lend it a salty sweetness. You can make your own puff pastry or take a shortcut and use frozen store-bought pastry. Although anchovies are a classic addition, many people prefer their pissaladière without them.

Preheat the oven to 425°F.

Heat a large skillet over medium-high heat. Add the olive oil and, when the oil is hot, add the onion, salt, and pepper. Sauté the onions, stirring them occasionally, until they are translucent, about 10 minutes. Turn the heat down to medium and cook the onions until they are golden brown and caramelized, about 15 minutes more. Remove from the heat and reserve.

Dust a work surface with flour and roll out half of the homemade puff pastry, or one sheet of the store-bought, using more flour as necessary to keep it from sticking. Roll it into a rectangle 11 by 13 inches. Place on a parchment-lined baking sheet and fold the edges ½ inch over the pastry to form a rim. Press the edges with the tines of a fork for a finished look. You now have the foundation for a pissaladière.

Arrange half of the tomato slices on the pastry. Season them with half of the salt and pepper. Top with half of the caramelized onions. Scatter half of the olives over the top, followed by half of the basil and parsley. Repeat the process with the remaining pastry.

Bake the pissaladières until the pastry is crisp and brown on the bottom and not soggy in the middle, 20 to 25 minutes. Cut into slices and serve hot or at room temperature.

Make-ahead: *The pissaladières can be assembled and frozen on a baking sheet wrapped in plastic wrap for 2 weeks. Bake without thawing, adding 5 minutes to the baking time.*

serves eight

Wild Mushroom Turnovers

ingredients

- *4 tablespoons unsalted butter*
- *2 tablespoons minced shallot*
- *8 ounces wild mushrooms, such as oyster, shiitake, cremini, or chanterelle, cleaned, trimmed, and sliced*
- *¼ cup dry sherry*
- *½ cup chicken stock*
- *¼ cup plus 1 tablespoon heavy cream, divided*
- *2 tablespoons minced fresh chives*
- *2 tablespoons chopped fresh Italian parsley*
- *5 ounces goat cheese*
- *Salt and freshly ground black pepper to taste*
- *Quick Puff Pastry (page 332), or one 17½-ounce package frozen puff pastry (2 sheets), thawed in the refrigerator*
- *1 egg yolk*

In the fall our cooking students clamor for new ways to cook the exciting varieties of wild mushrooms found in abundance at the grocery store. An elegant starter, these turnovers are deceptively easy to make and can be made either larger to be eaten on a plate or bite size to be eaten out of hand. If you can't find wild mushrooms, the button variety is a delicious substitute.

Melt the butter in a medium skillet over medium-high heat. Add the shallot and sauté for 2 minutes. Add the mushrooms and sauté until they exude their juices. Turn the heat down to medium and cook until the juices have evaporated.

Add the sherry to the mushrooms and cook until the pan is dry. Add the chicken stock and cook until dry again. Add ¼ cup of the cream and cook until the sauce is thickened. Add the chives, parsley, and goat cheese, and season to taste with salt and pepper. Set aside to cool.

Preheat the oven to 400°F. Roll the pastry out ⅛ inch thick on a floured surface. Cut each sheet of pastry into 8 squares (16 total). Spoon 1 tablespoon of the mushroom mixture slightly off-center onto one of the pastry squares. Fold over to enclose the filling and make a triangle. Seal the edges by pressing with the tines of a fork. Repeat with the remaining pastry squares and filling.

Mix the egg yolk with the remaining 1 tablespoon cream and brush over the top of the turnovers. Place the turnovers on a parchment-lined baking pan and bake until golden brown and crisp, about 10 minutes. Serve warm or at room temperature.

Make-ahead: *The mushroom filling can be made the day before and kept in the refrigerator until ready to use. The turnovers can be assembled and frozen on a baking sheet wrapped in plastic wrap for 2 weeks. Bake without thawing, adding 5 minutes to the baking time.*

Tip: *Most "wild" mushrooms found in your grocer's produce section aren't technically wild anymore. They are farmed much like the standard button mushrooms. Try searching your regional farmers' market in the fall for local varieties.*

makes two 16-inch pizzas

Artichoke Pizza with Roasted Garlic

ingredients

1 head garlic

2 tablespoons olive oil, divided

Basic Pizza Dough (page 108)

2 cans artichoke hearts, drained, squeezed dry, and chopped

¼ cup grated Parmesan cheese

½ cup grated Asiago cheese

½ cup grated fontina cheese

Salt and freshly ground black pepper to taste

In this unique take on white pizza, the roasted garlic adds depth, offset by the brininess of the artichoke hearts and topped off by a classic three-cheese combo. This recipe, like all pizza recipes, works best with a preheated pizza stone.

To roast the garlic: Preheat the oven to 350°F.

Cut off the top ½ inch of the garlic head and drizzle with about 1 teaspoon of the olive oil. Wrap in foil and bake until the garlic is soft, about 40 minutes. Allow to cool.

Reset the oven to 475°F, with a pizza stone in the lower section.

Shape and partially bake the pizza crusts as directed in the dough recipe.

Drizzle 1 tablespoon olive oil over each crust. Squeeze the roasted garlic from the head of garlic and spread over the pizzas. Arrange the artichoke hearts on the pizzas, and sprinkle with the cheese. Salt and pepper the pizzas and place them in the oven on top of the pizza stone. Bake until the bottom is crusty and the top is beginning to brown, 11 to 12 minutes. Allow to sit for a few minutes before cutting.

Make-ahead: *Pizza is best eaten directly from the oven, but if you have to make it earlier in the day, it can be reheated in a 375°F oven for 10 minutes.*

makes forty small turnovers

Moroccan-Style Lamb Turnovers

ingredients

- *1 teaspoon ground cumin*
- *1/2 teaspoon ground ginger*
- *1/4 teaspoon ground turmeric*
- *1/2 teaspoon ground cinnamon*
- *1 teaspoon salt*
- *1/4 teaspoon freshly ground black pepper*
- *1 tablespoon olive oil*
- *1/2 cup chopped onion*
- *2 cloves garlic, minced*
- *1 pound ground lamb*
- *1/3 cup white wine*
- *1 tablespoon tomato paste*
- *2 tablespoons golden raisins*
- *2 tablespoons pine nuts, toasted*
- *2 tablespoons chopped fresh cilantro*
- *1 egg*
- *1 tablespoon heavy cream*
- *Quick Puff Pastry (page 332), or one 17 1/2-ounce package frozen puff pastry, thawed in the refrigerator*

Moroccan cuisine is filled with the scent of sweet and savory spices intermingling together. We think that is part of what makes the dishes of this North African country seem to have so much depth and complexity. Redolent with cinnamon, ginger, and cumin, these fragrant lamb turnovers, cousins to the Spanish empanadas, are a great example of this spice marriage.

Mix together the cumin, ginger, turmeric, cinnamon, salt, and pepper in a small bowl. Set aside.

Heat the olive oil in a large skillet over medium heat. Sauté the onion until tender, about 2 minutes. Add the garlic and the spice mixture and continue to cook for another minute. Add the lamb and cook, breaking up any lumps with the back of a wooden spoon, until no longer pink, about 5 minutes. Add the wine and tomato paste and cook until most of the liquid has evaporated, about 4 minutes. Remove from the heat and add the raisins, pine nuts, and cilantro. Taste for seasoning. Let cool and set aside.

In a small bowl, beat together the egg and cream with a fork. Set aside.

Preheat the oven to 375°F. Line 2 large baking sheets with parchment paper. Divide the puff pastry in half. Work with half of the dough at a time, while keeping the other half chilled. On a lightly floured surface, roll half of the dough into a 12-by-15-inch rectangle. Cut into twenty 3-inch squares. Place a scant tablespoon of the filling in the center of each square. Brush the edges lightly with the egg wash. Fold each pastry into a triangle, enclosing the filling, and crimp the edges with a fork. Cut a small steam vent in the top of each turnover. Brush the tops lightly with more egg wash. Set on the prepared baking sheets. Repeat with the remaining dough and filling.

Bake the turnovers until golden brown, 15 to 20 minutes. Serve warm.

Make-ahead: *These can be frozen in a single layer on a baking sheet until solid, transferred to a freezer bag, and stored in the freezer for 1 month. They can be baked right from the freezer, adding 3 to 4 minutes to the baking time.*

makes about twenty breadsticks

Cornmeal Grissini with Fennel

ingredients

1 cup lukewarm water (105 to 115°F)

1 package active dry yeast (2¼ teaspoons)

1 teaspoon sugar

2½ cups all-purpose flour

⅔ cup yellow cornmeal

½ teaspoon fine sea salt

1 tablespoon fennel seed

¼ cup olive oil, plus additional for brushing the dough

Kosher salt, for sprinkling

Grissini are thin, crisp Italian breadsticks. Our fennel-scented version has a decidedly American twist with the addition of cornmeal, which gives them extra crunch. They're surprisingly easy to make because instead of forming individual snakes to make the sticks, you simply pat the dough into a rectangle, cut it into strips, and gently pull at either end to the desired length.

In small bowl, stir together the warm water, yeast, and sugar and let stand until foamy, about 5 minutes.

Stir together the flour, cornmeal, sea salt, and fennel seed in a large bowl, then stir in the yeast mixture and ¼ cup oil just until a dough forms.

Turn the dough out onto an unfloured work surface and knead until smooth and elastic, 8 to 10 minutes.

Transfer the dough to an oiled bowl and turn to coat. Cover the bowl with plastic wrap and let rise in a warm place until doubled in bulk, about 1 hour.

Preheat the oven to 425°F. Lightly oil two large baking sheets.

Punch the down dough and turn it out onto an unfloured work surface. Pat into a 14-by-10-inch rectangle. Cut crosswise into ½-inch-wide strips. Holding a strip with your fingers at each end, gently pull the strip to about 14 inches long. Place lengthwise on the oiled baking sheet, about ¾ inch apart.

Brush the sticks lightly with oil and sprinkle lightly with kosher salt.

Bake in the upper and lower thirds of oven, switching the position of the sheets halfway through baking, until the sticks are crisp and the ends are golden, 18 to 20 minutes total. Transfer to racks to cool.

Make-ahead: *Grissini keep in an airtight container at room temperature for 1 week.*

serves eight to ten

Walnut Focaccia with Red Grapes

dough

- $1\frac{1}{3}$ cups lukewarm water (105 to 115°F)
- 1 package active dry yeast ($2\frac{1}{4}$ teaspoons)
- 1 tablespoon sugar
- $3\frac{1}{4}$ cups unbleached all-purpose flour, plus more if necessary
- 3 tablespoons extra-virgin olive oil
- $1\frac{1}{2}$ teaspoons salt
- 1 cup toasted and chopped walnuts

topping

- $1\frac{1}{2}$ cups seedless red grapes
- 2 tablespoons extra-virgin olive oil
- 1 tablespoon chopped fresh rosemary
- Coarse sea salt, for sprinkling

Walnuts and grapes may seem like an unlikely combination for focaccia, but it's actually quite traditional. You'll see this type of focaccia all over Tuscany during grape harvest, before all the fruit is crushed and made into Chianti. It's often made as a sweet focaccia, but here we've added crunchy walnuts to the bread and rosemary to the topping to make a unique and surprisingly savory bread. This is wonderful served with goat cheese that has been drizzled with a fragrant Tuscan extra-virgin olive oil.

To make the dough: In a large bowl, stir together the water, yeast, and sugar and let stand until foamy, about 5 minutes. Add the flour, oil, and salt and beat with a wooden spoon until a dough forms. Turn out onto a lightly floured surface. Knead the dough until soft and velvety, about 10 minutes, adding a little more flour if it becomes too sticky to knead. Sprinkle the walnuts on top of the dough and continue to knead until they are evenly distributed. Form the dough into a ball.

Oil a large bowl. Add the dough, turning to coat with oil. Cover with a clean kitchen towel. Let rise in a warm area until doubled, about 1 hour and 15 minutes.

Press the dough evenly into a generously oiled 9-by-13-inch baking pan. Let rise, covered completely with a kitchen towel, until doubled in bulk, about 1 hour.

Preheat the oven to 450°F, using a baking stone if you have one.

Press the grapes into the top of the dough, and then brush the dough with the olive oil. Scatter the rosemary over the grapes, and sprinkle sea salt lightly over the focaccia. Bake in the middle of the oven until golden, about 25 minutes.

Using a large spatula, slip the focaccia out of the baking pan and onto a rack to cool. Cut into large squares. Serve warm or at room temperature.

Make-ahead: *Focaccia is really best eaten the day it's made, but you can refrigerate the unbaked dough, loosely covered in its bowl, for use the next day, or you can freeze it. To freeze the dough, flatten it into a disk and wrap tightly in plastic. If using cold dough from the refrigerator, let it sit on the counter for an hour or so to warm up. Allow frozen dough to sit in the refrigerator for 24 hours to thaw, and then let it sit on the counter for a few hours to finish warming up.*

Tip: *The sweetness of the grapes will make or break this bread. Taste one first to be sure they are at their sweetest.*

serves eight to ten

Focaccia with Roasted Red Peppers and Kalamata Olives

dough

1⅓ cups lukewarm water (105 to 115°F)

1 package active dry yeast (2¼ teaspoons)

1 teaspoon sugar

3¼ cups unbleached all-purpose flour, plus more if necessary

3 tablespoons extra-virgin olive oil

1½ teaspoons salt

topping

2 tablespoons extra-virgin olive oil

1 cup roasted red peppers from a jar, drained and roughly chopped

⅓ cup kalamata olives, pitted and chopped

Coarse sea salt, for sprinkling

Focaccia, like pizza, can be as simple or as elaborate as you wish. This version leans toward the simple side, with just a smattering of roasted peppers and chopped olives. Set out a big platter laden with squares of this soft, slightly salty focaccia next to a plate of cured meats, olives, and cheeses.

To make the dough: In a large bowl, stir together the water, yeast, and sugar and let stand until foamy, about 5 minutes. Add the flour, oil, and salt and beat with a wooden spoon until a dough forms. Turn out onto a lightly floured surface. Knead the dough until soft and velvety, about 10 minutes, adding a little more flour if it becomes too sticky to knead.

Oil a large bowl. Add the dough, turning to coat with oil. Cover with a clean kitchen towel. Let rise in warm area until doubled, about 1 hour and 15 minutes.

Press the dough evenly into a generously oiled 9-by-13-inch baking pan. Let rise, covered completely with a kitchen towel, until doubled in bulk, about 1 hour.

Preheat the oven to 425°F, using a baking stone if you have one.

Make shallow indentations all over the dough with your fingertips, and then brush with the oil, letting it pool in the indentations. Arrange the peppers and olives on top of the dough. Gently press the toppings into the dough. Sprinkle sea salt evenly over the focaccia and bake in the middle of the oven until golden, 25 to 30 minutes.

Using a large spatula, slip the focaccia out of the baking pan and onto a rack to cool. Cut into large squares. Serve warm or at room temperature.

Make-ahead: *Focaccia is really best eaten the day it's made, but you can refrigerate the unbaked dough, loosely covered in its bowl, for use the next day, or you can freeze it. To freeze the dough, flatten it into a disk and wrap tightly in plastic. If using cold dough from the refrigerator, let it sit on the counter for an hour or so to warm up. Allow frozen dough to sit in the refrigerator for 24 hours to thaw, and then let it sit on the counter for a few hours to finish warming up.*

makes thirty-five biscuits

Cheddar Biscuits with Ham and Chutney

ingredients

1 3/4 cups all-purpose flour

2 teaspoons baking powder

1 teaspoon salt

1/4 teaspoon cayenne pepper

3 tablespoons cold unsalted butter, cut into small pieces

1/2 cup grated cheddar cheese

3/4 cup buttermilk

2 tablespoons Dijon mustard

1 cup mango chutney (see Tips)

6 ounces thinly sliced Smithfield ham or Black Forest ham

Biscuits and ham bring a comforting, homey touch to any party. We've brought these country treasures uptown with the addition of sweet and tangy mango chutney.

To make the biscuits: Preheat the oven to 425°F. Line 2 large baking sheets with parchment paper. Combine the flour, baking powder, salt, and cayenne in a large bowl. Add the butter and, with your fingertips or a pastry blender, blend it into the flour mixture until the mixture resembles coarse meal. Stir in the cheese. Add the buttermilk and mustard and mix well.

Transfer the mixture to a lightly floured surface and gently knead about 3 times, until it just forms a dough. Roll out to a thickness of 1/2 inch. Cut out biscuits using a 1 1/2-inch round biscuit butter. Gather the scraps and reroll. Cut out additional biscuits. Transfer the biscuits to the prepared baking sheets. Bake until puffed and light golden on the bottom, about 12 minutes. Cool on a rack.

To assemble: Split each biscuit in half. Place a scant teaspoon of chutney on the bottom half of the biscuit, followed by a piece of ham, and then top with the other half of the biscuit. Transfer to a serving platter and serve at room temperature.

Make-ahead: *The biscuits can be made 8 hours ahead and kept, covered, at room temperature. The biscuits and ham can be assembled 1 hour ahead, covered, and kept at room temperature.*

Tips: *Because these biscuits are small, it's easy to overbake them. To check for doneness, peek underneath them to see if the bottom is slightly browned. If you wait for the top to be uniformly browned, you may go too far.*

Major Grey is a widely distributed type of mango chutney.

serves four to six

Crispy Corn Cakes with Smoky Black Bean Salsa

black bean salsa

- One 15-ounce can black beans, drained and rinsed
- 1 cup chopped tomatoes
- ½ cup chopped red onion
- 3 tablespoons minced fresh cilantro
- 2 tablespoons fresh lime juice
- ½ to 1 tablespoon finely chopped canned chipotle chiles in adobo sauce
- ½ teaspoon salt, plus more to taste

corn cakes

- 1 cup yellow or white cornmeal
- 2 teaspoons baking powder
- ½ teaspoon salt
- ½ teaspoon baking soda
- ½ cup grated sharp cheddar cheese
- 1 cup buttermilk
- 4 tablespoons unsalted butter, melted
- 1 cup fresh corn kernels, uncooked
- Oil for coating the skillet

- ½ cup sour cream, for serving

Crisp, hot corn cakes contrasting with cool, fresh salsa make this dish a delectable first course. The corn cakes alone make an interesting base for any number of toppings. Try them with sour cream and smoked salmon or with ham, cheddar cheese, and chutney.

To make the salsa: In a medium bowl, toss together all the salsa ingredients. Taste the salsa and season with more salt if necessary. Set aside to let the flavors blend while you make the corn cakes.

To make the corn cakes: In a large bowl, mix together the cornmeal, baking powder, salt, baking soda, and cheese. Add the buttermilk, butter, and corn kernels and stir until just blended.

Heat a large, nonstick skillet over medium-high heat. Lightly coat the pan with oil. Drop the batter by tablespoons into the skillet. Cook until bubbles break on top of each corn cake, and turn them over. Cook a few minutes more, or until the bottoms of the cakes are lightly browned. Place on a cookie sheet and keep in a warm oven until all the cakes are cooked.

To serve, arrange 3 or 4 cakes on a warm plate, top with a dollop of sour cream, and spoon on some of the salsa.

Make-ahead: *The salsa can be made up to 4 hours ahead and kept, covered, in the refrigerator. The corn cakes can be made up to ½ hour ahead and kept in a warm oven.*

serves six to eight

Rustic Goat Cheese Tart with Caramelized Balsamic Onions

Rich goat cheese makes the perfect backdrop for the sweet and tangy onions in this palate-pleasing tart. The addition of balsamic vinegar to the onions gives them sparkle and helps pull together the flavors of all the other ingredients. This savory tart is a cinch to take to a party, as it is terrific warm or at room temperature.

tart

½ recipe Quick Puff Pastry (page 332), or 1 sheet of frozen puff pastry, thawed in the refrigerator

filling

4 ounces goat cheese

3 ounces mozzarella cheese, grated

¼ cup sour cream

3 tablespoons grated Parmesan cheese

Salt and freshly ground black pepper to taste

1 egg

1 tablespoon water

balsamic onions

1 tablespoon unsalted butter

1 tablespoon oil

1 large onion, thinly sliced

Pinch of sugar

Salt and freshly ground black pepper to taste

1 tablespoon balsamic vinegar

Preheat the oven to 400°F.

Roll the dough out into a 14-by-10-inch rectangle on a lightly floured surface, and place it on a baking sheet covered with parchment. Refrigerate for 15 minutes.

Mix the filling ingredients together in a medium bowl and spread onto the dough, leaving a 1½-inch border. Fold the uncovered edge of the pastry over the filling mixture, making small pleats along the way.

Mix together the egg and water and brush around the edges of the pastry. Place in the oven and bake until golden brown, about 20 minutes.

To make the onions: While the tart is baking, heat the butter and oil in a skillet. Add the onions and sugar and cook over medium heat until the onions are a deep golden brown, about 20 minutes. Add the vinegar and season with salt and pepper.

Place the tart on a serving platter and arrange the onions on top. Slice and serve warm or at room temperature.

Make-ahead: *The tart can be made up to 4 hours ahead and kept, covered, at room temperature.*

serves eight to ten

Roasted Tomato and Mozzarella Tart

ingredients

Flaky Pastry (page 335)

1½ pints cherry tomatoes

2 tablespoons olive oil

¼ teaspoon salt, plus more for seasoning tomatoes

¼ teaspoon ground black pepper, plus more for seasoning tomatoes

1½ cups grated mozzarella cheese

6 tablespoons plus ¼ cup grated Parmesan cheese, divided

½ cup thinly sliced fresh basil

2 large eggs

1 cup half-and-half

During the time of the year when tomatoes are not at their peak, roasting cherry tomatoes can be a nice way to bring a bite of summer into your life. Roasting them intensifies their sweetness and depth of flavor. This tart matches them with mozzarella cheese and fresh basil and makes just as lovely a light lunch dish as it does an appetizer. Pair it with a salad and a crisp, dry white wine.

Roll out the pastry on a lightly floured surface into a 13-inch circle, about ¼ inch thick. Transfer to an 11-inch tart pan with a removable bottom. Fold in the overhang to form double-thick sides. Pierce with a fork. Cover and chill for 1 hour.

Meanwhile, preheat the oven to 375°F. In a medium bowl, toss the tomatoes with the oil and salt and pepper to taste. Arrange the tomatoes on a rimmed baking sheet. Drizzle any juices in the bowl over the tomatoes. Bake until the tomatoes are wrinkled and slightly browned in spots, 15 to 20 minutes. Remove from the oven, and increase the temperature to 400°F.

Line the tart shell with parchment paper; fill with dried beans or pie weights. Bake until the sides are set, about 20 minutes. Remove the paper and beans. Bake the shell until the bottom is set, pressing with the back of a fork if bubbles form, about 8 minutes. Cool for 5 minutes.

Sprinkle the mozzarella over the bottom of the shell. Top with 6 tablespoons of the Parmesan and the tomatoes and basil. Whisk together the eggs, half-and-half, ¼ teaspoon salt, and ¼ teaspoon pepper in a medium bowl. Pour the mixture into the tart shell. Sprinkle with the remaining ¼ cup Parmesan.

Bake until the custard is set and the crust is golden brown, about 35 minutes. Serve warm or at room temperature.

Make-ahead: *The tart can be made up to 4 hours ahead and kept, covered, at room temperature.*

makes twelve pieces

Kalamata Olive, Goat Cheese, and Roasted Red Pepper Bruschetta

bruschetta

Twelve ½-inch-thick slices Italian or French bread (from a loaf about 3 inches in diameter)

¼ cup olive oil

topping

4 ounces fresh goat cheese (such as Montrachet), softened

10 kalamata olives, pitted and finely chopped

2 tablespoons finely chopped fresh Italian parsley

Pinch of freshly ground black pepper

2 roasted red bell peppers, peeled and sliced lengthwise into ¼-inch strips

Extra-virgin olive oil, for drizzling

Kalamata olives have a bold flavor that gives these bruschetta an extra punch. If you're having a large party, think about making several different kinds of bruschetta and alternating them on one large serving platter. The colors will be striking, and the platter will make a nice centerpiece for your appetizer table.

To make the bruschetta: Prepare a grill or preheat the broiler. Brush the bread slices lightly on both sides with the olive oil. Grill or place the bread on a pan, 6 inches under the broiler, until lightly browned, turning once, 3 to 4 minutes total. Remove from the oven and let cool.

To make the topping: In a medium bowl, mix together the goat cheese, olives, parsley, and black pepper until well combined.

To assemble: Spread each piece of toasted bread with a layer of the goat cheese mixture, and then top with a few strips of the roasted red pepper. Drizzle the top with a little extra-virgin olive oil. Serve at room temperature.

Make-ahead: *The bread slices can be toasted up to 4 hours in advance and kept at room temperature in an airtight container. Topping can be made 1 day ahead and refrigerated.*

serves six to eight

Bruschetta Topped with White Bean and Gremolata Salad

bruschetta

- 1 baguette, cut on the diagonal into 3/8-inch-thick slices
- Olive oil, for brushing
- 1/2 cup extra-virgin olive oil
- 1/4 cup fresh lemon juice
- Salt and freshly ground black pepper to taste
- Two 16-ounce cans cannellini or navy beans, drained and rinsed

gremolata

- Grated zest of 2 lemons
- 1/2 cup finely chopped fresh Italian parsley
- 2 cloves garlic, minced

- Extra-virgin olive oil, for drizzling
- Lemon slices and parsley sprigs, for garnish

Gremolata is a powerhouse mixture of garlic, lemon, and parsley traditionally used as a garnish for osso buco. In this dish, it lends beautiful color and a burst of flavor to the white beans. This is the moment to break out your best olive oil to drizzle over the bruschetta. Its flavor will add an authentic finishing touch and give an attractive glisten to the white bean topping.

To make the bruschetta: Preheat the broiler. Brush both sides of the bread with olive oil and place on a baking sheet in a single layer. Place 6 inches under the broiler and brown on both sides, 3 to 4 minutes total.

In a medium bowl, mix together the olive oil, lemon juice, salt, and pepper. Toss with the beans and set aside.

To make the gremolata: Combine the zest, parsley, and garlic. Place on a cutting board and chop together until finely minced.

Mix the gremolata with the beans and place a large spoonful of the bean mixture on top of each slice of toasted bread. Drizzle the tops lightly with olive oil. Arrange the bruschetta on a large platter garnished with lemon slices and sprigs of parsley.

Make-ahead: *The bread slices can be toasted up to 4 hours in advance and kept at room temperature in an airtight container. The topping can be made up to 4 hours in advance. Assemble just before serving.*

Tip: *Canned beans can be a good substitute for dried. Look for brands whose beans are for the most part whole and not too mushy. Make sure you drain and rinse them well, or your dish may turn out too salty.*

makes thirty-six pieces

Tomato, Basil, and Fresh Mozzarella Bruschetta

bruschetta

1 baguette, about 22 inches long, ends trimmed, cut on the diagonal into 36 slices, ½ inch thick

½ cup olive oil

topping

3 large, ripe tomatoes (1½ pounds), cored, seeded, and cut into ¼-inch dice

8 ounces fresh mozzarella cheese, cut into ¼-inch dice, at room temperature

¼ cup chopped fresh basil

2 tablespoons cold-pressed extra-virgin olive oil

1 tablespoon balsamic vinegar

1 clove garlic, finely minced

¼ teaspoon salt

Freshly ground black pepper to taste

One of the true pleasures in life is going out to the garden on a hot August afternoon and picking a sun-warmed tomato right off the bush, cutting it up, tossing it with fragrant basil and olive oil, and piling it on crispy bread slices. Of course, you can use, as we often do, store-bought tomatoes, but wait until the season is at its peak, usually in August or September, to make this simple but flavorful dish.

To make the bruschetta: Prepare a grill or preheat the broiler. Brush the bread slices lightly on both sides with the olive oil. Grill or place the bread on a pan, 6 inches under the broiler, until lightly browned, turning once, 3 to 4 minutes total. Remove from the oven and let cool. The bread slices can be toasted several hours in advance.

To make the topping: In a medium bowl, stir together the tomatoes, mozzarella, basil, oil, vinegar, garlic, salt, and a generous grinding of pepper. Cover and let stand at room temperature for 30 minutes.

Adjust the seasoning, if necessary. Spoon some of the topping onto each slice of bread, or serve the topping in a bowl accompanied by the grilled bread slices, letting guests top their bruschetta to taste.

Make-ahead: *The bread slices can be toasted up to 4 hours in advance and kept at room temperature in an airtight container. The topping can be made up to 4 hours in advance. Assemble just before serving.*

serves six to eight

Bruschetta with Roasted Tomato, Pesto, and Mascarpone

ingredients

- 2 pints cherry tomatoes
- 2 tablespoons olive oil, plus more for brushing
- Salt and freshly ground black pepper to taste
- 1 baguette, cut on the diagonal into 3/8-inch-thick slices
- 8 ounces mascarpone or cream cheese
- 1/2 cup pesto, homemade (page 337) or store-bought

Certain dishes capture the spirit of a season, and every bite of these little toasts screams out "late summer!" The best thing about them, though, is that you don't have to make them in the summer. In this recipe, the tomatoes are oven-roasted, which brings out their sweetness and concentrates their flavor.

Preheat the oven to 425°F.

On a large, rimmed baking sheet, toss the cherry tomatoes with 2 tablespoons olive oil and sprinkle with salt and pepper. Roast the tomatoes until they collapse and are lightly browned, about 20 minutes. Set aside.

Preheat the broiler.

Brush both sides of the bread with olive oil and place on baking sheet in a single layer. Place 6 inches under the broiler and brown on both sides, 3 to 4 minutes total.

Spread a liberal amount of mascarpone on each slice of toasted bread. Top the mascarpone with a thin layer of pesto. Spoon a dollop of the roasted tomatoes in the middle of each slice, making sure not to completely cover up the pesto.

Make-ahead: *The bread slices can be toasted up to 4 hours in advance and kept at room temperature in an airtight container. Assemble just before serving.*

makes about seventy-two coins

Walnut Blue Cheese Shortbread Coins

ingredients

- *1 cup walnuts, toasted*
- *1 cup (2 sticks) unsalted butter, cut into tablespoon-size pieces*
- *4 ounces blue cheese, crumbled*
- *2 cups all-purpose flour*
- *1/4 teaspoon freshly ground black pepper*
- *Salt, for sprinkling*

Something about these savory, salty little rounds cries out for a martini.

Dump the walnuts into the bowl of a food processor and pulse 6 times. They should be chopped, but not ground.

Add the butter, blue cheese, flour, and black pepper to the nuts and process until the mixture forms a dough, about 6 seconds.

Remove the dough from the bowl and divide it in half. Transfer each half to a large piece of parchment paper. Form into a log approximately 1 1/2 inches in diameter. Wrap the log in the parchment and gently roll back and forth on the countertop to evenly round out the shape. Twist up the extra wrap on the ends and refrigerate for 8 hours.

Preheat the oven to 350°F.

Working with one log at a time, cut the dough with a sharp knife crosswise into 1/4-inch-thick slices and arrange them on a parchment-lined baking sheet. Bake in the oven until pale golden and crisp, 10 to 13 minutes. Cool on the baking sheet for a few minutes and then remove with a spatula to a rack. Sprinkle with salt. Serve warm or at room temperature.

Make-ahead: *The logs keep, chilled and tightly wrapped, for 3 days. They can also be frozen for up to 2 months. Thaw in the refrigerator overnight before slicing and baking.*

makes thirty-six pieces

Ham, Cheddar, and Apple Butter Bites

ingredients

- *9 slices home-style white bread, crusts removed*
- *3 tablespoons unsalted butter, at room temperature*
- *3 tablespoons apple butter*
- *9 thin slices ham*
- *9 thin slices cheddar cheese*

Although these bites are essentially dressed-up grilled cheese sandwiches (what could be wrong with that?), the technique is good to know and the filling possibilities are endless. Here we've combined the saltiness of ham and cheddar cheese with the sweetness of apple butter, but you could just as easily use pepperoni, mozzarella, and a smear of pizza sauce if pizza bites are what you crave.

Preheat the oven to 450°F. With a rolling pin, flatten each piece of bread. Spread one side of each piece with a teaspoon of butter. On the other side spread a teaspoon of apple butter, then top with a slice of ham and a slice of cheddar. Roll up, jelly-roll style, with the buttered side out, and secure each roll with toothpicks. Place on a parchment-lined baking sheet and bake until lightly browned, 10 to 12 minutes. Cool on racks for 5 minutes. Slice each roll crosswise into 4 pieces. Transfer to a serving plate and serve warm or at room temperature.

Make-ahead: *The uncooked rolls can be made 1 day ahead and kept, covered, in the refrigerator. Bake and serve as directed.*

Tip: *This easy recipe is made even easier if you use ham and cheese that has been sliced at the deli counter in your grocery store. The size of the slices seems to fit perfectly onto the bread, almost covering it completely, which is what you want.*

makes thirty-six turnovers

Picadillo Empanadas

ingredients

- *2 tablespoons vegetable oil*
- *1 cup finely chopped onion*
- *2 teaspoons minced garlic*
- *2 teaspoons ground cumin*
- *1 tablespoon chili powder*
- *1 teaspoon crumbled dried oregano*
- *3/4 teaspoon ground cinnamon*
- *1/4 teaspoon ground allspice*
- *1/4 teaspoon crushed red pepper flakes*
- *1/2 teaspoon salt*
- *1/4 teaspoon freshly ground black pepper*
- *1 pound ground beef*
- *1/4 cup tomato paste*
- *One 28-ounce can plum tomatoes, including the juice, chopped*
- *1/2 cup raisins*
- *1/2 cup finely chopped pimiento-stuffed green olives*
- *1 egg*
- *2 tablespoons water*
- *3 recipes Flaky Pastry (page 335)*

Although most people refer to these savory pies as empanadas, they are really empanadillas, a smaller, turnover version of the larger empanada. The ground beef is seasoned with a complex mix of spices, and the addition of raisins and olives gives the filling a subtly sweet and salty flavor. They're great for entertaining because they can be made ahead, frozen, and baked just before serving.

Heat the oil in a large skillet over medium heat. Add the onion, garlic, cumin, chili powder, oregano, cinnamon, allspice, red pepper flakes, salt, and pepper and cook over medium-low heat, stirring, until the onion is softened, about 3 minutes. Add the beef, and cook the mixture, stirring and breaking up any lumps, until the meat is no longer pink. Add the tomato paste, tomatoes with juice, raisins, and olives, and simmer the picadillo, stirring occasionally, until it is thickened and most of the liquid has evaporated, 20 to 25 minutes. Let it cool. Adjust the seasoning to taste.

Mix together the egg and water. Set aside. Preheat the oven to 425°F.

Work with one batch of dough at a time, while keeping the rest covered in the refrigerator. On a lightly floured surface, roll out the dough to a 12-by-8-inch rectangle. Cut it into twelve 4-by-2-inch rectangles. Using a pastry brush, lightly brush the egg wash around the edges of each rectangle. Put a scant tablespoon of the picadillo onto the bottom half of each rectangle and fold the top half over it, enclosing the filling. Crimp the edges with a fork to seal.

Transfer the empanadas with a spatula to a parchment-lined baking sheet. Using a sharp knife, make a small vent in the top of each one and brush lightly with the egg wash. Bake in the middle of the oven until they are golden, 10 to 15 minutes. Transfer the empanadas to a rack and let them cool. Serve warm or at room temperature.

Make-ahead: *The picadillo can be made 1 day in advance and kept covered and chilled. Let it return to room temperature before proceeding with the recipe. The unbaked empanadas can be frozen in a single layer on a baking sheet until solid, transferred to a freezer bag, and stored in the freezer for 1 month. They can be baked right from the freezer, adding 3 to 4 minutes to the baking time.*

serves ten to twelve

Brie en Croûte with Brown Sugar, Apples, and Almonds

ingredients

2 tablespoons unsalted butter

3 Granny Smith apples, peeled, cored, and cut into ¼-inch dice

⅓ cup brown sugar

Pinch of salt

Quick Puff Pastry (page 332), or one 17½-ounce package frozen puff pastry, thawed in the refrigerator

1 wheel Brie, about 17 ounces, chilled

3 tablespoons slivered almonds, toasted

1 large egg, lightly beaten

1 tablespoon heavy cream

There's really nothing more decadent than warm, creamy, oozy cheese, wrapped in a flaky, buttery crust. So when you're looking to gild the lily on any occasion, look no further than this dish.

In a medium skillet, melt the butter over medium heat. Add the apples and sauté until golden brown, about 8 minutes. Sprinkle in the brown sugar and salt and toss to coat the apples thoroughly. Continue to cook until the sugar is bubbly, about another minute. Remove the apples to a plate and let cool to room temperature.

Preheat the oven to 425°F. On a lightly floured surface, roll out half of the puff pastry or 1 sheet of frozen pastry to a rough circle about 15 inches in diameter. The dough should be ⅛ inch thick. Using the wheel of Brie as a guide, cut out a round of pastry the size of the Brie. Reserve the pastry round and keep refrigerated.

Trim off the rind from the top of the Brie. Roll out the rest of the pastry ⅛ inch thick (about 15 inches in diameter) and transfer to a large parchment-lined baking sheet. Center the Brie, cut side up, on the pastry in the pan and spread the sautéed apples on top, to within ½ inch of the edge of the Brie. Sprinkle with the almonds.

In a small bowl, mix together the egg and cream for an egg wash.

Carefully wrap the pastry up over the Brie and trim the excess to leave a 1-inch border on top of the Brie. Brush the border with the egg wash and place the reserved pastry round on top, pressing the edges of the dough together gently but firmly to seal. Brush the top of the pastry with egg wash and arrange the reserved cutouts decoratively on it. With the back of a table knife, gently score the side of the pastry with vertical marks, being careful not to pierce the dough. Chill the Brie, uncovered, for 30 minutes.

Bake in the middle of the oven until puffed and golden, 20 to 25 minutes. Let stand in the pan on a rack for about 20 minutes for very runny melted cheese, about 40 minutes for thicker melted cheese.

Make-ahead: *The Brie can be assembled, unbaked, 1 day ahead and kept chilled, covered loosely. It can also be frozen for up to 1 month, but it must be thawed overnight in your refrigerator before baking.*

makes about twenty-five twists

Cheddar Cheese and Rosemary Twists

ingredients

- *Quick Puff Pastry (page 332), or one 17½-ounce package frozen puff pastry, thawed in the refrigerator*
- *1 egg*
- *1 tablespoon water*
- *1¼ cups grated sharp cheddar cheese*
- *2 tablespoons minced fresh rosemary*

There isn't a caterer alive who doesn't appreciate the benefits of puff pastry. It can be made well in advance and pulled out of the freezer when needed to form the base of an endless variety of tidbits that are sure to please. Here we're using it as a vehicle for sharp cheddar cheese and fragrant rosemary that together create the most wonderful aroma in your house as they bake.

Preheat the oven to 400°F. Line 2 baking sheets with parchment paper.

On a lightly floured surface, roll out half of the puff pastry into an 18-by-10-inch rectangle. In a small bowl, beat the egg and water together with a fork. Lightly brush the pastry rectangle with some of the egg wash. Sprinkle the cheese and rosemary over it. Roll out the other half of the pastry into an 18-by-10-inch rectangle, and place it on top of the cheese. Gently roll over it with the rolling pin to fuse them together. Trim any uneven edges. Lightly brush the top with the egg wash. With a sharp knife or pizza cutter, cut the pastry crosswise into ½-inch-wide strips.

Arrange the strips about ½ inch apart on the baking sheets, pressing one end onto the baking sheet to secure it. Twist each strip a few times and press the other end onto the baking sheet to ensure that the strip will not unravel. Place the baking sheets in the refrigerator for 15 minutes to allow the puff pastry to chill again before baking.

Bake in the upper and lower thirds of the oven, switching the position of the sheets halfway through baking, until the sticks are crisp and the ends are golden, 10 to 12 minutes total. Transfer to racks to cool.

Make-ahead: *The twists can be made 2 days in advance and kept in an airtight container at room temperature. Rewarm them on a baking sheet for 5 minutes in a 350°F oven.*

Tip: *If the pastry warms up and becomes difficult to work with during assembly, simply place it in a baking pan and refrigerate for 10 minutes to allow it to firm up.*

makes about twenty-five straws

Parmesan and Cracked Pepper Straws

The sharpness of the black pepper and the earthy richness of the Parmesan make these easy-to-prepare straws a perfect match for predinner cocktails. Serve them standing up in glasses for an elegant presentation.

ingredients

- *Quick Puff Pastry (page 332), or one 17½-ounce package frozen puff pastry, thawed in the refrigerator*
- *1 egg*
- *1 tablespoon water*
- *¾ cup grated Parmesan cheese, divided*
- *½ tablespoon coarsely ground black pepper*

Preheat the oven to 400°F. Line 2 baking sheets with parchment paper.

On a lightly floured surface, roll out half of the puff pastry into an 18-by-10-inch rectangle. In a small bowl, beat the egg and water together with a fork. Lightly brush the pastry rectangle with some of the egg wash. Sprinkle ½ cup of the cheese and the black pepper over it. Roll out the other half of the dough into an 18-by-10-inch rectangle, and place it on top of the cheese. Gently roll over it with the rolling pin to fuse them together. Trim any uneven edges. Lightly brush the top with the egg wash and sprinkle with the remaining ¼ cup cheese. With a sharp knife or pizza cutter, cut the pastry crosswise into ½-inch-wide strips.

Arrange the strips about ½ inch apart on the baking sheets. Place the baking sheets in the refrigerator for 15 minutes to allow the puff pastry to chill again before baking.

Bake in the upper and lower thirds of the oven, switching the position of the sheets halfway through baking, until the sticks are crisp and the ends are golden, 10 to 12 minutes total. Transfer to racks to cool.

Make-ahead: *The straws can be made 2 days in advance and kept in an airtight container at room temperature. Rewarm them on a baking sheet for 5 minutes in a 350°F oven.*

serves four to six

Pita Nachos with Hummus and Greek Salsa

ingredients

- *1 serrano chile, minced*
- *½ cup diced red onion*
- *1 large tomato, seeded and diced*
- *½ medium cucumber, peeled, seeded, and diced*
- *2 tablespoons chopped fresh mint*
- *3 tablespoons olive oil*
- *2 teaspoons red wine vinegar*
- *½ teaspoon salt*
- *Pita Wedges (page 96)*
- *1½ cups Hummus (page 275)*
- *½ cup grated aged mizithra cheese*

We would tell you that this dish is a great low-fat alternative to "real" nachos (which it is), but it is so fresh and vibrant and as lovely to look at as it is good to eat, that the comparison doesn't seem fair. The pita chips are light and crisp, and the Greek salsa, while using many familiar salsa ingredients, employs mint rather than cilantro, which makes for a unique and refreshing topping.

In a medium bowl, combine the chile, onion, tomato, cucumber, and mint. Add the olive oil, vinegar, and salt and toss to coat. Taste and adjust the seasoning.

Arrange the pita wedges on a large platter. Scatter dollops of hummus on top of the pita chips. Spoon the tomato mixture over them, and sprinkle with the cheese. Serve immediately.

Make-ahead: *The salsa can be made an hour ahead, covered, and kept cool.*

Tips: *Although making your own hummus is quick and easy, feel free to use your favorite store-bought variety when you're really pinched for time.*

Mizithra is a Greek cheese made from the whey of feta. It is sold both fresh and aged. Fresh mizithra is soft, and the aged cheese is firm, with a pungent aroma and mild flavor. The aged cheese makes a perfect grating cheese. If you can't find mizithra in the market, substitute Romano.

makes thirty-six crackers

Bacon and Cheddar Shortbreads with Rosemary

ingredients

- *1 cup pecans, toasted*
- *4 slices bacon, cooked until crisp*
- *1 cup (2 sticks) unsalted butter, cut into tablespoon-sized pieces*
- *1 pound extra-sharp cheddar cheese, grated*
- *2 cups all-purpose flour*
- *1 tablespoon fresh rosemary leaves, or 1 teaspoon dried rosemary*
- *1 teaspoon cayenne pepper*
- *Kosher salt, for sprinkling*

Perfect for do-ahead dining, these crackers whip up quickly in your food processor and wait patiently in your freezer until you need them. Smoky bacon and fragrant rosemary combine to give sophisticated flavor to this savory shortbread, which partners well with sparkling wine.

Dump the pecans into the bowl of a food processor and process until finely chopped but not pasty.

Add the bacon, butter, cheddar, flour, rosemary, and cayenne to the nuts and process until the mixture forms a dough.

Remove the cracker dough from the bowl and divide it in half. Roll each half into a log about 3 inches in diameter. Wrap in parchment paper and refrigerate for 8 hours.

Preheat the oven to 350°F.

Working with one log at a time, cut the dough with a sharp knife crosswise into 1/4-inch-thick slices and arrange them on a parchment-lined baking sheet. Bake until pale golden and crisp, 10 to 13 minutes. Cool on the baking sheet for a few minutes and then remove with a spatula to a rack. Sprinkle lightly with kosher salt. Serve warm or at room temperature.

Make-ahead: *The logs keep, chilled and tightly wrapped, for 3 days. They can also be frozen for up to 2 months.*

makes two 12-inch flatbreads

Rosemary Flatbread with Onions, Walnuts, and Gorgonzola

dough

1 tablespoon sugar

1 package active dry yeast (2 1/4 teaspoons)

1 1/2 cups lukewarm water (105 to 115°F)

3 1/3 cups all-purpose flour

2 tablespoons chopped fresh rosemary, or 2 teaspoons dried

1 tablespoon salt

2 tablespoons olive oil

topping

3 tablespoons olive oil

2 medium red onions, thinly sliced

Salt and freshly ground black pepper to taste

3 tablespoons extra-virgin olive oil, divided

1 teaspoon chopped fresh thyme

1/2 cup chopped walnuts

1/2 cup crumbled Gorgonzola cheese

Coarse sea salt, for sprinkling

Focaccia is an Italian flatbread that can serve as part of a starter or a main dish, or as an unusual base for a sandwich or salad.

To make the dough: In a measuring cup with a pouring spout, add the sugar and yeast to the warm water and let sit until foamy, about 5 minutes. Place the flour, rosemary, and salt in a food processor and pulse to disperse the salt. Add the olive oil to the yeast mixture and pour the mixture into the processor through the feed tube while the machine is running. Process for 1 minute. The mixture should form a ball. If it is too loose, add more flour, a tablespoon at a time. The dough should be a little bit sticky. Transfer the dough to a bowl and cover with plastic wrap. Set in a warm place and let rise until doubled, 1 to 2 hours.

While the dough is rising, make the topping: Heat a sauté pan over medium-high heat and add the olive oil. When the oil is hot, add the onions, salt, and pepper and sauté until the onions begin to wilt. Turn the heat down and cook the onions slowly until brown and caramelized, about 30 minutes. Let sit in the pan until ready to assemble.

Place tiles or a baking stone in the oven and preheat to 425°F. Remove the dough from the bowl and place on a floured countertop. Cut the dough in half and place each half on a parchment-lined baking sheet. Drizzle the dough halves with some of the olive oil and press out the dough until it is a uniform thickness, about 1/2 inch. Spread the dough with the onions, thyme, walnuts, Gorgonzola, a drizzle of the remaining olive oil, and a sprinkle of sea salt.

Bake until lightly browned with bubbling cheese, 15 to 20 minutes. Remove from the oven and let cool for 5 minutes. Cut into wedges and serve warm.

Make-ahead: *Focaccia is really best eaten the day it's made, but you can refrigerate the unbaked dough, loosely covered in its bowl, for use the next day, or you can freeze it. To freeze the dough, flatten it into a disk and wrap tightly in plastic. If using cold dough from the refrigerator, let it sit on the counter for an hour or so to warm up. Allow frozen dough to sit in the refrigerator for 24 hours to thaw, and then let it sit on the counter for a few hours to finish warming up.*

Chapter 7 Meat

Poultry, *and* Eggs

makes forty-two chicken fingers

Chicken Fingers with Honey Mustard Dipping Sauce

ingredients

- *6 boneless, skinless chicken breast halves*
- *1 large egg, beaten*
- *2 tablespoons Dijon mustard*
- *1/8 teaspoon cayenne pepper*
- *1 1/2 cups panko crumbs or dried breadcrumbs*
- *1/2 cup grated Parmesan cheese*
- *1/4 cup chopped fresh cilantro*
- *1 teaspoon ground cumin*
- *4 tablespoons unsalted butter, melted*
- *2 bunches cilantro, for garnish*
- *Honey Mustard Dipping Sauce with Horseradish (facing page), for serving*

Chicken fingers aren't just for kids anymore. We've given this tired school-cafeteria classic an adult update with cayenne, Parmesan cheese, cilantro, and cumin. Using panko crumbs instead of regular breadcrumbs gives these juicy tidbits an extra crunch.

Preheat the oven to 425°F.

Cut each chicken breast on the diagonal into 7 strips. Mix the egg, mustard, and cayenne pepper together in a shallow bowl and toss the chicken strips to coat them.

In another bowl, mix the panko, Parmesan, cilantro, and cumin. Add half the chicken pieces and toss to coat them well. Line 2 baking pans with parchment and arrange the breaded chicken on the pan, leaving some space between the chicken pieces so that they will brown nicely. Drizzle with the butter. Repeat the process with the rest of the chicken.

Bake the chicken fingers until nicely colored and firm to the touch, about 25 minutes. For even browning, it helps to rotate the pans halfway through baking. Remove from the oven and cool for 5 to 10 minutes before serving. Serve the chicken fingers arranged on a platter, garnished with cilantro, with a bowl of the dipping sauce.

Make-ahead: *Before baking, the chicken fingers can be breaded and kept, uncovered, in the refrigerator for up to 8 hours.*

Tip: *Panko crumbs are Japanese dried breadcrumbs. They can be found at Asian markets and most grocery stores.*

Honey Mustard Dipping Sauce with Horseradish

(makes about one cup)

Horseradish gives this mustard-based dipping sauce an added kick. This dip is the perfect match for chicken fingers, crudités, breadsticks.

ingredients

- *½ cup Dijon mustard, grainy or smooth*
- *3 tablespoons honey*
- *3 tablespoons sour cream*
- *1 tablespoon prepared horseradish*

Mix all of the ingredients in a serving bowl. Refrigerate until needed.

Make-ahead: *This dip keeps, covered and refrigerated, for up to 3 days.*

serves ten

Chicken Skewers with Cranberry Dipping Sauce

marinade

- *1 thumbnail-sized piece fresh ginger, peeled*
- *3 cloves garlic, peeled*
- *¼ cup dry sherry or dry white wine*
- *3 tablespoons soy sauce*
- *2 tablespoons Asian (dark) sesame oil*
- *2 tablespoons hoisin sauce*
- *½ teaspoon Chinese chili sauce*

skewers

- *8 boneless, skinless chicken breast halves*
- *6 tablespoons sesame seeds*

Cranberry Dipping Sauce (facing page), for serving

Chicken skewers look and taste great on a holiday table. Guests will be intrigued by the red dipping sauce made from all-American cranberries with a touch of Asian influence in the ginger, soy, and sesame oil. We often make these up and freeze them on foil-lined trays a week in advance of a party. Just pop them into the oven frozen, being sure to give them a few more minutes of cooking time.

To make the marinade: Place the ginger, garlic, sherry, soy sauce, sesame oil, hoisin, and chili sauce in the bowl of a food processor and process until the garlic and ginger are shredded.

Cut each chicken breast half into 8 slices. Pour the marinade into a resealable plastic bag and add the chicken. Press out the air and seal the bag, laying it on a baking pan in the refrigerator to marinate for at least 2 hours and not more than 4 hours. Turn the bag over after 1 hour to evenly marinate the chicken.

Preheat the oven to 375°F. Remove the chicken from the marinade and thread it onto 6-inch wooden skewers that have been soaked in water for about 30 minutes. (The soaking keeps the skewers from burning up in the oven and also keeps the chicken moist.) Dredge one side of the chicken in the sesame seeds, and lay the prepared skewers on a foil-lined baking sheet.

Bake the chicken for about 10 minutes. Serve hot with the dipping sauce.

Make-ahead: *To freeze up to 2 weeks ahead, just toss the chicken in the marinade and do not allow it to sit before skewering. Once skewered, arrange it on a parchment-lined baking sheet wrapped in plastic and then a sheet of foil. The skewers can be baked frozen; just add a few more minutes to the baking time.*

ingredients

2 cloves garlic

1 thumbnail-sized piece fresh ginger

2 tablespoons soy sauce

2 tablespoons cider vinegar

1 teaspoon Asian (dark) sesame oil

1 can (8 ounces) whole-berry cranberry sauce

1 teaspoon Chinese chili sauce

Cranberry Dipping Sauce

(makes about two cups)

This sauce is a delicious accompaniment to roasted, grilled, or broiled chicken breasts, turkey, pork chops, and flank steak. You will be sure to find many uses for it, and it will keep in your refrigerator for a couple of weeks.

Process the garlic and ginger in the bowl of a food processor until finely minced. Add the remaining ingredients and process until smooth. Allow the sauce to sit for a few hours for the flavor to develop fully.

Make-ahead: *This sauce will keep, covered, in the refrigerator for up to 2 weeks.*

makes forty-eight pieces

Basil Crusted Chicken Fingers with Red Bell Pepper Aïoli

ingredients

2 pounds boneless, skinless chicken breast halves, each cut on the diagonal into 8 fingers

Salt and freshly ground black pepper to taste

Pesto (page 337)

2 cups panko crumbs

Red Bell Pepper Aïoli (see the Mayonnaise variation on page 334), for serving

We've ramped up the usual chicken fingers by marinating the chicken strips in pesto and then rolling them in panko crumbs (Japanese breadcrumbs). The aïoli is a colorful and tasty accompaniment for the adults, but don't forget to put out a bowl of ketchup for the kids.

Place the chicken in a large bowl, sprinkle with salt and pepper, and toss to mix well. Add the pesto and coat evenly. Let the chicken sit in the refrigerator for 30 minutes to flavor the meat.

Preheat the oven to 400°F.

Place the panko in another large bowl. Toss 3 or 4 pieces of chicken with the panko to coat, and transfer them to a parchment-lined baking sheet. Leave an inch or two between the chicken fingers so that they will cook evenly. Continue to coat the chicken pieces in the same way until all the chicken is coated with the crumbs. Bake until the chicken is firm to the touch, about 25 minutes. The coating will be soft and light but will crisp up as the chicken cools.

Serve the warm chicken fingers with the Red Bell Pepper Aïoli.

Make-ahead: *The breaded, unbaked chicken fingers can be kept, uncovered, in the refrigerator for up to 8 hours.*

Tip: *Panko crumbs are large flaked, unseasoned, dried Japanese breadcrumbs. If you can't find them, look for any larger flaked dried breadcrumbs at the grocery store.*

makes thirty-two pieces

Black Forest Ham and Pear Crescents

ingredients

- *2/3 cup sour cream*
- *2 teaspoons grated peeled ginger*
- *1/2 teaspoon salt*
- *Dash of freshly ground black pepper*
- *1 tablespoon finely minced fresh chives*
- *16 slices Black Forest ham, halved lengthwise*
- *2 Anjou or Bartlett pears, cored and each cut into 16 long slices, tossed with 1 tablespoon lemon juice to retard browning*
- *Finely minced fresh chives, for garnish (optional)*
- *Chive blossoms, for garnish (optional)*

Delectable sweet pears, salty ham, and rich sour cream with spicy fresh ginger make an easy and quick appetizer for busy hosts. When a recipe is this simple, only the best ingredients will do. Buy the highest quality ham available, and make sure the pears are sweet and juicy.

Mix the sour cream, ginger, salt, pepper, and chives in a small bowl. Taste for seasoning and adjust if necessary with salt and pepper.

Lay a piece of ham on a work surface and spread with about a teaspoon of the sour cream mixture. Lay a pear slice on one narrow end of the ham slice crosswise, so that the ends are sticking out from the sides of the slice of ham. Roll up the ham so that it encases all but the ends of the pear slice. Repeat with the remaining pear and ham slices.

Arrange the pear and ham crescents on a decorative platter and garnish with the minced chives or chive blossoms if desired.

Make-ahead: *The ginger sour cream can be made up to 8 hours in advance.*

Tips: *Try to buy the pears for this dish a few days in advance. We find that allowing hard, woody grocery store pears to ripen for a few days in a paper bag on the kitchen counter renders them succulent and juicy.*

Black Forest ham is a German smoked boneless ham that has a blackened skin from smoking or caramelization. If you can't find Black Forest ham for this appetizer, use any high-quality ham; your guests will still rave.

serves six

Caramelized Onion Frittata

ingredients

- *3 tablespoons olive oil*
- *2 cups thinly sliced onions*
- *3/4 teaspoon salt, divided*
- *1/4 teaspoon freshly ground black pepper, divided*
- *2 tablespoons balsamic vinegar*
- *6 large eggs, beaten*
- *2 tablespoons sour cream*
- *2 tablespoons unsalted butter*
- *3 tablespoons grated Parmesan cheese*

When onions are cooked slowly, they become meltingly tender and sweet. Sometimes we call them onion jam or a confit of onions. Whatever you call them, these onions make a simple, delicious frittata.

Heat a medium, heavy-bottomed skillet over medium heat. Add the olive oil and, when it is hot, add the onions to the pan, along with 1/2 teaspoon of the salt and 1/8 teaspoon of the pepper. Cook the onions over medium heat until they soften, then turn the heat to low and continue to cook very slowly, stirring occasionally, until the onions begin to brown and get very soft (the culinary term is "melted onions"). It should take about 30 minutes. Add the balsamic vinegar and continue to cook the onions until the vinegar has evaporated. Reserve.

In a medium bowl, whisk the eggs with the remaining 1/4 teaspoon salt and 1/8 teaspoon pepper. Whisk in the sour cream until incorporated.

Heat a 10-inch nonstick oven-safe skillet over medium heat. Add the butter, and when it sizzles, pour in the beaten eggs. Allow the skillet to sit undisturbed for 1 minute, then arrange the caramelized onion over the top. It will sink down into the frittata. Turn the heat to low and cook, covered and undisturbed, for about 3 minutes. In the meantime, preheat the broiler. Remove the skillet from the stove and place it on the second highest rack under the broiler, about 6 inches from the heat source. Broil the frittata until the top begins to brown, about 4 minutes. Sprinkle the cheese over the top and broil for another 2 minutes. Shake it to see if it has set. If it is still jiggly, leave it under the broiler for another minute.

Remove the frittata from the oven and let it sit for about 5 minutes. This will allow it to finish cooking and to set up. Cut the frittata into 12 wedges and serve warm or at room temperature.

Make-ahead: *The frittata can be cooked and kept, covered, at room temperature up to 1 hour before serving.*

makes about forty pieces, serving eight

Jerked Chicken and Melon Bites

ingredients

- ½ cup coarsely chopped onion
- 3 medium green onions, coarsely chopped
- 1 Scotch bonnet or habanero chile, cut in half lengthwise and seeded (see Tips)
- 2 cloves garlic
- 2 teaspoons Chinese five-spice powder
- 1 teaspoon ground allspice
- 2 teaspoons coarsely ground black pepper
- 1 teaspoon dried thyme
- ½ teaspoon ground nutmeg
- 1 teaspoon salt
- ¼ cup soy sauce
- 1 tablespoon vegetable oil
- 4 chicken breast halves, each cut into 10 square pieces
- ½ ripe honeydew melon, peeled, seeded, and cut into 1-inch squares

Jerk is a fiery Jamaican spice blend that can vary widely from island to island in the Caribbean. Although commercial blends of this spice mixture are available, the depth of flavor is better when it is freshly prepared. The cool, sweet melon really helps to put out the fire of these spicy chicken bites.

In a food processor, combine the onion, green onions, chile, garlic, five-spice powder, allspice, black pepper, thyme, nutmeg, and salt and process to a coarse paste. With the machine on, add the soy sauce and oil in a steady stream until combined. Pour the marinade into a large, shallow dish, add the chicken, and turn to coat. Cover and refrigerate for 1 hour or up to 3 hours.

Prepare a grill, or preheat the oven to 425°F. Soak the wooden skewers in warm water to cover for 30 minutes. Thread the chicken pieces onto 6-inch wooden skewers, one piece of chicken to a skewer, sliding the chicken onto the skewer so that about 2 inches of skewer is exposed at the pointed end. If grilling, cook the chicken for 2 minutes over hot coals, turn it, and cook for another 2 minutes. If using the oven, bake the chicken on a parchment-lined baking pan for about 7 minutes. Remove the chicken from the oven.

Add a piece of the melon to each chicken skewer and arrange the skewers artfully on a platter. Serve warm from the oven or at room temperature.

Tips: *Habaneros, the hottest of the hot chiles, are short, round chiles shaped like a mini pumpkin. They can be green, yellow, orange, or red when mature. Use gloves when handling these super-hot chiles to avoid burning your hands A serrated grapefruit spoon is a handy tool to use when removing the seeds from chiles. Just cut the chiles in half and scrape the seeds out with the tip of the spoon. Be sure to wash your hands thoroughly with soap after touching the chiles to avoid a transfer of the incendiary oils to other sensitive areas of your body.*

Chinese five-spice powder usually contains ground cloves, fennel seed, star anise, cinnamon, and Szechwan pepper.

makes twenty-four patties, serving six

Lamb Patties with Eggplant Relish

relish

- 3 tablespoons olive oil
- ½ cup diced onion
- 1 cup diced eggplant
- 1 cup diced yellow squash
- ¼ cup diced red bell pepper
- ½ teaspoon salt
- 2 cloves garlic, finely minced
- 1 teaspoon minced fresh thyme, or ½ teaspoon dried
- 3 tablespoons balsamic vinegar
- 1 tablespoon honey
- ¼ teaspoon freshly ground black pepper

lamb patties

- 1 pound lean ground lamb
- 1 egg
- ½ cup fresh breadcrumbs
- ¼ cup finely grated Parmesan cheese
- ¼ cup milk
- 1 teaspoon ground cumin
- 1 teaspoon ground coriander

Rich ground lamb and vinegary balsamic relish create a taste explosion in your mouth. These tender little burgers are sophisticated yet simple finger food that will surprise your guests with their Middle Eastern flavors.

Preheat the oven to 400°F.

To make the relish: Heat a medium nonstick frying pan over medium heat and add the olive oil. When the oil is hot, add the onion and sauté until it is soft, about 2 minutes. Add the eggplant and yellow squash and continue to sauté until the eggplant begins to soften, about 3 minutes more. Add the red bell pepper, salt, garlic, and thyme and cook for another 3 minutes to blend the flavors. Add the vinegar to the pan and cook until the vinegar has evaporated, about 3 minutes. Stir in the honey and pepper and taste the relish for seasoning. Adjust with salt and pepper as desired. Set aside to use later.

To make the lamb patties: In a medium bowl, mix with your hands the lamb, egg, breadcrumbs, Parmesan, milk, cumin, coriander, cinnamon, salt, pepper, and garlic. Heat a small nonstick frying pan over medium heat and cook about 1 tablespoon of the lamb mixture and taste to check the seasoning. Adjust the seasoning with salt and pepper if desired.

Divide the meat into 24 patties and arrange them on a parchment-lined baking pan. Make an indentation in the center of each patty with your thumb (this indentation will hold the relish later). Bake in the oven until the lamb patties are cooked to medium, about 8 minutes. They should be slightly pink inside when you remove them from the oven, and they will continue to cook for a few minutes as they sit.

1/2 teaspoon ground cinnamon

1 teaspoon salt

1/4 teaspoon freshly ground black pepper

2 cloves garlic, finely minced

1/3 cup mayonnaise, homemade (page 334) or store-bought

1/2 teaspoon ground cumin

24 slices narrow French baguette, lightly toasted

2 tablespoons finely minced fresh chives

Blend the mayonnaise and the cumin together and spread a small amount on each toasted baguette slice. This is the glue that will hold your appetizer together. Arrange a warm lamb patty on top of each slice, and top the lamb with the relish. Arrange the appetizers on a large serving platter, and sprinkle the chives over the top. Serve warm.

Make-ahead: *The lamb patties can be formed and kept, uncooked and covered, in the refrigerator overnight. The relish can be made 1 day ahead and kept, covered, in the refrigerator. Rewarm before serving.*

makes about twelve large wedges, serving six

Spanish Tortilla

ingredients

- *1½ cups diced peeled potatoes*
- *¼ cup plus 1 tablespoon olive oil, divided*
- *2 cups chopped onions*
- *3 cloves garlic, minced*
- *2 tomatoes, seeded and diced*
- *1½ teaspoons salt, divided*
- *½ teaspoon freshly ground black pepper, divided*
- *7 large eggs, beaten*
- *2 tablespoons minced fresh chives*

Spanish tortilla is an egg dish that resembles the Italian frittata. We've tinkered with the classic method here by steaming the potatoes instead of cooking them in a large amount of olive oil. Most tapas bars in Spain serve this in hearty wedges at room temperature. It is easy to eat out of hand while balancing a glass of sherry or other drink in the other.

Steam the potatoes over simmering water until they are tender and easily pierced with a fork, about 20 minutes. Remove from the steamer, transfer to a large bowl, and let cool slightly.

While the potatoes are steaming, heat a 10-inch nonstick, oven-safe skillet over medium-high heat and add ¼ cup of the olive oil. When the oil is hot, add the onions and sauté for 3 minutes. Turn the heat to medium and add the garlic to the pan. Sauté for another 3 minutes and add the tomatoes, ½ teaspoon of the salt, and ¼ teaspoon of the pepper. The mixture will become wet from the tomatoes. Turn the heat down if it cooks too fast and starts to spatter. Simmer until the tomatoes have reduced and the mixture is tender, about 10 minutes. Transfer to the bowl containing the potatoes and mix well. Wipe out the skillet with a paper towel.

In a large bowl, beat the eggs with the remaining teaspoon of salt and ¼ teaspoon pepper, and the chives.

Preheat the broiler. Heat the skillet over medium heat. Add the remaining tablespoon of olive oil and tilt the pan so that the oil covers the bottom. Add the potato-onion mixture and spread evenly in the pan. Quickly pour in the eggs and cook over low heat, covered, for 10 minutes. Turn off the heat and transfer the skillet to a broiler on the second highest rack, about 6 inches from the heat source. Broil until the tortilla is set, about 3 minutes. Remove from broiler and let stand, covered, for 15 minutes. Slide the tortilla onto a serving plate and cut into wedges. Serve warm or at room temperature.

Make-ahead: *The tortilla will keep for 2 days, covered and refrigerated. Let it come to room temperature before serving, or reheat, wrapped in foil, in a 350°F oven for about 10 minutes.*

Variations: *This recipe lends itself to many variations, such as substituting sun-dried tomatoes for fresh tomatoes or adding cooked sausage, ham, or bacon. Steamed broccoli, cauliflower, asparagus, or zucchini can be substituted for the potatoes or added with them for a substantial appetizer or luncheon entrée.*

makes about sixteen kabobs

Lemon Marinated Lamb Kebabs with Cilantro Yogurt Sauce

kebabs

2 tablespoons coriander seeds, ground in a mortar or spice mill

1 teaspoon salt

1/4 teaspoon freshly ground black pepper

1/4 teaspoon cayenne pepper

1 pound boneless leg of lamb, cut into 1-inch cubes

Grated zest of 1 lemon

1/2 cup fresh lemon juice (about 3 lemons)

yogurt sauce

1 cup yogurt

1 tablespoon fresh lemon juice

1/2 teaspoon salt

1/4 cup chopped fresh cilantro

salt and freshly ground black pepper to taste

We love the sharp brightness of lemon paired with the rich juiciness of lamb. These easy kebabs are terrific cooked on a hot grill on a warm summer night. Add some cold beer and call it a party.

Combine the coriander, salt, pepper, and cayenne in a bowl and add the lamb cubes. Toss to coat them evenly with the seasoning and add the zest and lemon juice. Let the lamb marinate at room temperature for 30 minutes.

To make the yogurt sauce: Combine the yogurt, lemon juice, salt, and cilantro in a small bowl. Set aside.

Prepare a grill or preheat a broiler. Soak 16 wooden skewers in water for 30 minutes. Thread 2 or 3 cubes of lamb loosely onto each skewer, and sprinkle with salt and pepper. Grill or broil the lamb for 3 minutes, then turn and cook for 2 minutes on the second side for medium doneness, or allow a minute longer per side for well done. Transfer the lamb to a platter and serve with the yogurt sauce for dipping.

Make-ahead: *The lamb can be cooked and kept, covered, at room temperature for 1 hour. Reheat in a 400°F oven for 3 minutes.*

makes about twenty-four wings

Spicy Teriyaki Wings

ingredients

- 1/4 cup soy sauce
- 1/4 cup chopped fresh cilantro
- 1/4 cup rice vinegar
- 1/4 cup brown sugar
- 2 tablespoons Asian (dark) sesame oil
- 2 tablespoons vegetable oil
- 2 tablespoons minced fresh ginger
- 1 tablespoon hoisin sauce
- 4 cloves garlic, minced
- 4 teaspoons Asian chili garlic sauce
- 2 pounds chicken drumettes
- Minced green onion, for garnish (optional)

Since chicken wings have so little meat on them, we tend to like the drumettes (the little drumstick-shaped part of the wing, the meatiest part) the best. That way, when your fingers are all messy from the wings, at least it was worth it. We've made our own version of teriyaki here with lots of chili garlic sauce for an extra kick.

Mix the soy sauce, cilantro, rice vinegar, brown sugar, sesame oil, vegetable oil, ginger, hoisin sauce, garlic, and chili garlic sauce together in a large bowl. Add the chicken wings and toss to coat. Refrigerate for at least 2 hours and up to 24 hours.

Preheat the oven to 425°F.

Arrange the wings on a parchment-lined baking sheet. Roast until golden brown, about 20 minutes, then turn and brown the second side, about 10 minutes.

While the wings are cooking, transfer the marinade to a small saucepan and reduce it over medium heat by half, about 5 minutes. Remove the marinade glaze from the heat and set aside.

When the wings have cooked for 30 minutes, brush them with the reduced marinade and set the oven to broil. Broil the wings until they are crispy, about 4 minutes. Turn them and brush the other side with the glaze. Broil on the second side until they are crispy, another 4 minutes.

Serve the wings hot on a large platter, garnished with green onion if desired.

Make-ahead: *The wings can be made up to 2 hours in advance and kept, covered, at room temperature. Broil the wings for 2 minutes on each side to reheat.*

Tip: *When serving appetizers with bones, it is considerate to leave ample dishes for guests to dispose of troublesome remainders.*

makes about sixteen kebabs

Tamarind Glazed Lamb Kebabs

ingredients

2 tablespoons olive oil

2 cloves garlic, minced

2 tablespoons honey

½ teaspoon Asian hot chili sauce

⅓ cup tamarind paste, chopped into small chunks

¼ cup water

1 tablespoon fresh lemon juice

½ teaspoon cardamom seed, ground in a mortar or spice mill

1 pound boneless leg of lamb, cut into 1-inch cubes

Salt and freshly ground black pepper to taste

Sliced lemons, for garnish

Italian parsley sprigs, for garnish

This treatment uses sweet honey, spicy chili sauce, and tangy, sharp tamarind paste to create a glaze perfect for the grill or barbecue. Try using this glaze on barbecued chicken or pork. Tamarind paste can be found in Asian grocery stores or at online specialty sites.

Prepare a grill or preheat the broiler.

Heat the olive oil in a medium skillet over medium heat. Add the garlic and sauté until fragrant, about 1 minute. Add the honey, chili sauce, tamarind paste, water, lemon juice, and cardamom and stir to combine the ingredients. The tamarind paste will break down as it heats up. Remove the glaze from the heat and let it cool. Strain through a fine-mesh strainer to remove the solids (there will be seeds and hard pieces in the tamarind paste). Set aside.

Place the lamb in a large bowl and toss with ¼ cup of the glaze. Allow to stand at room temperature for 1 hour.

Soak 16 wooden skewers in water for 30 minutes. Thread 2 or 3 cubes of lamb loosely onto each skewer and sprinkle with salt and pepper. Grill or broil the lamb for 3 minutes on the first side and 2 minutes on the second side for medium doneness; allow a minute longer per side for well done. Brush the lamb with the remaining glaze and arrange on a platter. Garnish with lemon slices and parsley sprigs.

Make-ahead: *The glaze can be made up to 2 days ahead and kept, covered, in the refrigerator.*

makes twenty-four pieces

Thai-Style Chicken Salad in Baby Pitas

ingredients

- 1/4 cup fresh lime juice, plus more as needed
- 1 tablespoon sugar
- 1 teaspoon Asian fish sauce
- 1/4 cup mayonnaise
- 2 cups cooked chicken, cut into 1/2-inch chunks
- 1 ounce bean sprouts
- 3 green onions, white and green parts, thinly sliced
- 1/3 cup coarsely chopped fresh cilantro
- 1/4 cup finely diced celery
- 2 tablespoons Thai red curry paste
- Salt and freshly ground black pepper to taste
- 12 baby pita breads, cut in half
- Cilantro sprigs and lime wedges, for garnish

East meets West in this lime- and cilantro-scented chicken salad. The filling would be great in rice paper wraps, but the ease and availability of baby pitas really speeds up the assembly process. Be sure to hide any leftover chicken salad in the refrigerator for lunch the next day.

In a large bowl, combine the lime juice, sugar, and fish sauce. Stir to dissolve the sugar and add the mayonnaise, chicken, sprouts, green onion, cilantro, celery, and red curry paste. Toss to combine. Taste and adjust the seasoning with salt, pepper, or more lime juice to your taste. Refrigerate for up to 4 hours, until ready to assemble the pitas.

Make a pocket in each pita half and stuff it with the chicken salad. Arrange on a serving platter and garnish with cilantro and lime wedges.

Make-ahead: *The pitas can be assembled up to 1 hour before serving, covered with a damp paper towel and then with plastic, and refrigerated.*

Tip: *When made with larger pitas, these chicken salad sandwiches make great picnic fare.*

makes one 9-by-5-inch loaf or three 4½-by-2¾-inch mini loaves

Veal and Ham Pâté

ingredients

- 3 tablespoons unsalted butter
- ¾ cup finely minced onion
- 2 teaspoons plus a dash of salt, divided
- 3 cloves garlic, minced
- ½ cup port or Madeira
- 2 carrots, peeled and cut into strips ¼ inch wide and 5 inches long
- 8 slices bacon
- 12 ounces ground lean pork
- 12 ounces ground veal
- 12 ounces ground pork fat
- 2 large eggs
- 1 tablespoon minced fresh chives
- 1 teaspoon dried marjoram
- ¼ teaspoon freshly ground black pepper
- ¼ teaspoon five-spice powder
- 2 tablespoons Cognac
- 4 ounces ham, sliced into 9 thin strips, ¼ inch wide by 5 inches long
- ½ cup shelled natural pistachios

Because it is almost impossible to find good store-bought pâté, you should make this dish at least once in your life. It will be a revelation, and you will be glad you found out how wonderful it is to have on hand. We like to make these in mini-loaf pans and freeze them a few weeks before the holiday craziness sets in.

Preheat the oven to 350°F.

Heat a medium skillet over medium heat and add the butter to the pan. When the butter melts, add the onion and a dash of salt. Sauté the onion until tender, about 10 minutes. Add the garlic to the pan and cook for another 2 minutes. Add the port or Madeira and cook until the liquid is reduced by half. Remove the pan from the heat and let it cool.

Bring 2 cups of water to a boil in a medium saucepan. Add the carrots and boil until crisp-tender, about 5 minutes. Remove from the water with a slotted spoon and pat dry on paper towels. Set aside. Add the bacon to the water in the pan and cook for about 5 minutes to remove some of the smoky flavor. Drain the water from the pan, pat the bacon dry on paper towels, and reserve.

Add the onion mixture, pork, veal, pork fat, eggs, chives, the remaining 2 teaspoons salt, marjoram, pepper, five-spice powder, and Cognac to a bowl and mix with your hands or a large spoon to combine. Sauté a tablespoon of the mixture in a skillet, taste to check the seasoning, and adjust if necessary.

If making a standard-size loaf, line the bottom and sides of a 9-by-5-inch loaf pan with the bacon. Divide the meat mixture into 3 parts and press 1 part into the bottom of the pan. Arrange 3 lengths of ham and 3 lengths of carrot lengthwise in the pan. Arrange pistachios between the rows. Top with another third of the meat mixture. Repeat the

Crusty bread, for serving

Mustard, for serving

Cornichons (tiny French pickles), for serving

process, ending with the remaining meat mixture. Cover the top of the pâté with the remaining bacon. If using mini-loaf pans, divide the meat mixture into 9 parts and layer the terrines in the same manner.

Cover the pâté with aluminum foil and set the pan or pans in the center of a 13-by-9-inch baking pan. Add boiling water to the pan so that the water comes halfway up the sides of the pâté pan(s). Place in the oven and bake until a meat thermometer inserted into the pâté reads 160°F, about 1 hour and 30 minutes for a standard-size loaf. The mini-loaf pans will be done in 45 minutes to 1 hour. The pâté will have shrunk from the sides of the pan and will be full of liquid fat. (The fat can be carefully drained off at this point and discarded or, if you prefer, left with the pâté. Many Europeans think of the fat as a delicacy, but most Americans will enjoy the pâté best without it.)

Carefully remove the pan of pâté from the water bath and set a piece of wood or cardboard that will fit inside the 9-by-5-inch pan over it. Top it with a 4-pound weight. This compacts the pâté and creates a better texture. Cool the pâté to room temperature and refrigerate it, still weighted, overnight.

Unmold the pâté from its pan, slice it, and serve on a platter, accompanied by rustic bread, grainy mustard, and cornichons.

Make-ahead: *If you keep the pâté in its pan, covered with its fat, it will keep for up to 1 week, refrigerated. Once the pâté is removed from the pan and the fat is disturbed, it will keep for 3 or 4 days, refrigerated. The pâté can be frozen, but the texture will suffer and become a bit grainy.*

makes about thirty-six kebabs

Smoke and Fire Beef Kebabs with Sour Cream, Lime, and Cilantro Dipping Sauce

ingredients

1/4 cup fresh lime juice

1 tablespoon chopped canned chipotle chiles in adobo sauce

2 large cloves garlic, minced

1/2 cup olive oil

1/2 teaspoon salt

1 1/2 pounds top sirloin beef, cut into 1-inch cubes

Sour Cream, Lime, and Cilantro Dipping Sauce (page 269), for serving

Chipotle chiles are what gives these kebabs their smoke and fire. These smoked, dried jalapeños are sold either in their dried form or canned in a vinegary tomato sauce called adobo. The flavor marries beautifully with beef, and although chipotles can be blazing hot, here they're cooled by the sour cream dipping sauce.

To make the kebabs: In a medium bowl, whisk together the lime juice, chipotles, garlic, olive oil, and salt. Pour into a resealable plastic bag. Add the beef cubes and marinate for 4 hours.

Meanwhile, soak about 36 wooden skewers in water for at least 30 minutes before grilling, to prevent burning.

Prepare a medium-hot fire in a grill. Place 1 or 2 cubes of beef on each wooden skewer, keeping them toward one end so that the other end can be used as a handle.

Place the kebabs on the grill. Grill for 2 to 3 minutes on each side for medium doneness. Serve warm with the dipping sauce on the side.

Make-ahead: *The marinade can be made a day ahead.*

makes thirty-six kebabs

Chicken Kebabs with Green Herb Sauce

kebabs

- 2 tablespoons fresh lemon juice
- 1/4 cup olive oil
- 1 clove garlic, minced
- 1/2 teaspoon salt
- 1/4 teaspoon freshly ground black pepper
- 1 1/2 pounds boneless, skinless chicken breast halves, cut into 1 1/2-inch cubes

sauce

- 1 tablespoon drained capers
- Grated zest of 1 lemon
- 1 teaspoon minced garlic
- 1/2 cup extra-virgin olive oil
- 1/4 cup chopped fresh mint
- 1/2 cup chopped fresh Italian parsley
- Salt and freshly ground black pepper (optional)

Our green sauce is really a takeoff on the Italian salsa verde. The Italian version often includes bread and anchovies and adds wonderful flavor to simple meat dishes. For this recipe we've left out the bread and anchovies and added mint to the parsley for a crisp, clean, and powerful sauce that enhances the chicken kebabs perfectly.

In a large bowl, combine the lemon juice, olive oil, garlic, salt, and pepper. Add the chicken and toss to coat. Cover and refrigerate for 1 hour. Meanwhile, soak 36 wooden skewers in water for 30 minutes to prevent burning during cooking.

To make the sauce: While the chicken marinates, chop the capers and, in a small bowl, whisk them together with the zest and garlic. Add the olive oil in a slow stream, whisking constantly until blended. Whisk in the herbs. Taste and season with salt and pepper if necessary. Set aside.

Prepare a grill or preheat a broiler. Thread 1 or 2 chicken pieces onto each soaked skewer, working the meat down toward one end. Grill or broil the kebabs until nicely seared and cooked through, 4 to 5 minutes on each side. Transfer to a serving platter and serve with the sauce.

Tip: *Don't try to make these too far ahead. The chicken should not sit in the acidic marinade for more than an hour, and the sauce will begin to darken if made more than an hour in advance.*

makes about thirty-two meatballs

Sweet and Spicy Sesame Lamb Meatballs

ingredients

- 1½ teaspoons olive oil
- ⅓ cup minced onion
- 1 large clove garlic, minced
- ½ teaspoon salt
- ½ teaspoon ground cumin
- ¼ teaspoon cayenne pepper
- ¼ teaspoon ground allspice
- ⅛ teaspoon ground cinnamon
- 1 pound ground lamb
- ½ cup fine fresh breadcrumbs
- 1 large egg, beaten lightly
- ¼ cup sesame seeds, lightly toasted
- 1 cup chutney (use your favorite)
- ¼ cup orange juice

Cucumber and Cilantro Yogurt Dip (page 251), for serving

For some reason, our students seem slightly intimidated by the thought of ground lamb, probably because its availability in the United States has been limited. But with the growing popularity of lamb, ground lamb can now be found in almost any good butcher shop. For these meatballs, we take advantage of its wonderful flavor by pairing it up with a Middle Eastern mix of spices and tossing them in an orange chutney glaze.

Heat the oil in a small, nonstick skillet over medium-low heat. Add the onion and garlic and cook, stirring, until softened. Transfer to a large bowl and stir in the salt, cumin, cayenne, allspice, and cinnamon. Add the lamb, breadcrumbs, egg, and sesame seeds and combine well. Form the mixture into 1¼-inch meatballs, arranging them on a tray.

Preheat the oven to 450°F. Bake the meatballs in the upper third of the oven until golden and just cooked through, 8 to 10 minutes.

Meanwhile, heat the chutney and orange juice in a large saucepan. Toss in the cooked meatballs and stir gently to coat. Remove the meatballs to a warm serving platter and serve with the yogurt dip.

Make-ahead: *The uncooked meatballs can be prepared 1 day ahead, covered loosely, and chilled. You can also freeze the uncooked meatballs in one layer on a baking sheet until solid, and then transfer them to a freezer bag where they will keep for a month. Thaw them in the refrigerator on a baking sheet and then bake as directed.*

Tip: *If you can't find ground lamb in your local butcher shop, ask your butcher to grind up some lamb shoulder for you. Any good butcher will be happy to do it.*

makes eighteen skewers

Chicken Satay with Thai Peanut Sauce

ingredients

1 cup unsweetened coconut milk

2 tablespoons Thai red curry paste

2 tablespoons dark brown sugar

2 tablespoons Asian fish sauce

2 teaspoons minced fresh ginger

1 clove garlic, minced

1 teaspoon ground coriander

1 pound boneless, skinless chicken breast halves, trimmed and cut into thin strips about 3 inches by 1/4 inch

Cilantro sprigs, for garnish

Thai Peanut Dip or Sauce (page 272), for serving

We're not sure what makes these so popular. Could it be their wonderfully warm Southeast Asian flavor, or could it be that they make the perfect vehicle (assuming that a large spoon would be too embarrassing) for the absolutely addictive peanut sauce? Either way, these spicy skewers are well worth tossing on the grill.

Combine the coconut milk, red curry paste, brown sugar, fish sauce, ginger, garlic, and coriander in a large bowl and mix well to dissolve the sugar. Add the chicken to the marinade and refrigerate for 3 hours. Soak 18 long bamboo skewers in water for at least 30 minutes.

Prepare a medium-hot fire in a grill, or preheat the broiler.

Thread the chicken strips onto the skewers and grill or broil until browned and just cooked through, 2 to 3 minutes per side. Watch closely to make sure they don't burn.

Transfer the skewers to a large platter, garnish with cilantro sprigs, and serve with the peanut sauce.

Make-ahead: *The marinade can be made 1 day ahead and kept, covered, in the refrigerator.*

Tip: *Thai red curry paste can be found in the Asian section of most grocery stores. Here we use it in the marinade, but it's also called for in the peanut sauce.*

makes about thirty meatballs

Mama's Meatballs in Marinara Sauce

meatballs

- 2 slices home-style white bread
- 3/4 cup milk
- 1 pound ground beef
- 1 pound bulk Italian sausage
- 1/3 cup grated Parmesan cheese
- 2 eggs
- 3 tablespoons minced fresh Italian parsley
- 2 cloves garlic, minced
- 1 teaspoon salt
- 1/2 teaspoon freshly ground black pepper

Good-quality Italian sausage, loaded with fennel and garlic, is the key to these tender, moist, and deeply flavorful meatballs. Look to your local Italian grocer for the best selection of homemade sausage. We like to serve these warm with small rolls, sautéed Italian peppers, and a heaping bowl of freshly grated Parmigiano-Reggiano and allow our guests to construct their own mini meatball subs.

To make the meatballs: Place the bread in a large bowl, and cover with the milk. Let stand until the bread is soft, about 10 minutes. Add the remaining meatball ingredients to the bowl. Using your hands, thoroughly combine the ingredients. Wet your hands and form the mixture into meatballs, slightly smaller than golf balls. Set on a baking sheet, cover with plastic wrap, and refrigerate until ready to use.

To make the sauce: Heat the olive oil in a large, heavy pot over medium heat. Add the onion and garlic and sauté until the onion begins to color, about 10 minutes. Add the oregano, salt, and pepper and cook for another minute. Add the tomatoes and bay leaves and bring the sauce to a boil. Reduce the heat to medium-low, cover, and simmer until the flavors blend, stirring often, about 30 minutes. Remove the bay leaves. Taste for seasoning and adjust if necessary.

Add the uncooked meatballs to the sauce and simmer, stirring occasionally to redistribute the meatballs in the sauce, until the meatballs are cooked through, another 25 minutes.

Place the meatballs and sauce in a serving bowl and sprinkle with Parmesan cheese. Serve warm.

Make-ahead: *The meatballs and sauce can both be made and stored separately up to 1 month ahead. Place the uncooked meatballs in a single layer on a tray and freeze until*

sauce

3 tablespoons olive oil

1 large onion, finely chopped

4 cloves garlic, minced

2 teaspoons dried oregano

½ teaspoon salt

¼ teaspoon freshly ground black pepper

Two 28-ounce cans crushed tomatoes with added purée

2 small bay leaves

Grated Parmesan cheese, for serving

solid. Transfer to a freezer bag. The cooked sauce can be cooled and then frozen. To cook: Defrost the sauce and bring to a simmer in a large pot. Add the frozen meatballs and continue to cook as directed in the recipe, adding 5 to 10 minutes to the cooking time.

Tips: *It may seem odd not to sauté or bake the meatballs, as many recipes call for doing before adding them to the sauce, but the results are wonderful. Besides saving you a messy step, we think this technique makes for a more tender meatball.*

The meatballs will seem overly crowded in the pot when added to the sauce. Don't worry; they will shrink after cooking for a bit and fit in the pot nicely.

serves eight to ten

Southwest Frittata

ingredients

- *8 eggs*
- *¼ cup sour cream*
- *1 teaspoon salt*
- *¼ teaspoon freshly ground black pepper*
- *1 cup grated cheddar cheese*
- *1 cup fresh or frozen corn kernels*
- *½ cup cherry tomatoes, halved*
- *4 corn tortillas, cut into ½-inch squares*
- *2 tablespoons chopped fresh cilantro*
- *2 tablespoons olive oil*
- *½ cup chopped onion*
- *Pico de Gallo (page 264), for garnish*

It's amazing what a little sour cream can do for scrambled eggs. In addition to adding flavor and moisture, the acid in the sour cream breaks down the protein in the eggs and makes them nice and tender. Leftovers of this cheesy Southwestern-flavored frittata are wonderful rewarmed as a taco filling.

Put the oven rack in the upper third of the oven and preheat to 425°F.

Whisk the eggs, sour cream, salt, and pepper in a medium bowl to blend. Mix in the cheese, corn, tomatoes, tortillas, and cilantro.

Heat the olive oil in a 12-inch heavy, oven-safe, nonstick skillet over high heat until hot but not smoking. Add the onion and sauté until just tender, about 5 minutes. Pour the egg mixture into the skillet and stir to blend. Transfer the skillet to the oven and bake until the frittata is set (the eggs should be just firm), 10 to 15 minutes. Preheat the broiler. Transfer the skillet to the top rack, about 6 inches from the heat, and cook until golden on top, about 1 minute.

Allow the frittata to sit for about 5 minutes to firm up. Slide it onto a cutting board and cut into small wedges. Spoon a dollop of pico de gallo on top of each wedge. Serve warm or at room temperature.

Make-ahead: *The frittata can be made up to an hour ahead and served at room temperature.*

serves eight to ten

Pasta Frittata

ingredients

- *8 ounces uncooked spaghetti*
- *2 tablespoons olive oil*
- *8 ounces sliced mushrooms*
- *6 oil-packed sun-dried tomatoes, drained and thinly sliced (about 3 tablespoons)*
- *8 large eggs*
- *3 ounces Parmigiano-Reggiano cheese, finely grated (about 3/4 cup)*
- *1/4 cup sour cream*
- *1 teaspoon salt*
- *1/4 teaspoon freshly ground black pepper*

When we teach our cooking classes, we try to emphasize to our students the importance of mastering technique as opposed to memorizing recipes. Once you understand the technique, you won't need the recipe. Frittatas are a perfect example. They're essentially large oven-baked omelets that can accommodate almost any ingredient you toss into them. Here we've combined pasta, which can be left over from last night's dinner, with sun-dried tomatoes, sautéed mushrooms, and Parmesan cheese for a quick but delightful appetizer.

Put the oven rack in the upper third of the oven and preheat to 425°F. Cook the spaghetti in a 6- to 8-quart pot of boiling salted water according to the package instructions. Drain and set aside.

Heat the oil in a 12-inch heavy, oven-safe, nonstick skillet over high heat until hot but not smoking. Add the mushrooms and sun-dried tomatoes and sauté, stirring frequently, for 2 minutes. Stir in the cooked spaghetti. In a medium bowl, whisk together the eggs, cheese, sour cream, salt, and pepper and pour over the pasta mixture. Transfer the skillet to the oven and bake until the frittata is set (the eggs should be just firm), 10 to 15 minutes. Preheat the broiler. Transfer the skillet to the top rack, about 6 inches from the heat, and cook until golden on top, about 1 minute.

Allow the frittata to sit for about 5 minutes to firm up. Slide it onto a cutting board and cut into small wedges. Serve warm or at room temperature.

Make-ahead: *The frittata can be made up to an hour ahead and served at room temperature.*

serves eight to ten

Chicken Liver Pâté

ingredients

1 pound chicken livers, trimmed

1 cup canned low-salt chicken broth

1 small onion, thinly sliced

3/4 cup (1 1/2 sticks) unsalted butter, at room temperature

1 tablespoon Cognac

1/4 teaspoon ground allspice

1/4 teaspoon freshly ground black pepper

1 teaspoon salt

Italian parsley sprigs, for garnish

Crackers, for serving

Cornichons, for serving

Even though chicken liver pâté may be considered the poor man's version of pâté made with foie gras (goose liver), we still think it can hold its own at any black tie affair. The best part is, for the price, you don't have to wait for a special occasion to serve it.

Spray a 3-cup soufflé dish or terrine with vegetable oil spray. Line the dish with plastic wrap, and spray the plastic with oil.

Combine the chicken livers, broth, and onion in a medium saucepan. Bring to a boil. Cover and simmer until the livers are cooked through, stirring occasionally, about 12 minutes. Drain off the cooking liquid, and transfer the chicken livers and onion to a food processor. Add the butter, Cognac, allspice, black pepper, and salt to the processor. Purée until smooth. Taste for seasoning and adjust if necessary. Transfer to the prepared dish. Cover and refrigerate until firm, at least 4 hours. Garnish with parsley sprigs and serve with crackers and cornichons on the side.

Make-ahead: *The pâté can be made 2 days ahead and kept, covered, in the refrigerator until ready to serve. Remove from the fridge about 30 minutes before serving. This will soften the texture somewhat and make it easier to spread.*

Tip: *Clean the livers by trimming and discarding any visible fat, green parts, or membrane. If you're uncomfortable working with the chicken livers, ask your butcher to trim them for you.*

serves four to six

Macho Nachos

ingredients

1 tablespoon olive oil

1 pound lean ground beef

½ cup minced onion

1 teaspoon salt

¼ teaspoon cayenne pepper

1 tablespoon chili powder

1 teaspoon ground cumin

1 tablespoon minced garlic

1 cup tomato sauce

One 12-ounce bag tortilla chips

4 ounces cheddar cheese, grated (about 1 cup)

4 ounces jalapeño Monterey Jack cheese, grated (about 1 cup)

¼ cup thinly sliced pickled jalapeños

1 cup peeled, seeded, and chopped Roma tomatoes

1 tablespoon chopped fresh cilantro

½ cup sour cream

Spicy Tomatillo Salsa (page 263) or Pico de Gallo (page 264), for garnish

Guacamole (page 265), for garnish

As a favorite menu item in every sports bar in the country, nachos are unavoidably macho, but what makes these nachos particularly so is the addition of the spicy ground beef topping. If you would like a vegetarian option, just replace the beef mixture with refried beans, or make a minimalist version with just the melted cheese and your favorite condiments.

In a large sauté pan, heat the olive oil. When it is hot, add the ground beef. Sauté, stirring constantly, until no pink remains and the beef is beginning to brown, about 3 minutes. Add the onion and continue to brown for 3 to 4 minutes. Stir in the salt, cayenne, chili powder, cumin, and garlic. Add the tomato sauce and bring the liquid to a simmer. Simmer until the liquid is reduced by a fourth, 2 to 3 minutes. Remove the pan from the heat.

Preheat the broiler. Place the chips on a large, heatproof platter. Spoon the beef mixture over the chips. Sprinkle the meat with the 2 cheeses and the pickled jalapeños. Place under the broiler until the cheese is melted and bubbly, about 1 minute. Watch carefully to avoid burning the exposed chips around the edges. Remove from the oven.

Sprinkle the tomatoes and cilantro on top of the cheese. Dollop spoonfuls of the sour cream, salsa, and guacamole around the edges of the serving platter. Serve hot.

Make-ahead: *The meat mixture can be made 2 days ahead and kept, covered, in the refrigerator. Reheat when ready to proceed with the recipe.*

makes sixteen

Devilishly Deviled Eggs

ingredients

8 large eggs

1/4 cup mayonnaise

2 teaspoons Dijon mustard

1/4 teaspoon cayenne pepper

Salt and freshly ground black pepper to taste

Paprika, for garnish

Chopped fresh chives, for garnish

Neither one of us can remember a childhood picnic or barbecue that didn't include a big platter of deviled eggs. A favorite of both adults and children, they're usually the first thing to go at a family get-together. Back then the recipe was basically the same no matter which aunt brought them. Now, though, the temptation to dress up deviled eggs can be overwhelming to some cooks (ourselves included). Here is the recipe we use when we're looking for a really good basic deviled egg.

Cover the eggs with cold water by 1½ inches in a heavy, 3-quart saucepan and bring to a rolling boil, partially covered. Reduce the heat to low and cook the eggs, covered completely, for 30 seconds. Remove from the heat and let stand, covered, for 15 minutes. Transfer with a slotted spoon to a bowl of ice and cold water to stop the cooking, and let stand for 5 minutes.

Peel the eggs and halve them lengthwise. Carefully remove the yolks and place them in a medium bowl. Set the egg whites cut side up on a serving platter. Mash the yolks with a fork. Add the mayonnaise, mustard, and cayenne and stir with a fork until smooth, then season with salt and pepper. Fill a pastry bag fitted with a ½-inch star tip with the yolk mixture and pipe it into the egg whites, or spoon the mixture into the egg whites. Garnish with a sprinkle of paprika and chives.

Make-ahead: *These can be made up to 8 hours ahead and kept, covered, in the refrigerator.*

makes sixteen

Niçoise Deviled Eggs

ingredients

- *8 large eggs*
- *Half of a 6-ounce can tuna packed in olive oil*
- *3 tablespoons extra-virgin olive oil*
- *2 tablespoons fresh lemon juice*
- *2 tablespoons capers, rinsed and drained*
- *Salt and freshly ground black pepper to taste*
- *8 kalamata olives, pitted and halved*

We know it's a cliché, but necessity really is the mother of invention. Meredith developed this recipe on an Easter day, when deviled eggs are an absolute requirement. (What else is one to do with an abundance of colored hard-boiled eggs?) Not having thought ahead, she found herself with no mayonnaise in the house, so in a moment of inspiration she concocted this takeoff on the niçoise salad. She uses tuna packed in olive oil along with the yolks and a splash of lemon juice to make a much lighter version of this retro classic.

Cover the eggs with cold water by 1½ inches in a heavy, 3-quart saucepan and bring to a rolling boil, partially covered. Reduce the heat to low and cook the eggs, covered completely, for 30 seconds. Remove from the heat and let stand, covered, for 15 minutes. Transfer with a slotted spoon to a bowl of ice and cold water to stop cooking, and let stand for 5 minutes.

Peel the eggs and halve them lengthwise. Carefully remove the yolks and place them in the bowl of a food processor. Set the egg whites cut side up on a serving platter.

Add the tuna to the food processor. Pulse several times until the yolks and tuna are well combined. Add the olive oil and lemon juice and pulse again until smooth. Add the capers and pulse 2 more times just to incorporate and chop the capers. You should still see bits of caper in the yolk-tuna mixture. Remove from the bowl and season with salt and pepper. Fill a pastry bag fitted with a ½-inch star tip with the yolk mixture and pipe it into the egg whites, or spoon the mixture into the whites. Decorate the top of each of the eggs with an olive half. Gently cover with plastic wrap and refrigerate until ready to serve.

Make-ahead: *These can be made up to 8 hours ahead and kept, covered, in the refrigerator.*

makes thirty pieces

Oven-Fried Chicken Lollipops

ingredients

- 30 chicken wing drumettes
- 2 cups buttermilk
- 1 teaspoon salt, divided
- 3 tablespoons unsalted butter
- 2 cups panko crumbs
- ½ teaspoon freshly ground black pepper
- 1 teaspoon paprika
- ¼ teaspoon cayenne pepper
- 1 teaspoon garlic powder

If you tell your friends you're bringing chicken lollipops to their party, you're bound to be met at the door by skeptics. You'll win them over quickly, though, once they see and, better yet, taste this fun alternative to standard chicken wings. The meat of a chicken drumette (the drumstick portion of the wing) is pushed down to one end of the bone, forming a ball; thus the name "lollipop." They're really quite practical, as they give your guests a handle to hold as they neatly nibble the crispy, tender meat off of one end.

Run a sharp paring knife around the bone at the narrow end of a drumette to separate the skin and tendons, and push the meat down toward the thick end to form a ball at the end of the bone. You now have a "lollipop." Repeat with the remaining drumettes.

Place the chicken, buttermilk, and ½ teaspoon of the salt in a large bowl and toss to coat. Cover with plastic wrap and refrigerate for 1 hour.

Preheat the oven to 400°F. Place the butter on a large baking sheet and place in the oven to melt. Remove from the oven and set aside.

Combine the panko crumbs, remaining ½ teaspoon salt, pepper, paprika, cayenne, and garlic powder in a large plastic bag. Lift the chicken pieces out of the buttermilk and, 3 at a time, drop into the bag and shake to coat.

Place the chicken on the pan, meat end down. Bake until golden, 20 to 25 minutes.

Make-ahead: *The chicken can be "lollipopped" and marinated in buttermilk a day ahead and kept, covered, in the refrigerator.*

makes thirty pieces

Hot and Spicy Buffalo Chicken Wings

blue cheese dip

3/4 cup mayonnaise

1 clove garlic, minced

2 tablespoons finely chopped fresh Italian parsley

1 1/2 cup sour cream

1 tablespoon fresh lemon juice

1 tablespoon white vinegar

1/2 cup crumbled blue cheese

Salt and freshly ground black pepper to taste

chicken wings

15 chicken wings

1/3 cup Tabasco sauce

Vegetable oil, for frying

1 3/4 cups all-purpose flour

1 teaspoon salt

1/4 teaspoon freshly ground black pepper

2 large eggs

1/4 cup water

1/2 cup Tabasco sauce

1/2 cup (1 stick) unsalted butter, melted

1 tablespoon cider vinegar

Celery and carrot sticks, for serving

Although this dish might not be ideal for a formal occasion that requires the use of the family linen, by all means don't save them only for Super Bowl Sunday. These zippy wings are an addictive, albeit messy, favorite with both family and friends. Serve them hot with plenty of cold beer and paper towels.

To make the blue cheese dip: In a medium bowl, mix together all of the dip ingredients with a wooden spoon until well incorporated. Refrigerate for 1 hour to allow the flavors to blend before serving.

To make the wings: cut off the wing tips and discard. Cut the remaining chicken wings in half at the joint and place in a large bowl. Toss with the hot sauce, cover, and refrigerate for 30 minutes.

Pour the oil for frying into a large pot to a depth of 2 inches, and heat over medium heat to 375°F.

Place the flour in a separate mixing bowl and mix together with the salt and pepper. In another bowl, whisk together the eggs and water until well blended. First dredge each wing piece in the flour mixture, then dip it in the egg mixture, and finally dredge it completely in the flour mixture, again coating it evenly.

Working in 3 batches so that you won't crowd your pot, deep-fry the wings until they are crispy and dark golden brown, about 10 minutes. When cooked through, set aside to drain on paper towels.

In a large bowl, combine the Tabasco sauce, melted butter, and cider vinegar. Add the hot cooked wings and toss quickly in the sauce to coat.

Place the hot wings on a serving platter and serve with the blue cheese dip and the celery and carrot sticks.

Make-ahead: *The dip can be made up to 1 day ahead and kept, covered, in the refrigerator. The wings are really best served while hot.*

Chapter 8 Savory

73 Endive *with* Herbed Cheese *and* Sprouts

75 Green Apple Slices *with* Tapenade

rovence *and* Micro Greens

79 Grilled Fennel *with* Truffle Oil *and* Parmesan Curls

82 Wild Mushroom Pâté

otato *and* Leek Pancakes *with* Applesauce *and* Sour Cream

Fruits *and* Vegetables

88 Roasted Vegetable Skewers *with* Yogurt Lemon Sauce

90 Zucchini *and* Fresh Herb Fritters

herry Tomatoes Stuffed *with* Feta, Green Onion, *and* Bacon

94 Sweet *and* Sour Cipollini Onions

96 Figs *with* Saga Blue *and* Prosciutto

98 Edamame

00 Jalapeño Poppers 201 Corn *and* Jalapeño Fritters

03 Chipotle, Black Bean, *and* Goat Cheese Nachos

makes thirty, serving six to eight

Baby Bellas with Prosciutto and Pine Nuts

ingredients

- *30 baby portobella or cremini mushrooms, wiped clean with a damp cloth*
- *2 tablespoons unsalted butter*
- *½ cup finely diced onion*
- *¼ cup finely diced celery*
- *2 cloves garlic, finely minced*
- *½ teaspoon dried thyme*
- *¼ cup finely diced prosciutto*
- *1 cup fresh breadcrumbs (about 4 slices of bread pulsed in a food processor)*
- *¼ cup minced fresh Italian parsley*
- *½ cup grated Parmesan cheese*
- *¼ cup chicken stock*
- *Salt and freshly ground black pepper to taste*
- *¼ cup pine nuts*

Baby portobella and cremini mushrooms are one and the same. They have more flavor than button (white) mushrooms and are readily available in grocery stores. Mushrooms are terrific containers for many different kinds of fillings, so we like to use our imaginations. Here we've taken a basic filling and elaborated on it with the addition of prosciutto and pine nuts.

Preheat the oven to 400°F.

Remove the stems from the mushrooms (a grapefruit spoon works nicely), mince them, and set them aside. You should have about ⅓ cup.

Lay out the mushroom caps, stem side down, on a parchment-lined baking sheet and bake them for about 10 minutes. The caps should have exuded some of their liquid. Remove from the oven and reserve.

Heat a large skillet over medium heat and add the butter to the pan. When the butter has melted and the pan is hot, add the onion, celery, garlic, thyme, and reserved mushroom stems. Sauté until the vegetables are tender, about 5 minutes. Add the prosciutto and cook for 1 minute longer. Remove the pan from the heat and transfer the vegetables to a large bowl.

Add the breadcrumbs, parsley, Parmesan cheese, and chicken stock to the vegetables and toss to mix. Season to taste with salt and freshly ground black pepper. The stuffing should hold together when squeezed.

Turn the mushroom caps over so that they are stem side up, and fill them with the bread filling, pressing gently and mounding the stuffing. Top each cap with a few pine nuts. Bake the mushroom caps until the mushrooms are tender and the stuffing is crispy on top, 10 to 15 minutes. Serve hot or at room temperature.

Make-ahead: *Uncooked stuffed mushrooms can be frozen for up to 2 weeks. Freeze on baking sheets wrapped in plastic and foil. They can be baked frozen; just add about 5 minutes to the cooking time.*

makes about twenty-four pieces, serving six

Endive with Herbed Cheese and Sprouts

ingredients

- *8 ounces Boursin or goat cheese*
- *2 tablespoons finely minced fresh Italian parsley*
- *2 teaspoons finely fresh minced chives*
- *1/4 teaspoon salt*
- *1/8 teaspoon freshly ground black pepper*
- *2 heads Belgian endive, leaves separated, washed, and dried*
- *2 cups sprouts, such as alfalfa, sunflower, broccoli, etc.*

The leaves of Belgian endive are usually about 4 or 5 inches long. They have a curvature to them that makes them the perfect edible spoon: they are easy to handle, and the fillings inside them stay put. These endives are quick to assemble, and the sprout garnish gives them a wispy visual appeal.

Add the cheese, herbs, salt, and pepper to the bowl of a food processor and process until creamy.

To assemble, transfer the cheese mixture to a pastry bag with a plain or fluted tip and squeeze about 1 tablespoon of cheese at the base of each leaf of endive. Top the cheese with a pinch of the sprouts, tucking them down a bit so that they adhere to the cheese. Arrange the filled leaves in a spoke pattern on a round platter for a decorative effect.

Make-ahead: *The filling can be stored in a tightly covered container in the refrigerator for up to 1 week. Allow it to soften at room temperature for 1 hour before using. The endives can be assembled up to 2 hours before service, covered, and refrigerated.*

Tip: *Belgian endive, or witloof, is the perfect vehicle to hold tasty bites of cheese, vegetable salads, seafood salads, chicken salads, and other fillings. Experiment with different cheeses or with colorful vegetable concoctions or shrimp salsa for a lower-fat alternative.*

serves four

Fettuccine of Zucchini and Carrot with Tomato Concassé

ingredients

4 medium carrots, peeled and trimmed

2 medium zucchini, trimmed

2 pints grape tomatoes

2 cloves garlic, minced

1 teaspoon minced fresh thyme

2 tablespoons olive oil

¼ teaspoon salt, plus more for seasoning

⅛ teaspoon freshly ground black pepper, plus more for seasoning

½ cup chicken stock

2 tablespoons extra-virgin olive oil

¼ cup thinly sliced fresh basil

2 tablespoons salt-packed capers, rinsed

Basil leaves, for garnish (optional)

Carla came up with this starter about 20 years ago and it is still a favorite, because its presentation is so stunning. A dish as simple as this is all about freshness, so make it when zucchini, tomatoes, and basil are in season and you won't be disappointed. This dish resembles a colorful fettuccine of vegetables, because the carrots and zucchini are sliced into thin strands.

Using a mandoline, peeler slicer, or chef's knife, cut the carrot and zucchini into long, thin fettuccinelike strands.

Blanch the carrot in 4 cups of boiling salted water for 2 minutes; blanch the zucchini for 1 minute. Immerse the vegetables in ice water to stop the cooking, and lay them out on a towel to dry.

Preheat the oven to 375°F.

Arrange the tomatoes, garlic, and thyme on a rimmed baking sheet and drizzle with the olive oil, salt, and pepper. Roast the tomatoes until they have shriveled slightly and begun to brown, about 15 minutes. Remove from the oven and deglaze the baking sheet with the chicken stock, scraping up any cooked-on bits. The tomatoes and stock will create a tasty sauce for the vegetables.

Heat the extra-virgin olive oil in a large sauté pan and add the blanched carrot and zucchini. Toss to coat with the olive oil and reheat the vegetables for 2 or 3 minutes. Add the tomato-chicken stock mixture, basil, and capers to the pan and toss to combine. Season with salt and freshly ground black pepper to taste. Serve on heated plates, garnished with basil leaves, if desired.

Variation: *Try tossing this vegetable medley with cooked pasta. Top with slivers of Parmesan cheese and more fresh basil.*

Tip: *A mandoline or Japanese slicer makes this dish easy to accomplish. There's also a new tool on the market from Kuhn Rikon that looks like a peeler but juliennes using the same motion. As a last resort you could use your trusty chef's knife, so if you must, go ahead and take it out of the drawer and give it a little exercise.*

makes forty-eight pieces

Green Apple Slices with Tapenade

ingredients

- *$1\frac{1}{2}$ cups kalamata olives, pitted*
- *$\frac{3}{4}$ cup oil-packed sun-dried tomatoes*
- *2 cloves garlic, minced*
- *1 teaspoon anchovy paste (more or less optional)*
- *$\frac{1}{4}$ cup capers, preferably salt-packed, rinsed*
- *Juice and grated zest of 1 lemon*
- *Grated zest of 1 orange*
- *$\frac{1}{4}$ cup chopped fresh Italian parsley*
- *1 teaspoon herbes de Provence, or 1 teaspoon dried thyme*
- *Freshly ground black pepper to taste*
- *$\frac{1}{4}$ cup extra-virgin olive oil*
- *3 Granny Smith apples, halved, cored, and each sliced into 16 slices*
- *2 tablespoons fresh lemon juice*
- *Lemon wedges and fresh parsley leaves, for garnish (optional)*

An abundance of apples and leftover tapenade after a cooking class sparked the idea of this dish. The tart apple plays well off the salty notes of the tapenade. The green, black, and white colors also look great on a decorative serving tray (very minimalist).

To make the tapenade: Place the olives, sun-dried tomatoes, garlic, anchovy paste, capers, lemon juice, zests, parsley, herbes de Provence, black pepper, and olive oil in the bowl of a food processor (or chop finely by hand and mix). Pulse a few times to incorporate and chop to the desired texture (we like it chunky).

Toss the apples with the lemon juice to keep them from browning. Spread a small mound of tapenade onto each of the apple slices and arrange them decoratively on a platter. Garnish with lemon wedges and parsley, if desired.

Make-ahead: *The tapenade can be kept, covered and refrigerated, for up to 2 weeks. Allow it to come to room temperature before serving.*

Tips: *It is easy to remove the pits from the olives. Simply lay the flat side of your knife on the olive and press. The olive opens up, and out pops the pit.*

Capers packed in salt have a better texture than those bottled in brine. They must be rinsed thoroughly before using.

The zest from the citrus is most easily removed using a Microplane, available at most cookware stores.

serves six

Grilled Apples with Herbes de Provence and Micro Greens

ingredients

- *3 Braeburn, Mutsu, or Crispin apples, peeled, halved, and cored*
- *3 tablespoons sherry vinegar*
- *1 large shallot, minced*
- *1/4 teaspoon salt*
- *Dash of freshly ground black pepper*
- *1/3 cup extra-virgin olive oil, plus more as needed*
- *1/2 teaspoon minced fresh thyme*
- *1/2 teaspoon minced fresh rosemary*
- *1/2 teaspoon minced fresh marjoram*
- *1/2 teaspoon minced fresh Italian parsley*
- *10 kalamata olives, pitted*
- *3 cups micro greens, washed and dried*

The presentation of this dish is visually striking, and your guests will surely never have eaten an apple prepared this way before. Marinating and then grilling apples is a novel way to use a fruit that is always at hand. The sugar in the apples caramelizes beautifully on the grill, on a grill pan, or in the oven under the broiler. The tapenade garnish really dresses up the plate, whether you squirt it from a squeeze bottle or just drizzle it over the top of the apples with a spoon.

Make about 8 slices lengthwise down the apple halves but not all the way through one end, so that they are still in one piece and will fan out when softened by cooking.

In a large bowl, combine the sherry vinegar, shallot, and salt and let sit for 5 minutes to let the flavors mellow. Add the pepper and whisk in the olive oil and herbs. Add the apples to the bowl and toss to coat them with the vinaigrette. Cover the bowl with plastic wrap and let the apples sit at room temperature for at least 1 hour and up to 2 hours.

Prepare a grill or heat a grill pan over medium-high heat. Remove the apples from the vinaigrette and reserve the vinaigrette. Lay the apples on the grill, flat side down, and grill them until browned, 4 or 5 minutes. Turn the apples and brown the other side for another 5 minutes. The apples should be caramelized and softened.

There should be about 8 tablespoons of vinaigrette left in the bowl. Remove 3 tablespoons of the vinaigrette and combine it with the olives in a food processor, mini chopper, or blender. Process until you have a fine paste. Thin the paste with water, if desired. Transfer the olive dressing to a squeeze bottle with a large opening, or reserve it in the work bowl.

In a medium bowl, toss the remaining vinaigrette with the micro greens. Arrange the greens on the center of 6 plates and top each with an apple half, slightly fanned out, cored side up. Drizzle some of the olive dressing over the top, or squirt it decoratively with the squeeze bottle. Serve immediately.

Make-ahead: *The apples can be grilled up to 4 hours before serving and kept at room temperature.*

Tip: *If you can't find micro greens in your grocery store, try using baby arugula or any other tender lettuce.*

serves six

Grilled Asparagus with Easy Orange Hollandaise

ingredients

1 bunch asparagus

2 tablespoons unsalted butter, melted

¼ teaspoon salt

Dash of freshly ground black pepper

easy orange hollandaise sauce

½ cup (1 stick) unsalted butter

2 large egg yolks

1 teaspoon sherry vinegar

2 teaspoons heavy cream

Grated zest of 1 orange

2 tablespoons frozen orange juice concentrate

¼ teaspoon salt

Dash of cayenne pepper

Dash of freshly ground black pepper

Grated or julienned orange zest, for garnish (optional)

Once you have tasted grilled or roasted asparagus, you will never boil it again. The dry heat from grilling or roasting leaves the asparagus crispy-tender and lightly caramelized for a more complex flavor. The rich orange hollandaise sauce is the perfect accompaniment to our favorite trumpet of spring.

Heat a grill or preheat the oven to 400°F.

Snap the tough ends from the asparagus and discard them. Arrange the spears on a baking sheet. Drizzle with the melted butter and season with the salt and pepper. Grill over a hot fire, turning once, for about 7 minutes, or roast the asparagus in the preheated oven for about 10 minutes. Remove from the oven and keep warm.

While the asparagus is cooking, make the hollandaise: Heat the butter to a simmer in a medium saucepan over medium-high heat. While it is heating, add the egg yolks, vinegar, cream, orange zest, orange juice concentrate, salt, cayenne, and pepper to the jar of a blender. Place the lid over the top and blend for 3 seconds. Remove the plastic stopper from the middle of the lid so that you can pour the hot butter into the blender while it is running. Turn the blender to blend, and pour the hot butter through the hole in a slow, steady stream. It should take about 15 seconds to get it all in. The sauce should thicken to a loose mayonnaise consistency. Taste the hollandaise for seasoning and adjust if necessary with salt, pepper, or more orange juice.

To serve, arrange the asparagus spears on 6 plates and nap them with the orange hollandaise. Garnish with orange zest, if desired. Serve warm.

Make-ahead: *The asparagus can be grilled up to 8 hours ahead of time and kept covered. The hollandaise can be made up to 1 hour before serving and kept warm in a bowl over a saucepan of warm water. Be careful not to let the bottom of the bowl touch the water or the sauce may overheat and break.*

Tip: *A bacterium known as* Salmonella enteritidis *can infect perfectly normal appearing eggs. Though the risk is small, the elderly, infants, and those with impaired immune systems can be affected more severely. To be safe, use pasteurized whole eggs when consuming raw eggs.*

serves six

Grilled Fennel with Truffle Oil and Parmesan Curls

ingredients

- *3 shallots, quartered*
- *3 tablespoons olive oil, divided*
- *1/4 teaspoon salt, plus more for seasoning*
- *Dash of freshly ground black pepper, plus more for seasoning*
- *2 medium heads fennel, trimmed and sliced crosswise into 1/8-inch slices*
- *3 tablespoons white wine vinegar or sherry vinegar*
- *1/2 teaspoon coarsely chopped fresh thyme*
- *1/3 cup extra-virgin olive oil*
- *4 ounces prosciutto, coarsely chopped*
- *1/2 cup Parmesan cheese curls (shave curls with a vegetable peeler)*
- *3 tablespoons white truffle oil*

Fennel is an Old World vegetable with New Age appeal. Roasted, grilled, or raw, fennel's clean taste adds sophistication and flair to savvy party menus. Roasting the shallots highlights their sweeter side and pairs nicely with floral thyme, anisey fennel, salty ham, and cheese topped with the pièce de résistance, earthy truffle oil.

Heat a grill or preheat the oven to 400°F.

Spread the shallots on a grill basket if grilling or in a baking pan if roasting in the oven. Drizzle the shallots with 1 tablespoon of the olive oil and sprinkle with salt and pepper to taste. Grill or bake until the shallots caramelize and soften, about 15 minutes. Cool the shallots, mince, and transfer to a small bowl.

Spread the fennel on a grill basket if grilling or in a baking pan if roasting in the oven. Drizzle the fennel with the remaining 2 tablespoons olive oil and sprinkle with salt and pepper to taste. Grill or bake until the fennel softens slightly, 7 or 8 minutes. Remove the fennel and divide it among 6 serving plates.

Add the vinegar, 1/4 teaspoon salt, a dash of pepper, and the thyme to the shallots and allow the mixture to sit for at least 5 minutes and up to 1 hour. Whisk in the extra-virgin olive oil.

Pour the vinaigrette over the fennel and top with a scattering of prosciutto and Parmesan curls. Drizzle the white truffle oil over the top. Serve warm or at room temperature.

Make-ahead: *The vegetables can be grilled up to 4 hours ahead of time and kept, covered, at room temperature. The vinaigrette can be made up to 4 hours ahead and kept, covered, at room temperature.*

serves six

Medley of Grilled Peppers with Capers and Pine Nuts

ingredients

1 red bell pepper

1 yellow bell pepper

1 orange bell pepper

1 green bell pepper

1 black or purple bell pepper

3 tablespoons sherry vinegar

½ teaspoon sea salt

2 cloves garlic, finely minced

3 tablespoons extra-virgin olive oil

Freshly ground black pepper to taste

2 tablespoons thinly sliced fresh basil

¼ cup pine nuts, toasted

¼ cup salt-packed capers, rinsed well

½ cup crumbled feta cheese

We like to make this dish in the summer, when peppers abound and the price is right at local farmers' markets. The visual appeal comes from the varied colors of the peppers, so try to pick up a few different colors when shopping. This dish is stunning served with fresh mozzarella or the Herbed Goat Cheese Bites on page 40.

Roast the peppers over an open flame on a grill or gas burner, or broil them, turning as they are blackened, so that the skin is charred evenly.

Transfer the peppers to a heatproof bowl and cover it with plastic wrap. Cooling the peppers in this way helps to separate the charred skin from the flesh of the peppers. When they are cool enough to handle, peel the charred skin from the flesh and remove the seeds and stems. Cut the peppers into strips about 4 inches long and 1 inch wide.

In a medium bowl, combine the sherry vinegar, salt, and garlic. Stir to dissolve the salt. Whisk in the oil and black pepper. Add the roasted peppers and toss to coat them with the vinaigrette. Set aside to marinate for at least 1 hour at room temperature or up to 2 days in the refrigerator. If chilled, allow the mixture to come to room temperature before serving.

Just before serving, stir in the basil, pine nuts, and capers. Divide the peppers among 6 serving plates and sprinkle cheese over the top. Serve at room temperature as part of a selection of antipasti.

Make-ahead: *The peppers can be roasted, peeled, and marinated up to 2 days ahead and kept, covered, in the refrigerator. Stir in the fresh herbs right before serving.*

Tips: *Basil is a tender herb that turns black and mushy if you chop it too vigorously. To get the best flavor and visual appeal from basil, roll the leaves together like a cigar and slice thinly. This is known as a chiffonade.*

To toast the pine nuts, heat a medium skillet over medium heat and add the pine nuts to the pan. Toss the pine nuts in the hot pan until they begin to brown and give off some of their oil. Be careful not to burn them. When they are lightly browned, transfer the nuts to a bowl or plate to cool.

makes about two cups

Wild Mushroom Pâté

ingredients

- 3 tablespoons olive oil
- 3 shallots or 1 medium onion, minced
- Pinch of salt, plus more to taste
- 12 ounces mixed wild mushrooms, chopped
- 2 cloves garlic, minced
- 1/4 cup dry white vermouth or dry white wine
- 2 tablespoons soy sauce
- 10 ounces goat cheese
- 1/4 cup chopped fresh herbs, such as parsley, thyme, marjoram, chives, or mint
- 1/2 cup walnuts, toasted
- Freshly ground black pepper to taste

- French or rustic Italian bread, thinly sliced and toasted, for serving

Wild mushrooms have an earthy, musky flavor totally unlike that of their generic cousin, the white button mushroom. We like to make this pâté up for large parties and serve it in a decorative crock with toasted baguette slices. For a more formal presentation it can be baked inside phyllo triangles, encased in puff pastry, or piped into gougères (see the recipe on page 92).

Heat the oil in a large sauté pan over medium heat. When the oil is hot, add the shallot with a pinch of salt, and sauté until it begins to look translucent, about 2 minutes. Add the mushrooms and sauté until they begin to give off some liquid, 3 or 4 minutes. Add the garlic and sauté until the mushrooms are dry, about 4 minutes.

Add the vermouth, along with the soy sauce. Cook until the pan is dry, about 2 minutes.

Transfer the mushrooms to the bowl of a food processor along with the goat cheese, herbs, and walnuts. Process in short bursts just to coarsely chop and mix the ingredients. Leave the mixture chunky.

Spoon the pâté into a decorative bowl and serve immediately with the toasted bread.

Make-ahead: *This pâté will keep, covered and refrigerated, for up to 3 days. Let it sit at room temperature for 1 hour to warm up before serving.*

makes forty pieces

New Potatoes with Crème Fraîche and Caviar

ingredients

- 20 small new potatoes, no more than 2 or 3 inches in diameter, washed and cut in half
- ½ teaspoon salt, plus a sprinkle of salt for each potato
- 8 ounces crème fraîche or sour cream
- ¼ cup finely minced fresh chives
- Freshly ground black pepper to taste
- 1 small jar caviar, black or orange, for garnish

New potatoes are one of the tastiest spring vegetables when plucked young and firm from the ground. Dense and buttery, they hardly need anything extra to taste fabulous. We've paired spring's best with crème fraîche or sour cream, fresh chives, and a touch of caviar for panache. If you aren't a fan of caviar, just leave it off or replace it with smoked salmon.

Using a small melon baller, remove the center of the cut side of each potato, leaving a crater to be filled later with crème fraîche. Arrange the potatoes in one layer in a steamer and steam them until the tip of a knife pierces the flesh easily, about 20 minutes. Remove the potatoes to a tray and sprinkle them lightly with salt. Let cool to room temperature before continuing.

In a small bowl, mix the crème fraîche with the chives, ½ teaspoon salt, and pepper. Add a dollop of this mixture to the indentation on each potato. Garnish each potato with caviar.

Make-ahead: *The new potatoes can be kept, covered and refrigerated, for up to 3 hours. They will taste better if allowed to sit at room temperature for 30 minutes before serving.*

makes six large or eighteen small pancakes, serving six

Sweet Potato and Leek Pancakes with Applesauce and Sour Cream

applesauce

4 cups diced Braeburn, Gala, or Mutsu apples (¼-inch dice)

⅓ cup light brown sugar

3 tablespoons fresh lemon juice

pancakes

2 tablespoons unsalted butter

1 cup thinly sliced leek, (white part only), washed

1 teaspoon plus a dash of salt, divided

¼ teaspoon plus a dash of freshly ground black pepper, divided

1 cup peeled and grated russet potato

2 cups peeled and grated sweet potato (yam)

Sturdy little pancakes topped with chunky applesauce and sour cream are our idea of the perfect comfort food. We think of this dish as a sit-down appetizer, but if you make the pancakes small, they could easily be passed or set out on a buffet table. These are best when served hot from the oven. Make lots. They will disappear fast.

To make the applesauce: Place the apples in a medium saucepan and cook over medium heat until they begin to give off water. Turn the heat to medium-low and cook, stirring occasionally, until the apples break down and become thick, about 20 minutes. (This technique concentrates the flavor of the apples.) Adjust the heat as necessary so that the apples don't brown or burn. Add the brown sugar and lemon juice and continue to cook for another 5 minutes. Remove from the heat and keep warm.

To make the pancakes: Heat a large skillet over medium heat and add the butter to the pan. When the butter has melted and the skillet is hot, add the leek and a dash each of salt and pepper and sauté, stirring, until tender, about 5 minutes. Remove the pan from the heat and transfer the leek mixture to a large bowl to cool.

Preheat the oven to 250°F.

To the leek mixture add the russet and sweet potatoes and egg and stir to mix. Add the flour, 1 teaspoon salt, baking powder, ¼ teaspoon black pepper, and nutmeg and mix thoroughly.

Heat 2 tablespoons of the oil in the skillet over medium heat. Drop the batter by quarter-cupfuls into the skillet. Using a fork or spatula, flatten each mound to a 4-inch round. If you want to make them smaller, add the batter by rounded tablespoons. Cook

1 large egg, beaten

⅓ cup all-purpose flour

½ teaspoon baking powder

¼ teaspoon ground nutmeg

About ⅓ cup vegetable oil

½ cup sour cream

2 tablespoons minced fresh chives, for garnish (optional)

the pancakes until brown, about 3 minutes, then turn to cook the other side for an additional 3 minutes. Transfer the pancakes to a baking sheet lined with parchment paper and keep warm in the preheated oven for up to 1 hour. Repeat with the remaining batter, adding more oil to the skillet as needed.

To serve the pancakes, transfer 1 large pancake or 2 or 3 smaller ones to each plate and top with applesauce and sour cream. Garnish with a sprinkling of chives, if desired.

Make-ahead: *The pancakes and applesauce can be made up to 24 hours before serving and kept, covered and refrigerated. Reheat the pancakes in a 350°F oven for 7 or 8 minutes. Rewarm the applesauce in the microwave or on the stove top.*

makes one 9-by-5-inch terrine, serving twelve

Terrine of Carrot, Leek, and Asparagus

ingredients

1 red bell pepper

2 carrots, peeled, trimmed, and cut lengthwise into 1/8-inch-thick lengths

4 tablespoons olive oil, divided

Salt and freshly ground black pepper to taste

20 stalks asparagus, woody ends trimmed

2 cups thinly sliced leeks (about 2 leeks)

1 teaspoon minced fresh thyme

11 ounces goat cheese, at room temperature

1/2 cup pitted and coarsely chopped kalamata olives

10 to 12 large fresh basil leaves

Chard or grape leaves, for lining platter

Flatbread crackers or toasted baguette slices, for serving

Terrines are usually rather time-consuming dishes to create, but this vegetable and goat cheese loaf is fast and easy to assemble. This dish is best when the carrots and asparagus still have a bit of texture to them, so be careful not to overcook them. One of our friends thought this dish was "so beautiful that it should be on the cover of a magazine." We think it tastes as good as it looks.

Char the pepper under a broiler or over a gas flame until the skin is blackened. Put it in a heat-resistant bowl and cover with plastic wrap. When cool enough to handle, peel the blackened skin from the flesh and cut away the seeds. Cut the pepper into 1-inch-wide strips. Set aside.

Preheat the oven to 425°F.

Place the carrots and asparagus on separate parchment-lined baking pans. Brush each with 1 tablespoon of olive oil and sprinkle with salt and pepper. Roast the vegetables until they are tender, about 15 minutes. (The carrots may take a few more minutes, depending on how thickly they were cut.) Remove from the oven and set aside.

Heat a medium skillet over medium heat and add the remaining 2 tablespoons olive oil. When the oil is hot, add the leek, thyme, and a dash each of salt and pepper. Sauté the leek until it is tender, about 10 minutes, turning the heat down if they begin to brown. Set aside.

Line a 9-by-5-inch loaf pan with plastic wrap, leaving an overhang. Trim the asparagus to fit the length of the pan, and reserve 5 asparagus spears for the last layer. Place a single layer of the best-looking asparagus spears decoratively on the bottom of the pan, covering it completely. This will be the top of the terrine. Spread one third of the cheese over the top of the asparagus, then cover with a layer of the sautéed leeks. Add a layer of carrot, trimmed to fit the pan, and top the carrot with half of the remaining goat cheese and a layer of olives. Top the olives with a layer of red bell pepper and the basil leaves. Finally, add the last of the cheese and then the remaining asparagus. Fold the plastic up over the top to enclose the terrine, and push down gently to compress the terrine and spread the cheese evenly. Refrigerate for at least 6 hours or up to 24 hours. Let stand at room temperature for at least 30 minutes before serving.

To serve, line a platter with decorative chard or grape leaves. Unwrap the top of the terrine and unmold it onto the platter. Peel off the plastic. Lightly salt and pepper the asparagus, if desired. Serve the terrine with flatbread crackers or toasted baguette slices.

Make-ahead: *The terrine can be made up to 24 hours before serving, covered, and refrigerated.*

Tip: *It can be difficult to cut this terrine, as the vegetables are a bit firm and the cheese is loose. We found a wide spreader with a serrated edge that works beautifully to cut and spread the cheese and vegetables. You probably have something in your gadget drawer that would work as well.*

makes eighteen skewers, serving six

Roasted Vegetable Skewers with Yogurt Lemon Sauce

ingredients

- 2 zucchini, halved lengthwise and cut into 1/4-inch-thick half-rounds
- 1 yellow squash, halved lengthwise and cut into 1/4-inch-thick half-rounds
- 1 small red onion, cut in half through the root and blossom ends, each half cut into 8 slices
- 1/2 head cauliflower, cut into florets
- 2 red bell peppers, trimmed, seeded, and cut into 1-inch squares
- Grated zest of 1 lemon
- 1/4 cup fresh lemon juice
- 1/4 teaspoon salt
- 1 clove garlic, finely minced
- 1/4 cup extra-virgin olive oil
- Freshly ground black pepper to taste
- 1 cup Greek or domestic plain yogurt
- 2 tablespoons minced fresh chives, for garnish

Vegetables never tasted so good as they do in this colorful vegetarian rendition of shish kebab. The bright lemon flavor of the easy-to-make yogurt sauce really enhances the vegetables. If you can, take the time to seek out Greek yogurt. It is thicker and richer tasting than the usual grocery store brands.

Soak eighteen 6-inch wooden skewers in water for 30 minutes. Thread some of each of the vegetables on the soaked skewers, alternating them for color and variety.

In a shallow, nonreactive pan, mix the lemon zest and juice, salt, and garlic and stir to dissolve the salt. Whisk in the olive oil and black pepper. Arrange the vegetable skewers in the pan and turn to them to coat with the marinade. Let the skewers sit for about 1 hour at room temperature for the flavors to develop.

Prepare a grill or preheat the oven to 400°F.

Transfer the skewers to a hot grill or roast them on a baking sheet until they are lightly browned and tender, about 7 minutes per side on the grill or about 20 minutes in the oven. Meanwhile, pour 1/4 cup of the marinade into the yogurt and stir to combine. Taste for seasoning and adjust with salt and pepper.

Serve the vegetable skewers with a generous drizzle of the yogurt sauce and a sprinkling of minced chives. Serve hot.

Make-ahead: *The vegetable skewers can be cooked and kept, covered and refrigerated, for up to 8 hours. Reheat in a 350°F oven for 7 or 8 minutes.*

Tips: *To serve this as a stand-up appetizer, thread only 1 or 2 pieces of vegetable on each skewer so that they can be dipped and nibbled.*

When making kebabs or anything on skewers, it is helpful to buy the flat wooden skewers. They serve as an anchor that will keep your food from swirling around the skewer as you try to turn it when cooking.

makes about thirty large chips

Windowpane Potato Chips

ingredients

3 large russet potatoes, scrubbed

1 bunch Italian parsley

¼ cup olive oil

Salt to taste

Your guests will rave about these sophisticated homemade potato chips featuring herbal silhouettes in their centers. A mandoline or Japanese slicer makes short work of slicing, and best of all, baking them in the oven eliminates the mess that comes with frying.

Preheat the oven to 400°F.

Slice the potatoes very thinly lengthwise by hand or using a mandoline or Japanese slicer. Make only 2 slices at a time to keep them from turning rusty. (You don't want to cover the potatoes with water because it will dilute the starch needed to hold them together.) Snip a leaf from a stem of parsley and lay it in the center of one of the potato slices. Top the potato with the next slice, matching the edges, and brush the outside of the potato on both sides with olive oil. Sprinkle with a little salt and place the potato slices on a parchment-lined baking pan. Slice 2 more thin layers of potato and repeat the process until you have made as many as you want. Bake until they are golden and crispy, 15 to 20 minutes. You may have to rotate the pan or remove some of the chips as they brown, while others will take longer to crisp up. Let the chips cool on the pan on a rack. The chips will be crisp if served within 2 hours. After that they begin to go stale and get a little rubbery.

***Variation:** Use sage, basil, or cilantro leaves instead of the parsley for a variety of decorative shapes.*

makes about eight fritters, serving four

Zucchini and Fresh Herb Fritters

ingredients

- *1 teaspoon salt, divided*
- *3 cups green and/or golden zucchini, coarsely grated and moderately packed*
- *2 eggs, beaten*
- *½ cup thinly sliced green onions, both white and green parts*
- *1 cup panko crumbs*
- *2 cloves garlic, finely minced*
- *½ cup chopped fresh Italian parsley*
- *¼ cup thinly sliced fresh basil*
- *1 teaspoon chopped fresh mint*
- *⅛ teaspoon freshly ground black pepper*
- *Vegetable oil, for frying*

- *½ cup crème fraîche or sour cream, for serving*

When brown grocery bags of fertile summer squash appear anonymously at your front door from neighbors' gardens, it's great to have recipe ideas beyond zucchini bread and ratatouille to use them up. These fritters are special because they consist largely of zucchini, not breading or batter. The bright yellow gold zucchini looks beautiful when mixed with the everyday green.

Toss the zucchini with ½ teaspoon of the salt, and set it aside in a colander to drain for 30 minutes. Meanwhile, in a large bowl, mix together the eggs, green onions, panko crumbs, garlic, parsley, basil, mint, remaining ½ teaspoon salt, and pepper.

Squeeze the zucchini with your hands and try to get as much water out of it as possible. Stir it into the batter. Taste for seasoning and correct with salt and pepper.

Add about ¼ cup vegetable oil to a large, nonstick skillet and heat over medium heat. When hot, drop the batter by quarter-cupfuls into the skillet. (Don't cook more than 3 at a time or they won't brown properly.) Flatten out the fritters and tidy up the sides with the back of a fork. Cook over medium heat until golden on the bottom, 3 or 4 minutes. Carefully turn the fritters with a wide spatula and cook on the second side, about 3 minutes. Remove the fritters from the pan and transfer them to a baking sheet. Cover to keep warm. Add more oil to the pan as needed and continue to fry the rest of the fritter batter in the same manner. Serve the fritters hot, with a dollop of the crème fraîche.

Make-ahead: *The cooked fritters can be kept in a 200°F oven for 30 minutes.*

Tip: *Summer squashes are thin skinned, tender, and versatile. They should be shiny and firm, not wrinkled and soft. Small to medium squash are always preferable, since large ones tend to be seedy, watery, and less flavorful.*

makes twenty-four pieces

Cherry Tomatoes Stuffed with Crab and Avocado

ingredients

- *24 large cherry tomatoes*
- *¼ teaspoon salt, plus more for seasoning tomatoes*
- *2 tablespoons fresh lemon juice*
- *3 tablespoons minced sweet onion*
- *2 tablespoons finely chopped fresh cilantro, plus 24 whole leaves*
- *2 tablespoons mayonnaise*
- *Pinch of freshly ground black pepper*
- *½ cup fresh lump crabmeat*
- *½ cup diced avocado*

Because crab and avocado are both delicate in structure and in flavor, they make a great partnership. Here we've added a hint of fresh cilantro and lemon juice, which bring out the best in both without overpowering either one.

Slice about ¼ inch off the top of each tomato. Using the small end of a melon baller, carefully scoop out some of the inside of each tomato, removing the seeds but leaving at least ¼ inch of the wall of the tomato intact. Lightly sprinkle the insides of the tomatoes with salt and place cut side down on paper towels to drain for 30 minutes.

In a medium bowl, mix together the lemon juice, onion, chopped cilantro, mayonnaise, ¼ teaspoon salt, and pepper. Gently fold in the crab and avocado. Taste for seasoning.

Fill each tomato with a spoonful of the filling and top with a cilantro leaf. Transfer to a serving platter and chill, covered in plastic wrap, until ready to serve.

Make-ahead: *The tomatoes can be made up to 4 hours ahead and kept, covered, in the refrigerator.*

Tip: *When fresh crabmeat isn't available, look for the plastic tubs of pasteurized crabmeat in the chilled seafood section of your grocery store.*

makes twenty-four pieces

Cherry Tomatoes Stuffed with Feta, Green Onion, and Bacon

ingredients

24 large cherry tomatoes

Salt, for sprinkling

1/3 cup mayonnaise

4 tablespoons finely chopped green onions, green part only, divided

3 slices bacon, cooked and finely chopped

3 tablespoons finely crumbled feta cheese

Freshly ground black pepper to taste

Whenever tomatoes and bacon are together, regardless of the format, you can't help but think BLT. This appetizer is no different. It has all the important components of the classic sandwich: tomatoes, mayo, and bacon. Here the cherry tomatoes also have the added pleasure of sharp, salty feta cheese and fresh green onions for company. As always, whenever you are serving a dish that is so reliant on fresh tomatoes, make sure they are ripe and in season.

Slice about 1/4 inch off the top of each tomato. Using the small end of a melon baller, carefully scoop out some of the inside of each tomato, removing the seeds but leaving at least 1/4 inch of the wall of the tomato intact. Lightly sprinkle the insides of the tomatoes with salt and place cut side down on paper towels to drain for 30 minutes.

Meanwhile, in a small bowl, mix together the mayonnaise, 2 tablespoons of the green onions, bacon, feta cheese, and pepper.

Fill each tomato with a spoonful of the filling and sprinkle with the remaining 2 tablespoons green onion. Transfer to a serving platter and chill, covered in plastic wrap, until ready to serve.

Make-ahead: *The tomatoes can be made up to 4 hours ahead and kept, covered, in the refrigerator.*

makes about forty-eight pieces

Roasted Mushrooms Stuffed with Bacon and Blue Cheese

ingredients

- 2 3/4 pounds button mushrooms (about 48, each about 1 1/2 inches in diameter)
- 8 ounces sliced bacon
- Olive oil, if necessary
- 1 medium onion, chopped
- 4 ounces blue cheese, crumbled (about 3/4 cup)
- 4 ounces cream cheese, at room temperature
- 2 cups fresh white bread cubes
- 1/2 teaspoon dried thyme
- Salt and freshly ground black pepper to taste

Roasting the mushrooms gives them a denser, meatier texture, somewhat reminiscent of steak. The addition of the blue cheese stuffing makes a lovely combination.

Preheat the oven to 375°F. Remove the stems from the mushrooms and chop the stems finely. Set aside.

Cook the bacon in a large, heavy skillet until crisp, about 8 minutes. Transfer to paper towels to drain. Coarsely crumble the bacon. Discard all but 1/4 cup plus 2 teaspoons of the bacon fat (adding olive oil if necessary to equal that amount).

Heat 2 teaspoons of the reserved bacon fat in a medium, heavy skillet over medium heat. Add the chopped onion and mushroom stems and sauté until tender, about 5 minutes. Transfer to a medium bowl and let cool; mix in the bacon, blue cheese, cream cheese, bread cubes, and thyme. Season the filling to taste with salt and pepper.

Line 2 large rimmed baking sheets with foil. Toss the mushroom caps and the remaining 1/4 cup bacon fat in a large bowl to coat. Sprinkle the mushrooms with salt and pepper. Place the mushrooms, rounded side down, in a single layer on the prepared baking sheets. Bake until the centers of the mushrooms fill with liquid, about 25 minutes. Turn them over and bake until brown and the liquid evaporates, about 20 minutes longer. Turn the mushrooms over again. Spoon 1 heaping teaspoon filling into each mushroom cavity.

Bake the stuffed mushrooms until heated through, about 10 minutes. Transfer to a platter and serve warm.

Make-ahead: *The mushrooms can be roasted and stuffed the day before and kept, covered, in the refrigerator. Bake as directed, adding a few minutes to the baking time.*

makes about two cups

Sweet and Sour Cipollini Onions

ingredients

2 pounds cipollini or small (1½-inch) white boiling onions, left unpeeled

1 cup sugar

¼ cup water

1 cup dry white wine

1 cup white wine vinegar

2 tablespoons extra-virgin olive oil

1 teaspoon salt

10 whole black peppercorns

1 bay leaf

3 tablespoons balsamic vinegar

An antipasto plate is easy to throw together for a party. In its simpler form, all it takes is a platter of Italian cold cuts, cheeses, and a handful of olives. But throw these sweet-tart onions into the mix and your antipasto plate goes from standard to stellar.

Blanch the cipollini in a large pot of boiling water for 1 minute, then drain in a colander and transfer to a bowl of cold water to stop cooking. Drain and peel.

Place the remaining ingredients in a large, heavy pot. Bring to a boil over high heat. Add the onions, reduce the heat to medium, and simmer until crisp-tender, about 10 minutes. Using a slotted spoon, transfer the onions to a jar with a lid. Increase the heat to high and boil until the liquid is reduced to 1¾ cups, about 20 minutes. Pour the liquid over the onions and let cool.

Cover the onion mixture and refrigerate for at least 2 days to allow the flavors to blend and the onions to absorb the syrup. Serve chilled or at room temperature.

Make-ahead: *These onions can be made up to 1 week ahead of time.*

Tip: *Cipollini onions, which are actually the bulbs of the grape hyacinth flower, are small, rather squat onions that have become increasingly available in the last few years. If you can't find them, pearl onions make a good substitute.*

makes twelve skewers

Melon, Prosciutto, and Mozzarella Skewers

ingredients

- *1/3 cup olive oil*
- *2 tablespoons chopped shallot*
- *2 tablespoons (packed) fresh mint leaves*
- *1/3 cup (packed) fresh basil leaves, plus sprigs for garnish*
- *1/4 teaspoon salt*
- *1 small (about 2 pounds) cantaloupe, halved crosswise, seeded, cut into 6 wedges, and peeled*
- *12 small balls fresh water-packed mozzarella, or one 8-ounce ball, drained*
- *12 thin slices prosciutto, cut in half lengthwise and gathered into ruffles*
- *Cracked black pepper, for sprinkling*

Salty prosciutto with sweet, cool melon is a classic combination that we've used as a springboard for this recipe. Instead of simply setting the ingredients out on a platter, we've made it more user-friendly by skewering them, along with fresh mozzarella, and drizzling them with a brightly flavored mint and basil dressing. The combination of the presentation along with the dressing breathes new life into this dish.

Place the olive oil, shallot, mint, basil, and salt in the bowl of a food processor. Pulse until the shallots and herbs are finely chopped.

Cut each cantaloupe wedge crosswise into 4 pieces. If using a large mozzarella ball, trim and cut into 12 cubes.

Pierce an 8-inch wooden skewer through one end of a prosciutto strip, add a piece of melon, and bring the prosciutto strip around the melon and onto the skewer again. Add a piece of mozzarella and lace the prosciutto strip around the cheese and back onto the skewer. Add one more piece of melon, bring the prosciutto strip around, and attach it at the end of the skewer. The prosciutto should appear to be ribboning through the melon and cheese. Repeat, making 12 skewers in all.

Arrange the skewers on a platter. Drizzle with the herb dressing and sprinkle with cracked black pepper. Garnish with basil sprigs.

Make-ahead: *The skewers can be prepared 2 hours ahead; cover and refrigerate. Remove from the refrigerator 15 minutes before serving, so they can come to room temperature.*

makes twenty-four pieces

Figs with Saga Blue and Prosciutto

ingredients

24 dried or fresh figs

1 cup Saga blue cheese

12 thin slices prosciutto, sliced in half lengthwise

What would a 1970s cocktail party be without one of the many variations of rumaki? Instead of wrapping bacon around almond-filled dates, we used prosciutto, figs, and blue cheese. The sweetness of the figs and the saltiness of the prosciutto play off against the bite of the blue cheese. Keep this one in mind when the champagne corks are popping and you're looking for something quick, easy, and festive.

Preheat the oven to 375°F.

With a knife, make a vertical cut into the figs, slicing down a little more than halfway.

Place a teaspoon or so of cheese into the cavity of each fig, and close the fig to enclose the cheese.

Wrap the fig tightly with a strip of prosciutto, and secure it with a toothpick.

Place the figs on a cookie sheet lined with parchment paper and place in the oven until the prosciutto is toasted and the cheese is warm, about 12 minutes.

Remove the toothpicks, place the warm stuffed figs on a platter, and serve.

Make-ahead: *The figs can be stuffed, wrapped in prosciutto, and frozen in a freezer bag for 2 weeks.*

Tip: *This is one of those baseline recipes that you can play with. Add fresh herbs to the cheese, or some toasted chopped walnuts for a nice textural contrast. Can't find good prosciutto? Use Black Forest ham or bacon. If you use bacon, make sure that you partially fry it before wrapping the figs so that it cooks adequately in the oven.*

makes twenty pieces

Italian Sausage Stuffed Mushrooms

ingredients

- *3 spicy or sweet Italian sausage links, casings removed (about 12 ounces)*
- *2 cloves garlic, finely minced*
- *2 ounces prosciutto, finely chopped*
- *1 cup grated Parmesan cheese (about 4 ounces), divided*
- *1 cup fresh breadcrumbs, divided*
- *One 8-ounce package cream cheese, at room temperature*
- *Salt and freshly ground black pepper to taste*
- *2 tablespoons finely chopped fresh Italian parsley*
- *20 large (about 2 inches in diameter) mushrooms, stemmed*
- *Olive oil, for drizzling*

It may sound trite, but everybody loves stuffed mushrooms. We've made them a million times, and it never ceases to amaze us how fast they disappear at a party. Some people have even been known to set up camp right in front of the platter. To give a twist to this basic recipe, try substituting goat cheese for the cream cheese.

Sauté the sausage in a large, heavy skillet over medium-high heat, breaking up the large lumps with the back of a wooden spoon, until the sausage is cooked through and brown, about 5 minutes. Add the garlic and prosciutto and continue to cook for another minute. Using a slotted spoon, transfer the sausage mixture to a large bowl and let cool. Add ½ cup of the Parmesan cheese, ½ cup of the breadcrumbs, and the cream cheese and mix together until well combined. Season to taste with salt and pepper.

In a small bowl, combine the remaining ½ cup Parmesan cheese and ½ cup breadcrumbs with the parsley. Set aside.

Brush a 9-by-13-inch baking dish with olive oil. Fill each mushroom cap with about 1½ tablespoons of filling. Make sure you have enough filling to mound nicely on top of the mushroom. Sprinkle with some of the cheese-breadcrumb mixture. Arrange the mushrooms, filling side up, in the prepared dish and drizzle lightly with olive oil.

Preheat the oven to 375°F. Bake, uncovered, until the mushrooms are tender and the filling is brown on top, 20 to 25 minutes.

Make-ahead: *The unbaked stuffed mushrooms can be made 1 day ahead. Cover and chill. They can also be frozen on baking sheets wrapped with plastic and foil for 2 weeks. Bake directly from the freezer, adding 7 to 10 minutes to the baking time.*

Tip: *When you get your mushrooms home from the market, wipe them with a damp towel to remove any dirt, and store them in a paper bag in the refrigerator. For a light luncheon entrée, use this filling in portobella mushrooms and serve with a green salad.*

serves six

Edamame

ingredients

1 tablespoon salt

One 1-pound bag frozen edamame

Coarse salt to taste

Potato chip addicts should thank their lucky stars for the newfound popularity of edamame. This equally addictive "good and good for you" snack can now be found in the frozen food section of almost any grocery store, and the ease with which it's prepared makes it possible to enjoy them with just a few moments' notice. If you have the time, try snipping one end off each pod. It's a nice touch for company and makes the edamame easier to eat.

Bring a large pot of water to a boil and stir in the tablespoon of salt. Have ready a bowl of ice and cold water. Cook the frozen edamame in boiling water until bright green, 2 to 3 minutes. Immediately drain and place the edamame in the ice water. Drain well.

Just before serving, toss the edamame with coarse salt to taste.

Make-ahead: *The edamame can be prepared 4 hours ahead and kept in a bowl, covered with a damp paper towel and plastic wrap, at cool room temperature.*

serves eight

Roasted Asparagus with Sesame Vinaigrette

ingredients

- 2 pounds asparagus, trimmed
- 2 tablespoons olive oil
- Salt and freshly ground black pepper to taste
- 2 tablespoons plus 2 teaspoons Asian (dark) sesame oil
- 1 tablespoon plus 1 teaspoon rice vinegar
- 1 tablespoon plus 1 teaspoon soy sauce
- 2 teaspoons sugar
- Toasted sesame seeds, for sprinkling

Roasting is a great way to prepare vegetables. It brings out their natural sweetness without losing valuable nutrients. This asparagus dish has a nutty, sweet and sour sesame dressing and makes a lovely, light first course to any meal.

Preheat the oven to 425°F.

Arrange the asparagus on a large baking sheet. Drizzle with the olive oil and toss to coat. Season with salt and pepper and roast until the asparagus is crisp-tender, 10 to 15 minutes. Arrange on a serving platter.

Mix the sesame oil, rice vinegar, soy sauce, and sugar in small bowl. Season to taste with salt and pepper. Spoon over the asparagus. Sprinkle with sesame seeds and serve.

Make-ahead: The dressing can be prepared 1 day ahead and kept, covered, in the refrigerator.

makes twelve large poppers

Jalapeño Poppers

ingredients

- *Vegetable oil, for frying*
- *12 large, fresh jalapeño chiles*
- *4 ounces cream cheese, at room temperature*
- *½ cup grated Monterey Jack cheese*
- *2 cloves garlic, chopped*
- *¼ cup chopped fresh cilantro*
- *1 cup plus 3 tablespoons all-purpose flour, divided*
- *½ cup milk*
- *1 large egg, lightly beaten*
- *1½ cups panko crumbs*

We've always had a soft spot in our hearts for bar food. After all, some of the best culinary creations in the world were first served alongside a mug of beer or glass of sherry. It's usually when a dish is mass-produced and prepackaged that its reputation becomes sullied. Here, we're happy to say, is a recipe that could bring these cheese-stuffed peppers the glory they deserve. The cream cheese filling is fresh and bold and positively oozing out of the hot pepper's crisp, light coating.

Pour oil into a medium, heavy saucepan to a depth of 1½ inches (the oil should not come more than halfway up the sides of the pan), and heat it to 375°F.

While the oil is heating, make a "T" in each pepper by cutting a slit lengthwise down one side and making another ½-inch cut parallel to the stem to create a pocket. Remove the seeds, being careful to leave the stem intact.

In a medium bowl, combine the cream cheese, Monterey Jack, garlic, and cilantro. Divide the mixture into 12 balls. Using your hands, form the balls into small cones (similar to the shape of the jalapeños). Gently open the jalapeños and place a cone of the cheese mixture into each one. Press the edges of the chiles together to close.

Working with 3 shallow bowls, place ½ cup of flour in one, combine another ½ cup flour with the milk and egg in another, and combine the remaining 3 tablespoons flour with the panko crumbs in the last bowl.

Dip the stuffed jalapeños into the flour and then into the milk batter, and finally roll them in the panko mixture, pressing to coat.

Working in batches if necessary, gently place the jalapeños in the preheated oil and fry until golden brown, 1 to 2 minutes. Remove from the oil and drain on a paper towel–lined plate. Cool slightly before serving, as the cheese is extremely hot.

Make-ahead: *The jalapeños can be stuffed with the cheese mixture 1 day ahead. They can be breaded, placed on a platter, and kept in the refrigerator up to 8 hours ahead.*

makes about thirty fritters

Corn and Jalapeño Fritters

ingredients

- 1 1/4 cups unsifted all-purpose flour
- 1/2 cup cornmeal
- 1 teaspoon baking powder
- 2 tablespoons sugar
- 1/2 teaspoon salt
- 2 large eggs, lightly beaten
- 1/3 cup milk
- One 13 1/4-ounce can creamed corn
- 1 cup fresh, frozen, or canned yellow corn kernels
- 1 jalapeño chile, minced
- 1/4 cup chopped fresh cilantro
- Vegetable oil, for frying
- Coarse salt, for sprinkling

Sour Cream, Lime, and Cilantro Dipping Sauce (page 269), for serving

These hot, crispy fritters were a childhood favorite of Meredith's. Her mother spent every family get-together standing at the stove trying to defend these golden treasures from hungry hands long enough to get them to the dinner table. For additional zip, we've added jalapeño and cilantro to her recipe and serve them with a dollop of Sour Cream, Lime, and Cilantro Dipping Sauce, which makes for a pleasant, cooling contrast.

Combine the flour, cornmeal, baking powder, sugar, and salt in a medium bowl. Stir in the eggs, milk, and creamed corn just until the flour mixture has all been moistened. The mixture should be lumpy. Fold in the corn, jalapeño, and cilantro. Heat 1/4 inch of vegetable oil in a large skillet over medium-high heat. Drop the corn batter by tablespoonfuls into the skillet and fry until brown on both sides. The centers should feel firm when gently pressed, about 1 minute per side. Remove and drain on paper towels. Sprinkle the fritters lightly with coarse salt immediately. Transfer to a serving platter and keep warm. Repeat until all the batter has been used, adding more oil as needed. Serve hot with dipping sauce on the side.

Make-ahead: *The fritters can be made and kept warm in a 200°F oven for 30 minutes.*

Tip: *Jalapeños are often thought of as a hot pepper, but over the years their heat has become less predictable. Some can be fiery hot, while others plucked from the same supermarket bin can be as harmless as a green bell pepper. In order to make your batch of fritters all the same, buy more than you need and try a tiny sliver as you're seeding them.*

makes about $3\frac{1}{2}$ cups

Eggplant Caviar

ingredients

- *2 medium eggplants*
- *1 large, ripe tomato*
- *1 red bell pepper, stem and seeds removed, quartered*
- *1 cup chopped onion*
- *2 cloves garlic, chopped*
- *2 teaspoons sugar*
- *3 tablespoons extra-virgin olive oil, plus more for drizzling*
- *2 tablespoons fresh lemon juice*
- *Salt and freshly ground black pepper to taste*
- *2 tablespoons chopped fresh Italian parsley*

Crackers or Pita Wedges (page 96), for serving

Referred to as "poor man's" caviar, this versatile dip or spread is just as at home on top of scrambled eggs as it is on a pita wedge. This recipe makes quite a bit, but its uses are endless.

Preheat the oven to 425°F.

Place the eggplant on a baking sheet. Pierce it several times with a fork. Bake until very soft and the skin wrinkles and cracks, about 45 minutes. Cool slightly. Cut the baked eggplant in half lengthwise. Peel off the skin. Place the eggplant in a sieve and let drain for 45 minutes.

Core the tomato and cut it in half crosswise; squeeze out the seeds.

Place the eggplant, tomato, red pepper, onion, garlic, and sugar in the bowl of a food processor (it may be necessary to do this in 2 batches). Pulse several times, until the vegetables are finely chopped but not puréed. Transfer to a bowl and stir in 3 tablespoons olive oil and the lemon juice. Season to taste with salt and pepper. Refrigerate for 2 hours before serving to allow the flavors to blend. Just before serving, sprinkle the top with the chopped parsley and drizzle with olive oil. Serve chilled or at room temperature with crackers or pita wedges.

Make-ahead: *The spread can be made up to 8 hours ahead and kept refrigerated.*

serves six

Chipotle, Black Bean, and Goat Cheese Nachos

ingredients

1 tablespoon olive oil

2 cups chopped onion

One 15-ounce can black beans, rinsed and drained

1 tablespoon chopped canned chipotle chile in adobo sauce

1/4 teaspoon salt

1 teaspoon balsamic vinegar

One 12-ounce bag tortilla chips

4 ounces goat cheese, crumbled

1/4 cup toasted pepitas

Easy Tomato and Chipotle Salsa (page 266), for serving

In this recipe, we use goat cheese as the perfect topper to a smoky, spicy black bean purée, made slightly sweet by the addition of caramelized onions and balsamic vinegar. Any leftover black bean purée will make a wonderful dip or spread for a tortilla wrap.

In a medium skillet, heat the oil over medium heat. Add the onion and sauté until golden, about 10 minutes. Transfer the onion to a food processor and add the beans, chipotle, salt, and balsamic vinegar. Process until smooth. Season with more salt, if necessary.

Preheat the broiler. Place the chips on a large, heatproof platter. Spoon the bean mixture over the chips. Sprinkle with the cheese and place under the broiler until the cheese is hot and lightly brown, about 1 minute. Watch carefully to avoid burning the exposed chips around the edges. Remove from the oven.

Sprinkle with the toasted pepitas and serve with the salsa.

Make-ahead: *The bean purée can be made 2 days ahead and kept, covered, in the refrigerator. Bring to room temperature before proceeding with the recipe.*

Tip: *Pepitas are hulled green pumpkin seeds that can be found at most specialty food stores.*

Chapter 9

07 Grilled Prosciutto-Wrapped Shrimp

09 Spicy Scallop Mango Ceviche

rab *and* Corn Cakes *with* Roasted Red Pepper Sauce

15 Grilled Spicy Thai Shrimp

oat Cheese Pinwheels **218** Clams Casino

Vontons **221** Crab-Mascarpone Cheesecake Bites

Seafood

epper Tempura *and* Beurre Blanc

25 Black Pepper Seared Tuna Skewers *with* Wasabi Aïoli

27 Coconut Shrimp *with* Red Curry Sauce

29 Crab Dip *with* Artichokes *and* Jalapeño

32 Potted Shrimp *with* Red Bell Peppers *and* Shallots

34 Oysters *on the* Half Shell *with* Mignonette

36 Salmon Mousse

39 Shrimp Salsa

almon *and* Caper Mousse *on* Endive Spears

andwiches *with* Dilled Mayonnaise

nd Melted Leeks **244** Tuna Carpaccio

ith Ginger Sesame Dipping Sauce

serves six to eight

Grilled Chipotle Shrimp

ingredients

- 2 tablespoons vegetable oil
- 1 cup tomato sauce
- 2 canned chipotle chiles in adobo sauce
- 2 tablespoons dark brown sugar
- 2 tablespoons fresh lime juice
- ½ teaspoon salt
- 2 pounds extra-large shrimp (16 to 20 per pound), peeled and deveined, tails left on

Shrimp is so easy to prepare for a party, especially when you can buy them already peeled and deveined. For a large crowd, we like to make several different marinades in advance and keep them in large, resealable plastic bags. Before the party, we pop our shrimp into the bags to marinate, skewer them, and onto the grill they go.

In a blender, purée the oil, tomato sauce, chipotles, brown sugar, lime juice, and salt. Pour into a large bowl, and toss gently with the shrimp to coat well. Cover and refrigerate for 30 minutes.

Meanwhile, soak about 15 wooden skewers in cold water for 30 minutes. Prepare a grill or preheat a broiler.

Thread 3 shrimp onto each skewer. Discard the remaining marinade.

Cook the shrimp over a medium-hot grill or broil until pink and firm to the touch, about 2 minutes per side. Transfer to a serving platter. Serve hot or at room temperature.

Make-ahead: *The marinade can be made 2 days ahead and kept, covered, in the refrigerator.*

Tip: *Strong iodine odors are an indicator that shrimp is not fresh. Shrimp should smell fresh, clean, and sweet—like the sea, not like chemicals.*

makes twenty-four pieces

Grilled Prosciutto-Wrapped Shrimp

ingredients

- *1/4 cup finely chopped garlic*
- *1/2 teaspoon salt*
- *2 tablespoons minced fresh rosemary leaves, plus sprigs for garnish*
- *3 tablespoons olive oil, plus more for brushing shrimp*
- *2 tablespoons fresh lemon juice*
- *24 extra-large shrimp (16 to 20 per pound)*
- *12 thin slices prosciutto, cut in half lengthwise*

Lemon wedges, for serving

Wrapping seafood in prosciutto makes such good sense. It not only helps to protect the seafood from drying out during the cooking process, it also lends its rich, salty flavor to whatever it encases. In this recipe, we've marinated the shrimp in garlic, rosemary, and olive oil, which stand up well to the earthiness of the prosciutto.

In a large, resealable plastic bag, combine the garlic, salt, minced rosemary, 3 tablespoons olive oil, and lemon juice. Add the shrimp and toss to coat. Marinate, chilled, for at least 4 hours or overnight.

In a shallow dish, soak 6 wooden skewers in water to cover for 30 minutes. Prepare a grill.

Wrap 1 strip of prosciutto around the middle of each shrimp. Thread 4 shrimp on each skewer and brush with additional oil. Grill the shrimp on an oiled rack, set about 5 inches over glowing coals, until just cooked through, 3 to 4 minutes on each side.

Alternatively, brush the shrimp with additional oil and grill on a hot, well-seasoned ridged grill pan, covered, over medium-high heat until cooked through, 3 to 4 minutes on each side.

Garnish the shrimp with rosemary sprigs and serve with lemon wedges.

Make-ahead: *The shrimp can be marinated, wrapped in prosciutto, and skewered and kept, covered, in the refrigerator for up to 8 hours before grilling.*

Tip: *Try this technique with other types of seafood as well. We like to wrap our salmon fillets or scallops in prosciutto and serve them alongside roasted root vegetables for an easy but impressive meal.*

serves six to eight

Grilled Ginger Shrimp

ingredients

2 tablespoons vegetable oil

Grated zest of 1 lemon

2 tablespoons fresh lemon juice

2 tablespoons peeled and grated fresh ginger

2 cloves garlic, minced

½ teaspoon salt

2 pounds extra-large shrimp (16 to 20 per pound), peeled and deveined, tails left on

Copious amounts of fresh ginger and lemon make the shrimp shine in this fast and easy dish. Ginger can be difficult to peel without wasting a good bit. We like to use the tip of a teaspoon to gently scrape the skin away. Using an Asian ceramic ginger grater further simplifies the process.

In a blender, purée the oil, lemon zest and juice, ginger, garlic, and salt. Pour the marinade into a large bowl and toss gently with the shrimp to coat well. Cover and refrigerate for 20 minutes.

Meanwhile, soak about 15 wooden skewers in cold water for 30 minutes. Prepare the grill or preheat the broiler.

Thread 3 or 4 shrimp onto each skewer. Discard the remaining marinade.

Cook the shrimp over a medium-hot grill or broil until pink and firm to the touch, about 2 minutes per side.

Transfer to a serving platter. Serve hot or at room temperature.

Make-ahead: *The marinade can be made 2 days ahead and kept, covered, in the refrigerator.*

makes about two cups

Spicy Scallop Mango Ceviche

ingredients

- 8 ounces diver, or dry-pack, sea scallops, cut into small dice
- 3 tablespoons chopped fresh cilantro
- 1 jalapeño chile, minced
- 1 tablespoon olive oil
- Juice of 1 to 2 limes
- ½ teaspoon salt
- Freshly ground black pepper to taste
- 1 mango, peeled, pitted, and cut into small dice

- Bibb lettuce leaves, for serving (optional)
- Tortilla chips, for serving

Ceviche is a seafood salad in which the seafood is "cooked" in the acid of the lime dressing. When buying limes remember that you're likely to get more juice from thin-skinned limes that yield to gentle pressure. The mango lends a floral, soft, sensuous element to an already exceedingly sexy dish.

In a medium bowl, combine the scallops, cilantro, jalapeño, and olive oil. Add enough lime juice to cover the scallops. Add the salt and season with pepper to taste. Marinate, covered, in the refrigerator at least 2 hours or up to 8 hours, stirring occasionally. The scallops should be firm and opaque.

Just before serving, add the mango and taste for seasoning. Serve either in a large bowl or, for a more dramatic effect, in individual martini glasses, each lined with a Bibb lettuce leaf. Serve tortilla chips on the side.

Tip: *Buying fresh seafood from a reputable seafood market is always important, but when you're working with a recipe that does not subject the seafood to the rigor of heat, it becomes even more critical. Make sure you're getting the best-quality seafood possible, and always give it the smell test. It should smell clean, like the sea, without a strong fishy odor.*

makes about thirty-six small crab cakes

Miniature Crab Cakes with Tomato Ginger Jam

tomato ginger jam

- 2 tablespoons unsalted butter
- 1/4 cup minced shallots
- 1 tablespoon finely grated peeled fresh ginger
- 1 large clove garlic, minced
- 3/4 teaspoon salt
- 1/4 teaspoon freshly ground black pepper
- 1/8 teaspoon crushed red pepper flakes
- 1 tablespoon sugar
- 1 1/2 pounds plum tomatoes, seeded and finely chopped
- 1 1/2 tablespoons fresh lime juice
- 2 tablespoons finely chopped fresh cilantro

We can't think of anyone we'd rather crack crab with than our good friend Fred Thompson. Not just because Fred knows his crab (he's the author of* Crazy for Crab *and* The Big Book of Fish and Shellfish*), but also because he likes to think outside the box. So when we were looking for a crab cake that was baked instead of fried, we knew he could help us out. What makes this recipe great for entertaining is that the cakes can be made in advance and baked as you need them. Fred pairs these crispy, golden cakes with a uniquely flavorful tomato and ginger jam.

To make the jam: Melt the butter in a 10-inch heavy skillet over medium-low heat. Add the shallots, ginger, garlic, salt, black pepper, and red pepper flakes and cook, stirring, until the shallots are softened, about 5 minutes. Add the sugar and cook, stirring, until dissolved. Add the tomatoes and simmer over medium heat, stirring occasionally, until thickened, 10 to 15 minutes.

Cool the jam to room temperature, then stir in the lime juice and cilantro.

To make the crab cakes: In a large bowl, whisk together the mayonnaise, egg, mustard, seafood seasoning, lemon juice, salt, pepper, and hot pepper sauce. Gently stir in the crabmeat, taking care not to break up the lumps. Chill, covered, for 2 hours.

Mix the cornflake crumbs and panko crumbs together in a shallow dish. Form 1 heaping teaspoon of crab mixture into a flat, round cake 1 1/2 inches in diameter (the mixture will be very moist). Repeat, making 36 cakes, placing the cakes on a greased baking sheet. Chill again, covered, for about half an hour. Gently dredge the cakes in the cornflake-panko mixture. The crab cakes can be refrigerated for up to 3 hours.

crab cakes

½ cup mayonnaise

1 large egg

1 tablespoon Dijon mustard

1 teaspoon Old Bay seasoning

1½ teaspoons fresh lemon juice

¼ teaspoon salt

⅛ teaspoon freshly ground black pepper

⅛ teaspoon hot pepper sauce

1 pound jumbo lump crabmeat, picked over for shell

2 cups cornflake crumbs

2 cups panko crumbs

Coarsely chopped fresh Italian parsley, for garnish

Preheat the oven to 400°F.

Bake the crab cakes in the middle of the oven until crisp and golden, 8 to 10 minutes. Transfer with a spatula to a platter, and top each with a taste of the tomato ginger jam.

Make-ahead: *The crab cakes can be made up to 3 hours ahead and kept, covered, in the refrigerator. The jam can be made 2 days ahead and chilled, covered. Stir in the lime juice and the cilantro when serving.*

makes about fourteen crab cakes and $1^2/_3$ cups sauce

Little Crab and Corn Cakes with Roasted Red Pepper Sauce

roasted red pepper sauce

One $7^1/_4$-ounce jar roasted red peppers, drained well

1 large shallot, coarsely chopped

2 teaspoons balsamic vinegar

$^1/_2$ cup heavy cream

Salt and freshly ground black pepper to taste

crab cakes

1 teaspoon Old Bay crab seasoning

$^1/_4$ teaspoon salt

1 egg

1 tablespoon fresh lemon juice

2 tablespoons unsalted butter, melted

$^1/_4$ cup mayonnaise

4 slices soft white bread, crusts trimmed, cubed

$^3/_4$ cup fresh corn kernels

Typically, our thinking on crab cakes is that the best ones consist of crab and little else, which is why we were both surprised at our delight with this recipe. The addition of corn does not come off as filler here; rather, its sweetness seems to enhance that of the crab, making the crab stand out even more. We use fresh corn kernels here, but in the summer when the grill is going nonstop, we like to throw on a couple of extra ears of corn and use the leftover grilled corn in this recipe.

To make the sauce: In a food processor, purée the roasted red peppers, shallot, and balsamic vinegar until almost smooth. Transfer to a small saucepan and add the cream. Stir over medium heat until warmed through; season to taste with salt and pepper.

To make the crab cakes: In a large bowl, mix together the crab seasoning, salt, egg, lemon juice, butter, and mayonnaise. Add the bread cubes, corn, green onions, and crab and toss gently to combine. Cover and refrigerate for 1 hour.

Place the breadcrumbs in a shallow bowl. Shape the crab mixture into round, flat cakes, using a scant $^1/_4$ cup for each. Gently roll the crab cakes in the breadcrumbs to coat. Place the formed cakes on a baking sheet, cover, and let rest in the refrigerator for 30 minutes.

When you are ready to cook, heat the oil in a large, nonstick skillet over medium-high heat. Working in batches, gently place about 5 cakes at a time in the skillet, being careful not to crowd them. Fry until the cakes are golden on one side, 2 to 3 minutes. Flip them carefully with a spatula, and fry on the other side for 2 to 3 minutes. Remove the cakes from the pan and place them on paper towels. Repeat with the remaining cakes. Serve warm with the sauce.

1/4 cup minced green onions

8 ounces back fin crabmeat from a refrigerated tin, picked over for shell and cartilage

8 ounces jumbo lump crabmeat from a refrigerated tin, picked over for shell and cartilage

3 cups fresh breadcrumbs

3 tablespoons vegetable oil

Make-ahead: *The sauce can be made a day ahead and kept, covered, in the refrigerator. The crab cakes can be formed and kept, covered, in the refrigerator for up to 3 hours.*

Tip: *If your corn is popping in the skillet, lower the heat slightly.*

serves eight to ten

Steamed Mussels with Wine and Garlic Butter

ingredients

- *3 pounds fresh mussels, scrubbed and debearded*
- *1 cup dry white wine*
- *½ cup (1 stick) unsalted butter*
- *⅓ cup finely chopped shallot*
- *6 large cloves garlic, minced*
- *4 tablespoons chopped fresh Italian parsley, divided*
- *2 tablespoons fresh lemon juice*
- *1 teaspoon grated lemon zest*

Whenever we serve these fragrant, buttery mussels, we always wonder whether we're making the dish for the mussels themselves or for the absolutely over the moon, to die for liquid that settles at the bottom of the mussel bowl. Make sure you serve this with lots of crusty bread for dipping, as it would be a crime to miss out on what is arguably the best part!

Place the mussels and wine in a large, heavy Dutch oven, cover, and cook over high heat until the mussels open, shaking the pan occasionally, about 5 minutes. Drain the mussels, reserving the liquid. Transfer the mussels to a large serving bowl; discard any that have not opened. Tent the bowl with foil to keep warm.

Melt the butter in the same Dutch oven over medium-high heat. Add the shallot and garlic and sauté until tender, about 3 minutes. Add 3 tablespoons of the parsley, lemon juice, zest, and reserved liquid from the mussels and bring to a boil. Season to taste with pepper. Drizzle the garlic butter over the mussels. Sprinkle with the remaining tablespoon of parsley.

Tip: All your mussels should be tightly closed before steaming to ensure that they are still alive. If you have a mussel that is slightly open, tap it on the counter. If it does not close, discard the mussel. Once you've steamed your mussels, if there are any that do not open, they should also be tossed.

serves four to six

Grilled Spicy Thai Shrimp

ingredients

12 extra-large shrimp (16 to 20 per pound), peeled and deveined

3 tablespoons sea salt dissolved in 3 cups water

Three 1- to 2-inch fresh red Thai chiles, minced

1 tablespoon minced garlic

2 tablespoons Asian fish sauce

¼ cup fresh lime juice

2 tablespoons brown sugar

2 tablespoons vegetable oil

2 stalks fresh lemongrass

2 green onions (white parts and half of greens), thinly sliced

¼ cup fresh mint leaves, torn into pieces, plus whole mint leaves for garnish

Lettuce leaves, for serving

After grilling, these fiery shrimp are tossed with an aromatic salad of lemongrass, green onions, and mint, which give it a delightful crunch and a lively, fresh flavor. Lemongrass is a staple in the Thai pantry and can usually be found in the produce section of your better grocery stores. It's important that you use the fresh lemongrass. Dried, jarred, or frozen lemongrass will have a completely different texture and taste.

Prepare a grill or preheat the broiler.

Soak the shrimp in the salt water for 10 minutes, then drain and rinse well in a colander.

In a blender, combine the chiles, garlic, fish sauce, lime juice, and brown sugar and process for a few seconds. Transfer half of the marinade to a large bowl. Add the oil and the shrimp and toss to coat.

Cook the shrimp over the medium-hot grill or broil until pink and firm to the touch, about 2 minutes per side.

Discard the tough outer leaves of the lemongrass and trim the root ends. Thinly slice the lower 6 inches of the stalks.

Toss the cooked shrimp with the remaining marinade mixture and stir in the sliced lemongrass, green onions, and torn mint leaves.

Serve on a bed of lettuce, garnished with mint leaves.

Make-ahead: *The marinade can be made 1 day ahead and kept, covered, in the refrigerator.*

Tip: *When working with fresh lemongrass, it's important to use the tender part of the inner stalk. At the root end of each stalk is a woody center that is too chewy to eat. The tender, more palatable part of the lemongrass is above this solid core. When you trim the root end, you should be able to see rings. If you still see a woody center, you're not far enough up the stalk. Once you trim the root end, you should have about 6 inches of tender stalk before the stalk becomes too tough again.*

serves six

Lemony Baked Crab Dip

ingredients

½ cup mayonnaise

4 ounces cream cheese, at room temperature

4 ounces goat cheese, at room temperature

Grated zest of 2 lemons

2 tablespoons fresh lemon juice

2 tablespoons minced fresh Italian parsley

8 ounces lump crabmeat, picked over for bits of shell

Salt and freshly ground black pepper to taste

2 tablespoons grated Parmesan cheese

Crackers, Pita Wedges (page 96), or toasted baguette slices, for serving

Call on this starter when you need something easy, fast, and delicious. A great substitute for the "been there, done that" hot artichoke, mayonnaise, and Parmesan dip, our version pairs lemon and crab with goat cheese for an upscale attitude.

Preheat the oven to 375°F. Brush a 1 ½-quart baking dish with olive oil.

In a medium bowl, mix the mayonnaise, cream cheese, goat cheese, lemon zest and juice, and parsley until well blended. Lightly fold in the crab. Season to taste with salt and pepper.

Spread the dip evenly in the prepared pan. Sprinkle with the Parmesan. Bake on the middle rack for 20 minutes.

Preheat the broiler. Broil the dip until the top is bubbly and golden, 3 to 5 minutes. Serve warm with crackers, pita wedges, or toasted baguette slices.

Make-ahead: *The unbaked dip can be assembled and kept, covered and refrigerated, for 8 hours. Bake as directed.*

Tip: *Use the best-quality crab you can find for this dish. We have good luck using the pasteurized crab located in the cold case seafood section at the grocery store.*

makes about twenty pieces

Smoked Salmon and Goat Cheese Pinwheels

ingredients

- *4 ounces soft fresh goat cheese (such as Montrachet), at room temperature*
- *2 tablespoons finely chopped shallot*
- *2 tablespoons finely chopped fresh chives, plus whole chives for garnish*
- *Grated zest of 1 lemon*
- *Salt and freshly ground black pepper to taste*
- *4 ounces thinly sliced smoked salmon*

Smoked salmon is so sophisticated that no matter how you serve it, people will think you worked hard to get it to the table. Operating on that premise, this elegant presentation of smoked salmon with goat cheese looks as though it took a long time to put together, when it's really very quick and easy. Just make sure you give it the proper chilling time so that it will firm up and be easy to slice into beautiful pinwheels.

In a medium bowl, mix together the goat cheese, shallot, chopped chives, and lemon zest. Season with salt and pepper.

Place a sheet of plastic wrap on a work surface. Lay the slices of smoked salmon on the plastic wrap to form a 12-by-4-inch rectangle, overlapping the salmon slightly. Spoon the goat cheese filling along 1 long side of the rectangle, leaving a ½-inch plain border. Using the plastic wrap as a guide, roll the salmon up into a tight log. Twist the plastic wrap at the ends to close.

Refrigerate until firm, at least 2 hours.

Unwrap the plastic from the log. Using a serrated knife dipped in water, cut each log crosswise into ½-inch slices. Arrange on a platter, garnish with chives, and serve.

Make-ahead: *The log can be made 2 days ahead of time and kept in the plastic wrap in the refrigerator. It can be sliced and arranged on a platter 8 hours ahead, covered, and kept in the refrigerator. Serve chilled.*

makes forty clams

Clams Casino

Clams casino sounds like a dish that Frank Sinatra or Dean Martin might have enjoyed between sets at The Sands. And if it was this version of the classic, they would have been happy to sing for their supper. Here is a retro dish that really does deserve a return engagement. The rich bacon-breadcrumb topping alone is worth the price of admission.

ingredients

- *4 slices bacon*
- *4 tablespoons unsalted butter, at room temperature*
- *2 large cloves garlic, minced*
- *2 tablespoons minced fresh Italian parsley*
- *1 teaspoon fresh lemon juice*
- *1/4 teaspoon salt*
- *1 cup fresh sourdough breadcrumbs*
- *Pinch of cayenne pepper*
- *1 cup white wine*
- *40 littleneck or cherrystone clams, scrubbed*
- *4 cups kosher salt, to hold the clams*

Cook the bacon in a medium skillet over medium heat until crisp. Drain on paper towels and let cool. In the bowl of a food processor, place the bacon, butter, garlic, parsley, lemon juice, salt, breadcrumbs, and cayenne and pulse until well combined. Set aside.

Place the white wine and the clams in a wide pot with a lid over medium heat. Allow the clams to steam until they open, about 10 minutes. Discard any that do not open. Remove the clams from the pot and, once they are cool enough to work with, remove the meat from the shells. Tear the shells in half and move the meat to 1 side of the shell, discarding the other.

Pour the kosher salt onto a large, ovenproof platter, and spread it out to make an even layer. (This will help the clams remain upright during baking and make for an attractive presentation when serving.) Evenly space the clams on the prepared platter. Top each clam with 1 teaspoon of the bacon-breadcrumb mixture.

Place a rack about 4 inches from the broiler element and preheat. Broil the clams until the crumbs are toasted and the butter is sizzling, 2 to 3 minutes. Serve warm.

Make-ahead: *The clams can be stuffed, covered, and refrigerated up to 4 hours before broiling.*

Tip: *All your clams should be tightly closed before steaming to ensure that they are still alive. If you have a clam that is slightly open, tap it on your counter. If it does not close, discard the clam.*

serves four

Italian Tuna Spread

ingredients

One 6-ounce can Italian tuna packed in olive oil

1 teaspoon fresh lemon juice

2 teaspoons balsamic vinegar

2 tablespoons heavy cream

1 tablespoon unsalted butter

¼ teaspoon salt

2 or 3 thin lemon slices, for garnish

Crackers or baguette slices, for serving

This spread has no business being as good as it is! Forget tuna salad or casseroles—once you try this satin-smooth spread you'll never want your tuna any other way.

In the bowl of a food processor, combine the tuna, lemon juice, and balsamic vinegar and process until smooth. Add the cream, butter, and salt and pulse until well blended. Transfer to a serving bowl and keep chilled until ready to serve. Top with the lemon slices as a garnish. Serve cold with crackers or baguette slices.

Make-ahead: *This spread can be made 1 day ahead and kept, covered, in the refrigerator.*

Tip: Buying Italian tuna packed in olive oil makes all the difference for this spread. We've tried it with domestic water-packed tuna, and both the texture and flavor just aren't as good.

makes fifty wontons

Crispy Crab Wontons

dipping sauce

1 cup prepared Asian plum sauce

½ teaspoon crushed red pepper flakes

1 tablespoon fresh lime juice

wontons

8 ounces cream cheese, at room temperature

½ teaspoon Worcestershire sauce

¼ cup finely minced green onion

1 clove garlic, finely minced

8 ounces lump crabmeat, picked over for shell

Salt and freshly ground black pepper to taste

50 wonton wrappers

Vegetable oil, for deep-frying

Anyone who ever ate at Trader Vic's will instantly recognize their famous Crab Rangoon as the inspiration for this dish. A creamy crab filling embraced by a crispy wonton wrapper is served alongside a semi-homemade plum dipping sauce. We've served this dish dressed up for New Year's Eve and dressed down for a poker party.

To make the sauce: In a small saucepan, combine the plum sauce and red pepper flakes. Heat over low heat until warmed. Remove from the heat and add the lime juice. Set aside.

To make the wontons: In a medium bowl, combine the cream cheese, Worcestershire sauce, green onion, and garlic. Stir until thoroughly mixed. Gently fold in the crab. Season to taste with salt and pepper.

On a flat surface, lay out a wonton wrapper in front of you so that it forms a diamond shape. Wet the edges of the wrapper. Add about 1 teaspoon of filling to the middle. Fold over the edges of the wrapper to make a triangle.

Keep the completed wontons covered with plastic wrap to keep them from drying out while preparing the remainder.

Pour about 2 inches of oil into a fryer or large, heavy pot and heat to 375°F. Working in batches of 6 wontons, carefully slide the wontons into the hot oil. Deep-fry until they are golden brown, about 3 minutes, turning once. Remove with a slotted spoon and drain on paper towels.

Transfer to a serving platter and serve with the dipping sauce.

Make-ahead: *The uncooked crab wontons can be made up to a month in advance. Freeze them in a single layer on a baking sheet. Once frozen, transfer them to a freezer bag. They can be fried directly from the freezer.*

makes thirty-six pieces

Crab-Mascarpone Cheesecake Bites

ingredients

- *Flaky Pastry (page 335)*
- *8 ounces mascarpone cheese, at room temperature*
- *8 ounces cream cheese, at room temperature*
- *2 tablespoons all-purpose flour*
- *2 eggs*
- *½ teaspoon salt*
- *Grated zest of 1 lemon*
- *1 tablespoon fresh lemon juice*
- *1 tablespoon minced fresh tarragon, plus several sprigs for garnish*
- *¼ cup chopped fresh Italian parsley*
- *8 ounces lump crabmeat, picked over for shell*

Mascarpone is cream cheese's sexy Italian cousin, and in this luscious, decadent cheesecake it really has a chance to shine. The lemon and fresh herbs add a brightness that cuts through the richness of the cheeses and crab beautifully.

Preheat the oven to 400°F.

Line an 8-by-8-by-1 ½-inch baking pan with foil, being sure to have a 2-inch overhang on 2 sides. Roll out the pastry to fit the pan. Fit the pastry into the pan, pressing gently to make sure it is all the way into the corners. The pastry should just come to the top edge of the pan. Trim off any excess. Refrigerate the crust for 15 minutes.

Meanwhile, in the bowl of a food processor, combine the cheeses and pulse until smooth. Add the flour and eggs and process again. Scrape the bowl down and add the salt and the lemon zest and juice. Pulse again to combine. Transfer to a large mixing bowl and add the herbs and crabmeat. Gently fold into the cheese mixture with a large rubber spatula.

Pour the filling into the prepared crust. Bake in the lower third of the oven for 15 minutes. Reduce the heat to 325°F and continue to bake until the top is lightly browned but still just slightly jiggly in the center, 25 to 35 minutes. Let cool on a baking rack for 30 minutes. Cover loosely with plastic wrap and chill in the refrigerator for at least 2 hours.

When ready to serve, grasp the foil overhang and gently lift the cheesecake out of the pan. Cut the cheesecake into 1½-inch squares. Arrange on a serving platter with fresh tarragon sprigs as garnish. Allow the squares to come to room temperature for half an hour before serving.

Make-ahead: *The cheesecake can be made 2 days ahead, covered, and refrigerated. Allow it to come to room temperature before serving.*

Tip: *The mascarpone gives this cheesecake a richer, denser consistency. If you cannot find mascarpone, you can substitute cream cheese (for a total of 16 ounces of cream cheese).*

serves six

Seared Scallops with Crispy Zucchini and Red Pepper Tempura and Beurre Blanc

parsley oil

1 bunch Italian parsley

½ cup extra-virgin olive oil

beurre blanc

6 tablespoons fresh lemon juice

6 tablespoons water

¼ cup finely diced shallots

2 tablespoons heavy cream

10 tablespoons chilled unsalted butter, cut into tablespoon-size pieces

Salt and freshly ground white pepper to taste

Everybody ought to have one recipe in their repertoire that makes them feel like a chef. This impressive scallop dish will surely fit the bill. We developed this dish for a wine and food pairing class as the perfect starter with champagne. The bubbles of the wine cut through the rich sweetness of the scallops and the crispy tempura coating of the vegetables.

To make the parsley oil: Bring a small saucepan of water to a boil and immerse the parsley in the boiling water. Blanch for 30 seconds. Remove from the pan and immerse the blanched parsley in a bowl of ice water to stop the cooking and set the color. When cool, dry in a cotton towel. Place the parsley and the oil in a blender or food processor. Process for about 10 seconds and allow the oil to sit for at least 1 hour and preferably 2 or 3 to get the best color. Strain the oil through a fine-mesh strainer and use the parsley oil for drizzling decoratively on the plates. We like to put it in a squeeze bottle.

To make the beurre blanc: Place the lemon juice, water, and shallot in a medium skillet and cook over medium-high heat to reduce it to about 1 tablespoon. Add the cream and heat until it bubbles. Off the heat, add the butter 1 tablespoon at a time, melting the butter just enough so that it doesn't separate. Add the next piece of butter before the first one has completely melted. Continue in this manner until all the butter has been added and has melted into the sauce. Return the pan to the heat when necessary. Season the sauce with salt and white pepper. Keep warm.

To make the tempura: Add the oil to a skillet or wok and heat it to 350°F. In a medium bowl, mix the flour with the salt and whisk in the sparkling water to make a batter. Dip the zucchini into the batter to cover it, allowing the excess to drip off. Fry the zucchini

tempura

3 cups vegetable oil, for frying

1 cup all-purpose flour

½ teaspoon salt

1 cup chilled sparkling water

2 zucchini, sliced ¼ inch thick on the diagonal

2 red bell peppers, seeded and cut lengthwise into ½-inch-wide strips

1¼ pounds diver, or dry-pack, sea scallops

Sea salt and freshly ground white pepper to taste

in the hot oil, turning once, for 2 to 4 minutes. Remove to a tray lined with paper towels. Cook the peppers in the same manner. Keep the vegetables in a warm oven until serving time.

Heat a large, nonstick skillet over medium-high heat. Dry the scallops and add them to the hot skillet. You may have to cook them in 2 batches. Cook the scallops for about 1½ minutes on each side. They should be golden brown and just opaque in the center. Sprinkle the scallops as they are cooked with sea salt and white pepper.

To serve, divide the beurre blanc among the plates. In the center of each plate, arrange some of the zucchini and red pepper tempura. Top the vegetables with the scallops and drizzle the parsley oil over all.

Make-ahead: *The parsley oil can be made up to 24 hours ahead and kept in the refrigerator.*

serves four to six

Crispy Calamari with a Lemon-Basil Aïoli

lemon basil aïoli

- 1/3 cup finely chopped fresh basil
- Grated zest of 1 lemon
- 1 1/3 cups mayonnaise, homemade (page 334) or store-bought

calamari

- 1 pound whole small squid, bodies cleaned and cut into 1/4-inch-wide rings, tentacles reserved
- 1 cup milk
- 1 large egg
- Vegetable oil, for frying
- 1 cup all-purpose flour
- 1 cup cornmeal
- 1 teaspoon salt, plus more for sprinkling
- 1/4 teaspoon freshly ground black pepper

- 1 tablespoon chopped fresh Italian parsley, for garnish
- Lemon wedges, for serving

Light, crispy calamari is something we often enjoy in restaurants but rarely attempt to make in our own kitchens. Now that fresh, quality squid can be found in most good fish markets, there is no reason not to enjoy this addictive dish at home.

To make the aïoli: Fold the basil and lemon zest into the mayonnaise. Chill, covered, until ready to use.

To make the calamari: Rinse the squid under cool water and pat dry with paper towels. Combine the milk and egg in a medium bowl, mixing with a fork until lightly beaten. Add the prepared calamari to the milk mixture and stick it in the refrigerator while getting everything else set up; it fries better if marinated and chilled for about 15 minutes.

Pour about 2 inches of oil into a fryer or large, heavy pot and heat to 375°F. Mix the flour, cornmeal, 1 teaspoon salt, and pepper in a large, shallow bowl. Toss the calamari in the seasoned flour-cornmeal mixture to coat, shaking off the excess. Fry until golden brown, 1 to 3 minutes.

Using a slotted spoon, transfer the fried calamari to paper towels to drain, and season with salt to taste. Drizzle some of the aïoli onto the serving plates or platter. Top with the calamari, sprinkle with the parsley, and serve immediately with lemon wedges and more aïoli on the side.

makes twenty-four pieces, serving six

Black Pepper Seared Tuna Skewers with Wasabi Aïoli

wasabi aïoli

- 2 tablespoons wasabi powder
- 1 teaspoon soy sauce
- 2 teaspoons fresh lemon juice
- 1 cup mayonnaise, homemade (page 334) or store-bought

skewers

- 1 pound tuna steaks, cut into 1-inch cubes (about 24 pieces)
- 2 tablespoons soy sauce
- 1 tablespoon vegetable oil
- 24 slices pickled ginger
- 2 tablespoons coarsely ground black pepper

Tuna and pepper are frequently paired, but when you add pickled ginger and wasabi it all adds up to a flavor explosion. The wasabi aïoli isn't very hot—go ahead and add more wasabi powder if you like. The tuna is best when not overcooked, so be careful with the heat. The middle of the tuna should be rare.

To make the aïoli: In a medium bowl, mix the wasabi powder, soy sauce, and lemon juice. Add the mayonnaise and stir to combine. Chill, covered, for at least 1 hour to let the flavors develop.

Combine the tuna, soy sauce, and vegetable oil in a large bowl and let marinate for 30 minutes at room temperature. Soak 24 wooden skewers in water for 30 minutes. Prepare a grill or preheat a broiler.

Thread a piece of pickled ginger onto each skewer 3 inches up from the tip. Drain the tuna and thread a cube onto each skewer. Grind the pepper over a plate and dip one side of the tuna in it to coat it with the pepper. Grill over high heat for 1 minute on each side, or slip under the broiler for 2 minutes on each side. The tuna should be pink in the center.

Arrange the skewers on a platter and serve the hot tuna skewers with a bowl of the wasabi aïoli.

Make-ahead: *The aïoli can be made up to 24 hours in advance and kept, covered, in the refrigerator.*

serves six

Chilled Shrimp with Bloody Mary Cocktail Sauce

ingredients

- 8 cups water
- 1 lime, cut in half
- 1 tablespoon salt
- 1 pound medium shrimp (31 to 35 per pound) in the shell, thawed if frozen
- One 14½-ounce can Italian San Marzano whole tomatoes
- 2 tablespoons fresh lime juice
- ⅓ cup finely diced celery
- 2 tablespoons vodka
- 1 tablespoon Worcestershire sauce
- 1 tablespoon prepared horseradish
- 1 teaspoon Tabasco or hot pepper sauce, or more to taste
- ½ teaspoon salt
- 1 teaspoon freshly ground black pepper
- ¼ cup finely chopped fresh cilantro (optional)
- Celery stalks with leaves attached, cut into 4-inch lengths, for garnish

In their college days, Carla and her friends would concoct a version of these amazing Bloody Marys on springtime Sunday afternoons. Lots of pepper, lime, Tabasco, Worcestershire, and the ubiquitous celery all play supporting roles to the bloody part of the Mary: the tomato. Instead of using tomato juice, which can be loaded with sodium, we are using the most flavorful canned tomatoes you can buy and blending them up to create a thicker sauce.

In a large saucepan over high heat, bring the water to a boil. Squeeze in the juice of the lime and then add the squeezed lime to the water, along with the salt. When the water comes back to a boil, add the shrimp in their shells. Cover the saucepan with a lid and remove it from the heat. Let the shrimp sit in the covered pan for 3 minutes. They will cook perfectly. When they are opaque, drain them and plunge them into an ice bath to stop the cooking. Peel the shrimp when they are cool enough to handle, and keep them in the refrigerator until ready to assemble.

Add the whole tomatoes and their juice to a food processor work bowl and process to a smooth sauce consistency, about 10 seconds. Pour into a large bowl and add the lime juice. celery, vodka, Worcestershire sauce, horseradish, Tabasco, salt, and pepper. Taste the sauce for seasoning and add more of whatever you like, if desired. Chill in the refrigerator for at least 2 hours to let the flavors develop.

To assemble, toss the chilled shrimp with the sauce. Add the cilantro, if using. Arrange the shrimp and sauce in large martini or margarita glasses, and garnish with the celery stalks. Serve cold.

Make-ahead: *The sauce can be made 24 hours in advance and kept, covered, in the refrigerator.*

serves six

Coconut Shrimp with Red Curry Sauce

curry sauce

One 14½-ounce can unsweetened coconut milk

¼ cup chopped fresh cilantro

2 cloves garlic, minced

2 tablespoons fresh lime juice

2 tablespoons red curry paste

1 tablespoon Asian fish sauce

1 tablespoon light brown sugar

½ teaspoon crushed cardamom seeds

batter

½ cup all-purpose flour

½ cup cornstarch

2 teaspoons red curry paste

1 teaspoon salt

¾ cup beer

About 6 cups peanut or canola oil, for frying

¼ cup cornstarch

3 cups sweetened flaked coconut

18 large shrimp (21 to 30 per pound), peeled, deveined, and butterflied, tails left intact

Fresh cilantro leaves, for garnish (optional)

Coconut shrimp is one of those dishes that most everyone loves. There is something about that crunchy, sweet, chewy coconut covering tender, sweet shrimp that makes you keep popping them in your mouth long after you've become full. This recipe pairs the shrimp with a lightly spiced red curry sauce. We've even put some of the red curry paste in the batter for extra flavor.

To make the sauce: Combine the coconut milk, cilantro, garlic, lime juice, red curry paste, fish sauce, brown sugar, and cardamom in a medium saucepan and bring to a boil over high heat. Turn the heat down to medium and simmer for 2 or 3 minutes to let the flavors develop. Strain the sauce into a clean saucepan and keep hot.

To make the batter: Combine the flour, cornstarch, curry paste, and salt in a medium bowl. Slowly whisk in the beer until well mixed. Refrigerate the batter if not frying the shrimp right away.

Add enough oil to a large saucepan to measure 2 inches deep. Heat it to 370°F.

Place the cornstarch in a large bowl, and place the coconut in a second large bowl. Dredge the shrimp in the cornstarch, shaking off the excess. Dip the shrimp into the batter to coat them lightly, and then dredge in the coconut. Fry 4 or 5 shrimp in the hot oil until the coconut is golden and the shrimp is cooked through, about 2 minutes. Drain on paper towels. Continue to fry the shrimp in batches.

Arrange the shrimp on a decorative platter and serve the curry sauce in a bowl to the side. Garnish with cilantro, if desired. Or divide some of the sauce among 6 plates and stand 3 of the shrimp on top of each plate. Serve hot.

Make-ahead: *The sauce can be made 2 days ahead and kept, covered, in the refrigerator. The batter can be made 2 hours before using. The shrimp can be cooked and kept warm on a baking sheet in a 200°F oven for 20 minutes.*

serves six

Coquilles St. Jacques

ingredients

- 1 cup milk
- 5 tablespoons unsalted butter, divided
- 1½ tablespoons all-purpose flour
- ¼ teaspoon salt
- Dash of ground nutmeg
- Dash of freshly ground black pepper
- 1 teaspoon sherry vinegar
- ⅓ cup fresh breadcrumbs
- 12 diver, or dry-pack, scallops, about 1 pound
- ⅓ cup grated Gruyère cheese

Years ago, Carla picked up scallop shells at a garage sale. She couldn't wait to host the next dinner party and make coquilles St. Jacques. There is just something over the top about tender, briny scallops in a rich cream sauce served in beautiful shells. If you haven't seen scallop shells at a garage sale lately, any oven-to-table gratin dishes or ramekins will work just fine.

Heat the milk to a simmer in a small saucepan over medium-high heat.

While the milk is heating, melt 3 tablespoons of the butter in a medium saucepan over medium heat. Add the flour and cook, stirring, until foamy, about 3 minutes. Add the hot milk all at once while whisking. Stir the sauce until it is thick and bubbly. Remove from the heat and add the salt, nutmeg, black pepper, and sherry vinegar. Taste the sauce for seasoning and adjust if necessary. Let cool slightly before continuing.

Heat a medium skillet over medium heat and melt the remaining 2 tablespoons butter. Remove the skillet from the heat and stir in the breadcrumbs to coat them evenly with the butter. Reserve.

Preheat the broiler and arrange one of the oven racks at the highest position.

Set out the shells or ramekins on a baking sheet. Arrange 2 scallops in each. Top each scallop with about 3 tablespoons of the sauce. Sprinkle some of the cheese over the sauce and top with a tablespoon or so of the buttered breadcrumbs. Broil the scallops for about 7 minutes. The sauce and cheese should be golden brown. The scallops should be tender and juicy, not overcooked. Carefully transfer the hot scallops in their shells or ramekins to a serving plate. Serve immediately.

Tip: *If you are fortunate enough to have scallop shells, pour about ¼ cup kosher salt onto the center of each serving plate and set a scallop shell securely in the center of it. The salt will provide a nest for the scallop shell to fit into, making it more secure.*

makes about six cups, serving sixteen

Crab Dip with Artichokes and Jalapeño

ingredients

- 2 tablespoons vegetable oil
- ½ cup finely diced red bell pepper
- ⅓ cup chopped green onion
- ¼ cup finely diced celery
- 2 cloves garlic, minced
- 2 serrano chiles, seeded and minced
- Two 14-ounce cans artichoke hearts, drained, squeezed dry, and chopped
- 1 cup mayonnaise, homemade (page 334) or store-bought
- 1 cup grated Parmesan cheese
- ¼ cup Worcestershire sauce
- ½ teaspoon celery salt
- ¼ teaspoon freshly ground black pepper
- 1 pound lump crabmeat, drained, preferably the pasteurized type sold in the refrigerated seafood section
- ½ cup sliced almonds, toasted

Pita Wedges (page 96), for serving

We love to serve this dip during the holidays when something especially rich and delicious is in order. Don't be put off by the list of ingredients in this creamy seafood dip. Everything adds up to delicious.

Preheat the oven to 350°F.

Heat the vegetable oil in a large sauté pan. Add the red pepper, green onion, and celery and sauté until the vegetables begin to soften, 3 or 4 minutes. Add the garlic and chiles and cook for another 2 minutes. Remove from the heat and transfer to a large bowl.

Add the artichoke hearts, mayonnaise, Parmesan, Worcestershire, celery salt, pepper, and crabmeat to the bowl and toss to combine.

Transfer the dip to a 2-quart baking dish and bake until it is hot all the way through, about 40 minutes. Remove the dip from the oven and top with the toasted almond slices. Serve hot with the pita wedges as an accompaniment.

Make-ahead: *The unbaked dip can be kept, covered, in the refrigerator for up to 24 hours. Add 10 minutes to the baking time if baking it straight from the refrigerator.*

Tip: *Garlic is a flavor, and it can be lessened or increased according to taste. If your garlic cloves are large and the recipe calls for 2, add 1 and then taste to see if more is required.*

serves six

Crispy Scallops with Pineapple Chile Salsa

ingredients

- *1 cup finely diced pineapple*
- *1/3 cup finely diced red bell pepper*
- *1/4 cup minced fresh cilantro*
- *1 clove garlic, minced*
- *1 tablespoon fresh lime juice*
- *1 tablespoon honey*
- *1/2 teaspoon minced fresh thyme*
- *1/4 teaspoon minced habanero or Scotch bonnet chile*
- *1/4 teaspoon salt*
- *Freshly ground black pepper to taste*
- *18 diver, or dry-pack, sea scallops, about 1 1/2 pounds*
- *Fleur de sel or sea salt to taste*
- *2 tablespoons finely chopped fresh cilantro, for garnish*

The spicy, sweet pineapple is a nice counterpoint to the rich, briny sweetness of the sea scallops. To save time, buy the pineapple already peeled and cored. Remember, the visual appeal of most salsas is enhanced when all the fruits and vegetables are cut the same size. Try to be consistent, and cut with attention to detail.

In a medium bowl, toss together the pineapple, red pepper, 1/4 cup cilantro, garlic, lime juice, honey, thyme, chile, and salt. Taste for seasoning, and adjust with more lime juice, habanero, salt, or pepper. Let sit at room temperature for at least 30 minutes.

Heat a nonstick skillet over medium heat. Place the scallops on a clean kitchen towel or paper towel, and pat them dry. When the pan is hot, add 6 scallops to it, and sprinkle a little fleur de sel over them. Cook until the scallops are golden on the bottom, about 3 minutes. Turn and cook on the other side for about 2 minutes. Remove the scallops from the pan and transfer them to a platter. Cover the platter to keep them warm. Repeat with the next batch of scallops, making sure that the skillet is hot before adding them to the pan. Cook all the scallops in the same manner.

Arrange 3 of the hot scallops in the center of each plate, and place a small mound of the pineapple salsa in the middle. Garnish each plate with the finely chopped cilantro. Serve hot.

Make-ahead: *The salsa can be made and refrigerated up to 4 hours before serving. Allow it to come to room temperature before serving.*

Tips: *Sea scallops are usually 1 to 2 inches in diameter and about 1½ inches thick. Their peak season is in the winter. There are two types of fresh scallops on the market, dry-pack (diver) scallops and wet scallops. Wet scallops are treated with a chemical phosphate that can extend their shelf life up to a few weeks. When cooked, wet scallops leach water and will not brown. Frozen sea scallops would be a better choice than wet, but the best choice is dry-pack, or diver, scallops. They have a superior taste and texture and are harvested in a more eco-friendly manner than wet scallops. Dry scallops can be stored on ice in your refrigerator for up to 2 days. Other kinds of scallops are calico and bay scallops, which are much smaller and are usually sold already cooked.*

Fleur de sel is generally regarded as the finest of sea salts, with a fine texture and superior taste. It comes from French salt basins south of the Brittany coast.

makes about two cups

Potted Shrimp with Red Bell Peppers and Shallots

ingredients

- *2 tablespoons unsalted butter*
- *½ cup finely diced shallots*
- *¼ cup finely diced red bell pepper*
- *8 ounces shrimp (any size), shelled, deveined, and coarsely chopped*
- *1 teaspoon minced fresh thyme*
- *¼ teaspoon salt, plus more to taste*
- *¼ cup dry white wine*
- *4 ounces goat cheese, at room temperature*
- *2 teaspoons fresh lemon juice*
- *1 tablespoon minced fresh chives*
- *Freshly ground black pepper to taste*

Assorted crackers or flatbread, for serving

Potted shrimp is an old-fashioned appetizer that we've updated with the color of red peppers and the flavor of goat cheese. No longer a snack for dowagers or your great-aunt Marie, potted shrimp is a delicious appetizer that can be made the day before you serve it.

Melt the butter in a large sauté pan over medium heat. When hot, add the shallots and red bell pepper and sauté until softened, about 2 minutes. Add the shrimp, thyme, salt, and white wine and cook until only about 1 tablespoon of the liquid remains, about 2 minutes.

Remove the pan from the heat and stir in the goat cheese, lemon juice, and chives. Taste and adjust the seasoning with salt and pepper. Transfer the potted shrimp to a decorative crock and chill, covered, for at least 4 hours before serving.

To serve, place the chilled crock on a decorative platter and surround with assorted crackers.

Make-ahead: *This dish can be made up to 24 hours ahead and kept, covered and refrigerated.*

makes twenty-four pieces, serving six

Halibut Skewers with Moroccan Herb Sauce

ingredients

- 1/4 cup chopped fresh cilantro
- 1/4 cup chopped fresh Italian parsley
- 2 cloves garlic, minced
- Grated zest of 1 lemon
- 2 tablespoons fresh lemon juice
- 1/2 teaspoon ground cinnamon
- 1/2 teaspoon ground cumin
- 1/2 teaspoon paprika
- 1/2 teaspoon salt
- 1/8 teaspoon cayenne pepper
- 1/8 teaspoon freshly ground black pepper
- 1/4 cup olive oil
- 1 pound halibut, skinned and cut into 1 1/2-inch cubes (about 24 pieces)

Halibut is a firm-fleshed white fish that adapts to many sauces and cooking techniques. It is the perfect foil for this green sauce, redolent with the herbs and spices of North Africa.

Prepare a grill or preheat the oven to 400°F. Soak 24 wooden skewers in water for 30 minutes.

Place all the ingredients but the halibut in a food processor or blender and process until smooth. Place the halibut in a medium bowl and toss with 3 tablespoons of the herb sauce. Marinate for 15 minutes or no longer than 30 minutes in the refrigerator.

Thread the halibut onto the skewers and grill for 5 minutes over the hot fire, turning once, or roast them on a parchment-lined baking pan in the oven for 8 minutes. Arrange on a platter and drizzle with the remaining herb sauce. Serve hot.

Make-ahead: *The sauce can be made and kept, covered, in the refrigerator for 24 hours.*

serves six

Oysters on the Half Shell with Mignonette

ingredients

- *¼ cup sherry vinegar*
- *½ teaspoon coarsely ground black pepper*
- *2 tablespoons finely chopped shallot*
- *⅛ teaspoon salt*
- *3 cups crushed ice, to hold the oysters*
- *18 fresh oysters, shells scrubbed, shucked, on the half shell*

Our love affair with the tender mollusk began with Aphrodite, the Greek goddess of love. Ever since she rose from the sea on an oyster shell and the term "aphrodisiac" was coined, oysters have been synonymous with romance. Aficionados of raw oysters believe that a drop or two of sharp mignonette sauce is the ultimate accompaniment to their clean, briny crispness.

Combine the vinegar, pepper, shallot, and salt and chill in the refrigerator for at least 1 hour.

Spread at least ½ inch of crushed ice in each of 6 shallow bowls. Arrange the chilled oysters on the half shell, 3 to a bowl. Sprinkle about ¼ teaspoon of the mignonette sauce on each oyster. Serve immediately.

Tips: *When serving oysters on the half shell, quality is of the utmost importance. Search out Olympic oysters from the Pacific Northwest, or Belon, Blue Point, or Wellfleet oysters from the East Coast, for the most succulent flavor.*

Most fish purveyors will shuck your oysters for you, but if you want to try it yourself, all you need is an oyster knife. Hold the oyster cupped side down with the hinged end in your hand. Insert the knife between the shells, a third of the way from the wide end of the oyster, and pry it open. Cut the muscle attaching it to its shell. Once the meat is free, place it in the cupped side of the shell and serve it on ice.

serves six

Oysters Rockefeller

ingredients

- 3 slices bacon
- ¼ cup thinly sliced green onion, both white and green parts
- 1 clove garlic, minced
- 2 cups finely chopped arugula, stems removed
- 1 tablespoon finely chopped fresh Italian parsley
- 1 tablespoon Pernod or other anise-flavored liquor
- 1 teaspoon hot pepper sauce
- ½ cup dry breadcrumbs
- ¼ cup finely grated Parmigiano-Reggiano cheese
- About 3 pounds kosher salt, for baking and serving
- 18 fresh oysters, shells scrubbed, shucked, on the half shell
- ⅓ cup unsalted butter, cut into 18 pieces

Back in 1899, Antoine's in New Orleans served the first oysters Rockefeller. Most restaurants that delve into bivalves serve a version of this sinfully rich take on John D. Rockefeller's namesake dish. We've substituted peppery arugula for the spinach that is regularly used in this savory first course.

Preheat the oven to 450°F.

Heat a large skillet over medium heat and add the bacon. Cook, turning, until crisp. Drain on paper towels and crumble into small pieces. Pour off all but 2 tablespoons of the fat in the pan. Reserve.

To the hot fat in the pan, add the green onion and garlic and cook for 1 minute. Add the arugula, parsley, Pernod, and hot pepper sauce and toss over medium heat until the arugula wilts. Remove the greens from the pan and cool.

In a medium bowl, toss the breadcrumbs with the cheese.

Spread kosher salt over a baking sheet to a depth of about ½ inch (reserve some salt for serving). Arrange the oysters in half shells on top of the salt, making sure that they are stable and won't roll over. Top each oyster with a teaspoon of the arugula mixture and a crumble of bacon, and sprinkle with a teaspoon or so of the bread-cheese mixture. Top each with a piece of butter.

Bake the oysters in the upper rack of the oven until the crumbs brown and the edges of the oysters begin to curl, 8 to 10 minutes.

While the oysters are cooking, pour about ½ cup of the kosher salt onto each of 6 serving plates. Carefully arrange 3 hot oysters on top of the salt on each plate (make sure they are stable before you carry them to the table), and serve immediately.

Tip: *Store-bought breadcrumbs are just not good enough for this dish. To make dried breadcrumbs, tear up a day-old baguette and process the pieces in a food processor until they are fine crumbs. Spread the crumbs evenly over a baking sheet and bake in a 350°F oven until they are dried, about 10 minutes. Breadcrumbs can be frozen fresh or dried so that they are ready when you are.*

serves twelve

Salmon Mousse

poached salmon

2 cups dry white wine

1 cup water

½ small onion, peeled and quartered

½ small carrot, peeled and quartered

½ stalk celery, peeled and quartered

½ teaspoon whole black peppercorns

1 bay leaf

Five 1-inch pieces of parsley stem

½ teaspoon dried thyme leaves

½ teaspoon salt

1 pound salmon, cut into 4 fillets and skinned

When chilled in a fish mold, salmon mousse makes a classic presentation, perfect for a wedding or bridal shower. We've added a bit of heat to this otherwise smooth and delicate mousse. This recipe is sure to become a favorite special-occasion appetizer.

To poach the salmon: Add the wine, water, onion, carrot, celery, peppercorns, bay leaf, parsley stems, thyme, and salt to a large saucepan. Heat the mixture over medium-high heat until it comes to a boil. Turn the heat to low and simmer the liquid, covered, for 30 minutes. Add the salmon to the pan and cover again. Poach the salmon until you can flake it with a fork, about 10 minutes. Remove the salmon from the poaching liquid and transfer to a plate to cool.

Meanwhile, strain the poaching liquid into a clean saucepan and reduce the liquid over medium heat until ¼ cup remains. It will take about 30 minutes. Watch the pan when the liquid has reduced to ½ cup, as it will reduce quickly from that point on. It will look slightly syrupy when it has reduced sufficiently. Remove from the heat and reserve.

Add the water and lemon juice to a small saucepan and sprinkle the gelatin over it. Let the gelatin soften for 5 minutes.

Heat the gelatin over medium heat until it dissolves and is no longer grainy. Reserve.

Add the salmon to the work bowl of a food processor, along with 3 tablespoons of the reduced poaching liquid, the gelatin mixture, sour cream, green onion, dill, hot sauce, salt, and pepper. Process until smooth. Add the heavy cream through the feed tube while processing. The mixture will become lighter. Taste and correct the seasoning with more dill, hot sauce, salt, pepper, or lemon juice.

2 tablespoons water

1 tablespoon fresh lemon juice

1 envelope gelatin

1 cup sour cream

½ cup chopped green onion

2 tablespoons minced fresh dill

2 teaspoons Tabasco or hot pepper sauce

2 teaspoons salt

⅛ teaspoon freshly ground black pepper

½ cup heavy cream

Dill sprigs, for garnish

Crackers and toast points, for serving

Pour the mousse into a 1½-quart decorative mold or bread pan and cover with plastic wrap. Refrigerate the mousse for 6 hours or overnight. To unmold it, dip the mold or pan into hot water for 5 seconds and turn out onto a decorative platter. Garnish with dill and serve with crackers or toast points.

Make-ahead: *The mousse will keep for up to 2 days, covered and refrigerated.*

Tip: *If using a loaf pan or plain mold for the mousse, line the mold with a large piece of plastic wrap. Fill the mold and cover the top with the loose ends of plastic wrap. To unmold, uncover the top pieces of plastic, lay a plate upside down on top of the mold, and invert. The mousse will unmold cleanly. Just pull the plastic off and serve.*

makes about twenty-four pieces

Sautéed Salmon Cubes with Watercress Aïoli

ingredients

- 1 pound salmon fillet, skinned and cut into 1-inch cubes
- ½ teaspoon salt
- ⅛ teaspoon freshly ground black pepper
- 2 tablespoons olive oil
- Juice of 1 lemon
- 1 cup mayonnaise, homemade (page 334) or store-bought
- 1 bunch watercress, washed and thick stems removed
- Watercress, for garnish (optional)

Watercress aïoli is one of the classic sauces to pair with fish. The peppery watercress adds a bit of a bite to the rich mayo. Because this is such a simple recipe, the quality of the salmon is critical. It should be firm and smooth, with no fishy smell. Ask your seafood vendor when shipments arrive so that you can buy it as fresh as possible.

Season the salmon with the salt and pepper. Heat a large, nonstick skillet over medium heat, and when it is hot add the oil and salmon cubes to the pan. Cook, turning the salmon cubes gently so that they don't fall apart, until they are almost cooked through, about 3 minutes. Turn the salmon cubes out onto a paper towel–lined tray, and drizzle with the lemon juice.

Place the mayonnaise in a food processor.

Bring 4 cups of water to a boil over medium-high heat. Fill a medium bowl with 1 cup ice cubes and 1 cup water. Add the watercress to the boiling water and blanch it, stirring, for 30 seconds. Remove with a slotted spoon and plunge it into the bowl of ice water to stop the cooking. When cold, remove the watercress and squeeze it dry with your hands. Add the dried watercress to the work bowl of the food processor containing the mayonnaise, and blend. The mayonnaise will turn a bright green. Taste for seasoning and adjust with salt and pepper, if desired. Fill a pastry bag fitted with a fluted tip with the watercress aïoli.

Arrange the salmon cubes on a decorative tray. Pipe a teaspoon of the mayonnaise on top of each salmon cube. Stick a toothpick into the center of each salmon cube. Garnish the platter with fresh watercress, if desired. Serve warm or at room temperature.

Make-ahead: *The cooked salmon cubes, drizzled with lemon juice, can be kept at room temperature for 1 hour.*

makes five cups

Shrimp Salsa

ingredients

1 lime, halved

1 pound medium (31 to 35 per pound) shrimp, peeled, deveined, and cut into thirds

2 cups seeded and diced tomatoes

1/3 cup minced red onion

1/4 cup chopped fresh cilantro

1 ripe avocado, peeled, pitted, and diced

1/4 cup fresh lime juice

3 tablespoons chopped pickled jalapeño, or to taste

1 teaspoon chopped fresh thyme

1 teaspoon chopped fresh oregano

1 teaspoon salt

Freshly ground black pepper to taste

Lettuce leaves, for lining the serving bowl

Assorted tortilla chips (blue corn and white corn), for serving

The bright lime flavor of this shrimp salsa is sure to satisfy. The sweet shrimp really sings with the ripe tomato and rich avocado. Using the pickled jalapeño makes it easy to get the heat where you want it.

Squeeze the juice from the lime into a medium saucepan, add the squeezed lime halves, and fill it with 4 cups of water. Bring the water to a boil over high heat. As soon as the water comes to a boil, add the shrimp, cover the pan, and remove from the heat. Let the shrimp cook in the covered pan for 3 minutes. Drain the shrimp and plunge them into a bowl of ice water to stop the cooking and chill them. Refrigerate the shrimp until ready to assemble the salsa.

In a large bowl, mix the shrimp with the tomatoes, onion, cilantro, avocado, lime juice, jalapeño, herbs, salt, and pepper. Mix thoroughly. Taste for seasoning and adjust with more lime juice, salt, or pepper.

Line a decorative bowl with lettuce leaves and add the shrimp salsa to the bowl. Serve the salsa with a mix of regular and blue corn tortilla chips.

Make-ahead: *This dish can easily be made and refrigerated up to 3 hours before serving. It should be made the day it is served. Although it doesn't go bad, the vegetables become watery, and it isn't as good the next day.*

makes twenty-four pieces

Smoked Salmon and Caper Mousse on Endive Spears

ingredients

1 tablespoon fresh lemon juice

1 tablespoon water

1 teaspoon gelatin

4 ounces smoked salmon, skin removed and chopped

½ cup sour cream

¼ teaspoon freshly ground black pepper

2 teaspoons prepared horseradish, drained

3 heads Belgian endive, leaves separated

2 tablespoons capers, rinsed and dried

Endive spears make a crunchy, peppery vehicle for the creamy, smoky salmon mousse. The capers and horseradish give it the zing necessary to balance the richness of the dish.

Add the lemon juice and water to a small saucepan. Sprinkle the gelatin over the liquid and let it soften for 5 minutes.

Heat the gelatin mixture over medium heat, stirring, until the gelatin has dissolved. Set aside.

Add the smoked salmon to the work bowl of a food processor and process until it is very smooth. Add the sour cream to the bowl and continue to process until blended. Stir in the black pepper, horseradish, and gelatin mixture. Taste and correct the seasoning with more lemon juice, salt, or pepper. Transfer the mixture to a bowl and refrigerate until it is firm, about 2 hours. Transfer to a pastry bag with a star tip.

Lay out the endive leaves on a work surface and pipe a mound of the chilled mousse onto the flat end of each leaf. Top with a few capers and arrange on a decorative platter.

Make-ahead: *The mousse can be made up to 24 hours in advance and kept, covered and refrigerated. The filled endive spears can be kept, covered with plastic and refrigerated, for up to 2 hours.*

Tip: *Belgian endives are pale white spears with light green around the edges. Cut the root bottom to free the leaves without tearing them.*

makes thirty small sandwiches

Smoked Trout and Cucumber Sandwiches with Dilled Mayonnaise

ingredients

- *8 ounces smoked trout, boned from head and tail and skin removed*
- *½ cup (1 stick) unsalted butter, at room temperature*
- *2 tablespoons fresh lemon juice, plus more to taste*
- *Salt and freshly ground black pepper to taste*
- *1 cup mayonnaise, homemade (page 334) or store-bought*
- *½ cup minced fresh dill, divided*
- *20 slices dense home-style white bread (1½ pounds), crusts removed*
- *1 English cucumber, very thinly sliced*

These crowd-pleasing, dainty sandwiches are deceptively simple to put together, and finding high-quality smoked trout is easier than ever. Look for the type smoked with apple wood or pecan.

Flake the trout and go over it very carefully with your fingers to make sure no bones remain. Place in a food processor along with the butter, lemon juice, salt, and pepper. Process the mixture until it is smooth. Taste and adjust the seasoning with more lemon juice, salt, or pepper.

In a small bowl, combine the mayonnaise with ¼ cup of the fresh dill. Set aside.

Spread 10 slices of the bread with the trout mixture. Top the trout with slices of cucumber, at least 4 thin slices to a sandwich. Season with salt and pepper. Spread the remaining slices of bread with the dilled mayonnaise. Press the sandwiches together and, using a serrated knife, cut each into 3 fingers. Place a dab of mayonnaise on each short end and dip into the remaining minced dill. Arrange the sandwiches on a tray and cover with a damp paper towel to prevent them from drying out. Cover the tray with plastic wrap and refrigerate until chilled. Serve the sandwiches cold.

Make-ahead: *The sandwiches can be wrapped as described and refrigerated for up to 2 hours. The trout mixture can be made a day ahead and refrigerated. Let it come to room temperature before attempting to spread it.*

Variation: *Instead of cucumbers, try using peeled and thinly sliced Granny Smith apples on the sandwiches for a tart and crispy alternative.*

makes eight 4-ounce servings

Timbales of Scallop and Sole with Lemon Beurre Blanc and Melted Leeks

A timbale is a dish, usually custard based, mixed with vegetables, meat, or fish baked in a mold. In this rendition we are using a scallop mousseline as the timbale's base and finishing it off with velvety melted leeks and a tart, sinfully rich butter sauce. This elegant starter will make any meal feel like a black-tie affair.

scallop mousseline

- 14 ounces sea scallops, rinsed, patted dry, and refrigerated until ready to use
- 1 large egg
- ½ teaspoon salt
- ¼ teaspoon freshly ground white or black pepper
- ⅛ teaspoon freshly grated nutmeg
- Dash of cayenne pepper
- ½ cup heavy cream, chilled

leeks

- 4 tablespoons unsalted butter
- 2 cups thinly sliced leeks (white part only), rinsed well
- ½ teaspoon salt
- ⅛ teaspoon freshly ground black pepper

- 14 ounces sole, skinned and bones removed
- Salt and freshly ground black pepper to taste

To make the mousseline: Add the scallops, egg, salt, pepper, nutmeg, and cayenne to the work bowl of a food processor and process for about 10 seconds. Add the cream through the feed tube while processing for another 10 seconds. Be careful not to over-process, or the mixture will be rubbery.

Bring a small pan of water to a boil and add a teaspoon of the mousseline to the water to poach it for 1 minute. Taste the mousseline and correct the seasoning with salt and pepper if necessary. Refrigerate until ready to assemble the timbales.

To make the leeks: Melt the butter in a medium skillet over medium heat and add the leeks, salt, and pepper. Sauté until they are soft and very tender, turning the heat down to low so that they don't brown and get crispy. It will take about 20 minutes. Add a few tablespoons of water to the pan if it becomes dry and they start to brown. You want the leeks to become velvety soft and melted. They will reduce to about ½ cup. When the leeks are soft, remove them from the heat and set aside. They can be reheated just before serving.

To assemble the timbales: Butter eight 4-ounce timbale molds or ramekins. Pound the sole fillets with the flat side of a meat pounder to a uniform thickness of about ⅛ inch. Using a sharp, round cookie cutter the same circumference as your molds, mark circles onto the fish and cut them out with kitchen shears. You will need 3 rounds for each mold. Save the scraps, as they can be pieced together as the center rounds of the molds.

Using the 8 nicest rounds, lay 1 round, flesh side down, in each mold. Lightly salt and pepper.

lemon beurre blanc

1 large shallot, thinly sliced

1 cup dry white wine

1 tablespoon white wine vinegar

3 whole black peppercorns

1/4 teaspoon dried thyme

1/2 cup (1 stick) cold unsalted butter, cut into 1/2-inch pieces

Salt and freshly ground black pepper to taste

Black caviar, for garnish (optional)

2 tablespoons minced fresh chives, for garnish (optional)

Transfer the mousseline to a pastry bag fitted with a 1/4-inch plain tip and pipe a 1/2-inch layer into each mold. Add another layer of sole, using the scraps if necessary, so that you have 8 whole rounds left to place on the top of each. Season the sole with salt and pepper and pipe mousseline once again on top. Cover the mousse with the remaining whole sole rounds, seasoning lightly. Refrigerate until ready to serve.

To make the beurre blanc: Place the shallot, wine, vinegar, peppercorns, and thyme in a medium skillet and reduce the mixture over high heat until only a tablespoon of liquid remains in the pan. Remove the pan from the heat and add the butter in bits, whisking constantly and adding another piece of butter before the first one melts completely. The pan should be cooling off as you add the butter, and you should have a nice, thick emulsion. Taste for seasoning and adjust with salt and pepper. Keep the skillet of sauce over a pan of warm water (not touching the water) until ready to serve, no longer than 1 hour.

To bake the timbales: Preheat the oven to 350°F. Bring a teapot of water to a boil.

Place the ramekins in a roasting pan lined with a kitchen towel so that they are not touching each other. Cover with a sheet of foil, leaving a space open through which to pour the hot water. Place the pan on a rack in the oven and carefully pour the boiling water into the pan until it reaches a third of the way up the sides of the ramekins. Close the foil over the pan and bake until the sides of the timbale mixture pull away from the ramekins, 20 to 25 minutes. Remove from the oven and carefully remove the hot ramekins from the water bath with tongs or, if you have them, canning tongs.

To serve: Place a few tablespoons of warm melted leeks on each of 8 plates. Invert the timbales onto the leeks and spoon some of the butter sauce around the edge of the leeks. Top each timbale with a few grains of caviar, or sprinkle with chives. Serve hot.

Make-ahead: *The unbaked ramekins can be assembled up to 8 hours in advance and kept, covered, in the refrigerator. The leeks can be made up to 4 hours in advance and kept, covered, at room temperature.*

serves four

Tuna Carpaccio

ingredients

- *12 ounces sushi-grade ahi tuna steaks, at least 1 inch thick*
- *2 tablespoons cracked black pepper*
- *2 tablespoons olive oil*
- *2 cups arugula*
- *2 tablespoons fresh lemon juice*
- *2 tablespoons extra-virgin olive oil*
- *Dash of salt*
- *Freshly ground black pepper to taste*
- *2 tablespoons salt-packed capers, rinsed and drained*
- *2 tablespoons truffle oil*
- *Shavings of Parmesan cheese for top of salad*

Carpaccio generally consists of thinly sliced raw beef drizzled with lemon juice and olive oil with capers scattered over it, but tuna is also a candidate for the carpaccio treatment. Here we've paired thin slices of rare tuna with peppery arugula, earthy truffle oil, and salty Parmesan cheese. No one will be asking, "Where's the beef?"

Rub the tuna with the cracked pepper and 2 tablespoons olive oil. Heat a medium, nonstick skillet over medium-high heat and add the tuna to the pan. Sear for 30 seconds; turn and sear the other side for 30 seconds. Remove the tuna to a plate and let it cool for a few minutes. Slice the tuna as thinly as possible. You should have about 16 slices.

Toss the arugula with the lemon juice and 2 tablespoons extra-virgin olive oil. Season with salt and black pepper.

Arrange the dressed arugula in the center of each of 4 plates. Arrange the tuna in a spoke pattern on top of it, and sprinkle the capers over the tuna. Drizzle the tuna with the truffle oil and top the salad with the Parmesan cheese shavings. Serve immediately.

makes about forty skewers, serving ten

Tuna Skewers with Ginger Sesame Dipping Sauce

dipping sauce

3 tablespoons tahini

2 tablespoons hot water

1½ tablespoons Asian (dark) sesame oil

1 tablespoon soy sauce

1 tablespoon honey

2 teaspoons hoisin sauce

1 teaspoon peeled and grated fresh ginger

½ to 1 teaspoon Asian chili oil

2 teaspoons rice vinegar

2 pounds sushi-grade tuna steaks, preferably 1 inch thick

3 tablespoons soy sauce

2 tablespoons black sesame seeds

Nothing is easier than this Asian-inspired tuna dish. The nutty, rich sesame sauce holds its own with the tuna, which we consider to be the "steak" of seafood. A meal can easily be made with these tuna skewers; Cucumber, Carrot, and Wasabi Mayo Rolls (page 76); and Roasted Asparagus with Sesame Vinaigrette (page 199).

To make the sauce: Add the tahini, hot water, sesame oil, soy sauce, honey, hoisin sauce, ginger, chili oil, and rice vinegar to the bowl of a food processor and process until completely smooth, scraping down the bowl as necessary. If the sauce is too thick, add a little more hot water to thin it. Transfer to a bowl and let it sit at room temperature for at least 2 hours to allow the flavors to blend and develop, or refrigerate overnight. Use at room temperature.

Heat a grill or preheat an oven to 400°F. Soak forty 4-inch wooden skewers in cold water for 30 minutes.

Cut the tuna steaks into 1-inch square cubes and toss in a medium bowl with the soy sauce. Pour the sesame seeds onto a plate.

Thread 1 piece of fish onto each soaked wooden skewer, leaving it close to the tip (for dipping), and then dip one side in the sesame seeds. Grill on the hot grill for 2 minutes on each side, or arrange them on a parchment-lined baking sheet and bake for 7 minutes.

Arrange the hot tuna skewers on a decorative platter and serve with the bowl of dipping sauce. Serve warm or at room temperature.

Make-ahead: *The dipping sauce can be made up to 24 hours in advance and kept, covered and refrigerated.*

Chapter 10 Salsas

oasted Walnut Spread **250** Caponata
52 Curried Lentil Dal
Walnut Tapenade *with* Goat Cheese
55 Mango Habanero Salsa
57 Spicy Ham Spread

Dips, *and* Spreads

59 White Bean *and* Roasted Garlic Spread
heese, Roasted Red Pepper, *and* Pine Nut Dip
63 Spicy Tomatillo Salsa **264** Pico *de* Gallo
66 Easy Tomato *and* Chipotle Salsa
horizo, *and* Cheddar Dip
69 Sour Cream, Lime, *and* Cilantro Dipping Sauce
ubes **271** Spicy Thai Dipping Sauce
73 Sesame-Soy Dipping Sauce
ean, Rosemary, *and* Pancetta Spread
oasted Pine Nuts *and* Garlic Oil
78 Buttermilk Ranch Dipping Sauce
pinach *and* Bacon Dip

makes $2\frac{1}{2}$ cups

Apple Chile Salsa

ingredients

2 Crispin, Braeburn, Gala, or other sweet-tart, firm apples, peeled, cored, and diced into small cubes, about 2 cups

¼ cup finely diced red bell pepper

Grated zest of 1 lemon

2 tablespoons fresh lemon juice

2 tablespoons citron tea (see Tip)

3 green onions, white and green parts, finely chopped

½ serrano chile, seeded and minced, plus more to taste

¼ cup chopped fresh cilantro

¼ teaspoon salt, plus more to taste

Freshly ground black pepper to taste

It's a good idea to use crispy apples for salsa, since they are available year round. The red bell pepper gives this salsa visual pizzazz, while the citron tea adds citrusy notes.

In a medium bowl, toss together the apple, bell pepper, lemon zest, lemon juice, tea, green onions, chile, cilantro, salt, and black pepper. Taste for seasoning and adjust with more chile, salt, or black pepper. Let sit at room temperature for at least 30 minutes.

Make-ahead: *The salsa can be kept, covered and refrigerated, for up to 4 hours. Allow it to come to room temperature before serving.*

Tip: *Citron tea is a marmaladelike product made from citron, a citrus fruit native to China. It can be found in Asian markets and is most often used to flavor hot water as a tea. If you can't find citron tea, just use orange marmalade, though it may make your salsa a bit on the sweet side. You can counter the sweetness by adding another teaspoon or so of lemon juice.*

makes four cups

Blue Cheese and Toasted Walnut Spread

ingredients

- *1 cup crumbled Gorgonzola or Saga blue cheese, at room temperature (about 5 ounces)*
- *8 ounces cream cheese, at room temperature*
- *1 cup sour cream*
- *1/2 cup mayonnaise, homemade (page 334) or store-bought*
- *1 cup chopped toasted walnuts*
- *1/2 cup finely diced celery*
- *1/4 cup chopped green onion, white and green parts*
- *2 tablespoons minced fresh Italian parsley*
- *1/2 teaspoon coarsely ground black pepper*
- *1/2 teaspoon salt*
- *1/4 teaspoon cayenne pepper*
- *Milk to thin the dip, if desired*

For a change of pace, serve this savory dip with slices of fresh apples or pears that have been dipped in lemon water to keep them from browning.

Mix all ingredients in a large bowl until blended. If desired, thin the dip with a tablespoon or so of milk. Refrigerate, covered, for at least 1 hour.

Make-ahead: *This dip can be made up to 3 days ahead and kept, covered and refrigerated.*

makes about three cups

Caponata

ingredients

1/4 cup olive oil

8 ounces spicy Italian sausage, crumbled

1 cup diced red onion

2 cloves garlic, minced

1 1/2 pounds eggplant, diced

1 teaspoon salt

1/4 teaspoon freshly ground black pepper

1/4 teaspoon crushed red pepper flakes (optional)

6 plum tomatoes, quartered, seeded, and sliced into strips

1/4 cup currants, soaked in hot water for 20 minutes

1/4 cup red wine vinegar

1/4 cup chopped fresh Italian parsley

1/4 cup orange juice

1/4 cup pine nuts, toasted

10 kalamata olives, pitted and chopped

2 tablespoons capers, rinsed and drained

2 tablespoons brown sugar

Toasted bread or pita rounds, for serving

Many cuisines of the Mediterranean feature some variation of caponata. Whether it is flavored with capers, olives, and tomatoes, as in the Italian versions, or spiced with chiles, garlic, and coriander in the Indian style, versatile eggplant is the main ingredient. Our unique version includes spicy sausage, salty olives and capers, sweet currants, tart wine vinegar, and lots of onions, garlic, and tomatoes for a sweet-savory spread that is terrific on toasted bread.

Heat the olive oil in a large sauté pan over medium heat. When hot, add the crumbled Italian sausage. Cook, stirring and breaking up the large chunks of sausage, until they are no longer pink. Add the onion and garlic and cook for about 3 minutes. Add the eggplant, salt, pepper, and red pepper flakes, if using, and cook, stirring, until the eggplant is soft, about 4 minutes.

Add the tomatoes, currants, vinegar, parsley, orange juice, pine nuts, olives, capers, and brown sugar. Cook over medium-low heat, stirring every now and then, until the tomatoes have softened and the mixture is thick, about 10 minutes. Remove the caponata from the heat and allow it to cool. Serve at room temperature with toasted bread or pita rounds as an accompaniment.

Make-ahead: *Caponata is better made a day ahead and refrigerated overnight. Let it warm up on the counter for 1 hour before serving.*

makes three cups

Cucumber and Cilantro Yogurt Dip

ingredients

- *2 cups plain whole yogurt*
- *1 English cucumber, peeled, halved lengthwise, seeded, and coarsely grated*
- *1 teaspoon salt*
- *2 cloves garlic, minced*
- *½ cup sour cream*
- *2 tablespoons fresh lemon juice*
- *¼ cup chopped fresh cilantro*
- *¼ teaspoon freshly ground black pepper*

Crudités or Pita Wedges (page 96), for serving

In Indian cuisine, this dip is referred to as raita, and it is served with spicy foods. The coolness of the dairy is refreshing and goes well with everything from crudités to chips and spicy kebabs. Draining the yogurt of its excess moisture thickens the dip but does require that you start this dish one day ahead.

Line a fine-mesh strainer with a double thickness of cheesecloth that has been rinsed and squeezed dry. Pour the yogurt into the strainer and place the strainer over a bowl to catch the liquid. (Make sure that the bottom of the strainer is high enough so that the liquid won't reach the strainer as it drains.) Cover with plastic wrap and refrigerate overnight, discarding the liquid.

Mix the grated cucumber, salt, and garlic and place in a strainer over a bowl to catch the juice. Refrigerate for at least 2 hours or overnight. Discard the juice.

In a large bowl, combine the drained yogurt, sour cream, lemon juice, cilantro, and pepper. Squeeze the cucumber dry and add to the yogurt. Season to taste with more salt and pepper, if desired. Cover and chill for at least 2 hours.

Make-ahead: *This dip can be made up to 24 hours ahead and kept, covered and refrigerated.*

Tip: *It is easy to seed a cucumber with the curved edge of a spoon. Simply cut the cucumber lengthwise to expose the seeds, and scrape them out.*

makes about three cups

Curried Lentil Dal

ingredients

- *3 cups water*
- *2 cups chopped onion, divided*
- *3 cloves garlic, minced, divided*
- *1 cup dried red lentils (see Tips)*
- *3 teaspoons curry powder, divided*
- *1¾ teaspoons salt, divided*
- *2 tablespoons vegetable oil*
- *2 plum tomatoes, seeded and chopped*
- *¼ cup olive oil*
- *¼ cup chopped fresh cilantro*
- *1 serrano chile, seeded and chopped*
- *¼ teaspoon freshly ground black pepper*

Chapati or sliced vegetables, for serving (see Tips)

Dal is an Indian dish made with colorful red lentils. We use it as a healthy dip to be served with chapati (Indian flatbread) or crudités.

In a large saucepan, combine the water, 1 cup of the onions, a third of the garlic, lentils, 2 teaspoons of the curry powder, and 1 teaspoon of the salt. Bring to a boil over medium-high heat. Reduce the heat to low and cover the pot with a lid. Simmer the lentils until they are tender, about 15 minutes.

In a medium skillet, heat the vegetable oil over medium heat. When hot, add the remaining 1 cup onions and sauté until soft, about 3 minutes. Add the remaining garlic and the remaining teaspoon of curry powder and continue to sauté until the onions are browned and soft, about 10 minutes. Reserve.

Drain the lentils and transfer them to a food processor. Purée until smooth. Return the purée to the saucepan and combine with the browned onions. Simmer the mixture for 5 minutes or so to blend the flavors. Transfer the dal to a decorative bowl and add the tomatoes, olive oil, cilantro, chile, remaining ¾ teaspoon salt, and the pepper. Serve with crudités or chapati.

Make-ahead: *The dal can be made 1 day ahead and kept refrigerated. It may need to be thinned with a little water to bring it back to the desired consistency. Let come to room temperature before serving.*

Tips: *Red lentils can be found in most grocery stores or specialty stores in the Asian aisle. If you can't locate red lentils, regular brown lentils will work fine. They just won't be as attractive.*

Chapati is a fried Indian flatbread that is also found in most Middle Eastern grocery stores. Pita bread is a good substitute.

serves eight

Fig and Walnut Tapenade with Goat Cheese

ingredients

1 cup dried Calimyrna figs, stems removed, quartered

1/3 cup port wine

1/2 cup pitted, chopped kalamata olives

2 tablespoons extra-virgin olive oil

1 tablespoon balsamic vinegar

1 tablespoon chopped capers, preferably salt-packed, rinsed (see Tip)

2 teaspoons minced fresh thyme

2 teaspoons minced fresh Italian parsley

Salt and freshly ground black pepper to taste

Two 4-ounce logs goat cheese, cut into 1/2-inch-thick rounds

1/2 cup toasted, chopped walnuts

Toasted baguette slices or crackers, for serving

One of our favorites, this dish offers a great contrast in flavors. Tapenade is a Provençal spread made of olives, herbs, and garlic. We've taken it one step further and added figs for a California twist. A great year-round appetizer, this dish can be expanded to serve a crowd.

Combine the figs and port in a medium saucepan. Cook over medium heat until the liquid evaporates and the figs are soft, about 4 minutes. Transfer to a medium bowl to cool.

To the bowl add the olives, olive oil, vinegar, capers, thyme, and parsley. Season with salt and freshly ground black pepper.

On a large platter, arrange overlapping cheese rounds in the center of the plate. It is easier to cut the cheese while still cold from the refrigerator. Let the cheese warm up for 15 minutes if it is cold, and spoon the tapenade over the top. Garnish with the toasted walnuts. Serve with baguette slices or crackers.

Make-ahead: *The tapenade can be made up to 3 days ahead and kept, covered and refrigerated. Allow it to come to room temperature before serving.*

Tip: *Capers come packed in brine or salted. We prefer the salted capers because they have a firmer texture than the mushier brined variety. The salted capers should be rinsed well and then soaked in clean water for a few minutes to remove excess salt.*

makes three cups

Jalapeño Jack and Andouille Dip

ingredients

- *8 ounces jalapeño Monterey Jack cheese, grated*
- *8 ounces Colby cheese, grated*
- *2 tablespoons all-purpose flour*
- *1 tablespoon olive oil*
- *6 ounces uncooked andouille sausage*
- *2/3 cup beer*
- *1/4 cup chopped fresh cilantro*

Tortilla chips, for serving

Cheese and beer just naturally go together. When you add spicy sausage and chips, you've got a party on your hands.

Add the grated cheese and flour to a large bowl and toss to combine.

Heat a medium skillet over medium heat and add the olive oil to the pan. Add the sausage and cook, breaking it up into small pieces until it is no longer pink. Drain any grease from the sausage, and set the sausage aside.

In a large saucepan, bring the beer to a simmer over medium heat. Add the cheese mixture in 1/2-cup increments, stirring until melted before adding more cheese. The mixture will become thick and creamy. Stir in the sausage and cilantro. Transfer the dip to a fondue pot or other flameproof dish. Set over candles or Sterno to keep hot. Serve with tortilla chips.

Make-ahead: *The dip can be made up to 1 day ahead and kept, covered and refrigerated. If you are going to reheat the dip, you may need to add some extra beer to achieve a smooth consistency. Reheat slowly and add the beer by the tablespoon, stirring constantly over low heat.*

makes two cups

Mango Habanero Salsa

ingredients

- 1 ripe mango, peeled, pitted, and cut into ½-inch dice
- ⅓ cup diced red onion (½-inch dice)
- ⅓ cup diced red bell pepper (½-inch dice)
- ¼ cup chopped fresh cilantro
- ¼ cup habanero jelly or other spicy jelly
- 2 tablespoons fresh lime juice
- ¼ teaspoon finely minced habanero chile
- Salt and freshly ground black pepper to taste

A ripe mango is a thing of beauty. If you buy them a few days before you need them, they will have a chance to ripen on your countertop. Habaneros are not only hot, they also have a fruity flavor that pairs nicely with the mango.

Add all ingredients to a medium bowl and mix. Transfer to the refrigerator to allow the flavors to develop. Let sit at room temperature for 30 minutes before serving, for the best flavor.

Make-ahead: *This salsa can be made 4 hours ahead and kept at room temperature.*

Tip: *Habaneros are the hottest of the hot chiles, so be careful when handling them. Try not to touch the cut part of the chile or the heat can literally burn your hands. To be on the safe side, wear gloves when handling habaneros, and carefully dispose of the gloves as soon as you are finished working with them.*

makes about three cups

Not Your Mama's Onion Dip

Back in the day, everybody's mom made onion dip using that sodium-loaded onion soup mix. We figured we could do better, so here is our version, much lighter on the salt but still packed with oniony flavor.

ingredients

- *2 tablespoons olive oil*
- *3½ cups chopped red onion*
- *1 teaspoon salt, divided, plus more to taste*
- *¼ teaspoon freshly ground black pepper, plus more to taste*
- *3 cloves garlic, minced*
- *¼ cup dry white wine*
- *8 ounces cream cheese, at room temperature*
- *1 cup sour cream*
- *1 teaspoon Worcestershire sauce*
- *¼ teaspoon cayenne pepper*
- *¼ cup minced fresh chives*

Potato chips, crackers, crudités, or Pita Wedges (page 96), for serving

Heat the olive oil in a large skillet over medium heat and add the onion, ½ teaspoon of the salt, and ¼ teaspoon black pepper. Sauté the onion, stirring, until it begins to soften, about 3 minutes. Add the garlic, turn the heat to medium-low, and continue to cook slowly, stirring every now and then, until the onion begins to brown, about 10 minutes. Turn the heat to low and cook until the onions are meltingly tender and brown, about 15 minutes longer. Add the wine to the pan and cook until the liquid has evaporated and all the brown bits on the bottom of the pan are mixed into the onions.

In a medium bowl, mix the onions, cream cheese, sour cream, Worcestershire sauce, ½ teaspoon salt, cayenne, and chives until combined. Correct the seasoning with salt and pepper to taste. Serve the dip with chips, crackers, crudités, or pita wedges.

Make-ahead: *The dip can be kept, covered and refrigerated, for up to 3 days.*

makes about two cups

Spicy Ham Spread

ingredients

- *1 tablespoon unsalted butter*
- *1 tablespoon all-purpose flour*
- *½ cup milk, heated*
- *¼ teaspoon cayenne pepper*
- *¼ teaspoon salt*
- *⅛ teaspoon ground nutmeg*
- *1 pound ham, diced*
- *1 tablespoon Dijon mustard*
- *1 tablespoon Worcestershire sauce*
- *¼ cup minced green onion, white and green parts*

Cocktail bread slices (mini loaves) or crackers, for serving

A ham spread is quick and easy to make and, in addition to being an appetizer, can serve as a ready-on-the-spot sandwich filling when hungry people abound. Those little loaves of bread called cocktail loaves make a terrific base for this boldly flavored ham spread. When warmed in the oven, these hearty little sandwiches are guaranteed to keep the wolf at bay.

Melt the butter in a medium saucepan over medium heat and, when it is hot, add the flour. Stir the flour and butter until it becomes foamy and hot. Add the hot milk and stir vigorously with a whisk to keep lumps from forming. The sauce should thicken immediately if your milk is hot enough. Add the cayenne, salt, and nutmeg and cook for 2 minutes at a simmer. Remove from the heat and set aside.

Add the ham, mustard, and Worcestershire sauce to the work bowl of a food processor. Add the white sauce and process until the ham spread is smooth. Transfer the spread to a medium bowl and stir in the green onion.

When ready to serve, preheat the broiler. Spread the ham mixture over slices of bread or crackers and broil until the topping is hot and lightly browned.

Make-ahead: *The spread keeps for up to 5 days, covered and refrigerated.*

makes one cup

Sun-Dried Tomato Spread

ingredients

- *8 ounces goat cheese, at room temperature*
- *1/3 cup minced oil-packed sun-dried tomatoes*
- *1/4 cup toasted, chopped pine nuts*
- *1/4 cup chopped kalamata olives*
- *1/4 cup sour cream*
- *2 teaspoons minced fresh Italian parsley*
- *1/2 teaspoon minced fresh thyme*

Crackers, toasted bread, or crudités, for serving

There is a reason that goat cheese, sun-dried tomatoes, fresh herbs, and olives are combined with such regularity: They are simply so good together. No one is ever bored by this smashing combo.

Mix the goat cheese, sun-dried tomatoes, pine nuts, olives, sour cream, parsley, and thyme together in a medium bowl. Pack into a decorative crock and refrigerate for 2 hours to let the flavors blend. Remove from the refrigerator 30 minutes before serving, to soften the spread.

Make-ahead: *This spread will keep, covered, in the refrigerator for up to 5 days.*

makes about two cups

White Bean and Roasted Garlic Spread

ingredients

- 1 head garlic
- 1 tablespoon olive oil
- 2 cans white kidney beans or cannellini beans, drained and rinsed
- 2 tablespoons fresh lemon juice
- 1/4 cup plus 2 tablespoons extra-virgin olive oil, divided
- 1 teaspoon salt, plus more to taste
- 1/4 teaspoon freshly ground black pepper, plus more to taste
- 1/4 cup chopped fresh Italian parsley

- 24 baguette slices, toasted, for serving

White beans are nutritious and delicious. We love to put out this spread as an alternative to fatty cream-based dips and spreads. The roasted garlic is subtle, but definitely there. The lemon and parsley keep it fresh, and the drizzle of extra-virgin olive oil on top gives it just a little richness.

Preheat the oven to 375°F.

Cut off the top 1/2 inch of the garlic. Drizzle 1 tablespoon olive oil over the top of it and wrap in aluminum foil. Place the garlic in the oven and bake until it is soft, about 45 minutes. Let the garlic cool until you can handle it.

Add the beans to a food processor along with the lemon juice, 1/4 cup extra-virgin olive oil, salt, and pepper. Squeeze the garlic into the work bowl. The soft garlic should squish out from the papery husk. Process until smooth, about 1 minute. Some canned beans are drier than others. If the mixture is too thick, add some water to thin it. Add the parsley and pulse 3 times to blend. Taste the spread and adjust the seasoning with salt and pepper.

Transfer the spread to a decorative bowl and drizzle the remaining 2 tablespoons olive oil over the top. Arrange the toasted baguette slices around it. The spread can also be served as a dip with carrots and celery.

Make-ahead: *The spread keeps for up to 3 days, covered and refrigerated.*

makes three cups

Yogurt Green Onion Dip

ingredients

- *2 cups whole plain yogurt*
- *8 ounces cream cheese, at room temperature*
- *3 green onions, white and green parts, trimmed and sliced*
- *1/3 cup chopped fresh Italian parsley*
- *2 teaspoons fresh lemon juice*
- *1 teaspoon salt, plus more to taste*
- *1/4 teaspoon freshly ground black pepper, plus more to taste*
- *1/8 teaspoon cayenne pepper*

Yogurt makes a lighter alternative to heavier sour cream-based dips. This rendition has hints of green onion, parsley, and lemon and is the perfect dip to serve with The Ultimate Crudités Tray (page 42). Save the extra for a baked potato topping.

Add all ingredients to the work bowl of a food processor and blend until smooth. Taste for seasoning and adjust with salt and pepper.

Make-ahead: *The dip keeps, refrigerated, for up to 5 days.*

makes about 2½ cups

Feta Cheese, Roasted Red Pepper, and Pine Nut Dip

ingredients

6 ounces feta cheese

¼ teaspoon minced garlic

1 cup sour cream

4 ounces cream cheese, at room temperature

1 roasted red bell pepper, diced

½ cup finely chopped fresh Italian parsley

Salt and freshly ground black pepper to taste

¼ cup pine nuts, toasted

Pita chips, crackers, or crudités, for serving

The generous scattering of toasted pine nuts on the top of this boldly flavored dip makes it look as luxurious as it tastes.

Combine the feta, garlic, sour cream, and cream cheese in a food processor. Pulse until the ingredients are just combined. Scrape the feta mixture into a bowl and stir in the red pepper and parsley. Season to taste with salt and pepper.

Just before serving, spoon the dip into a serving bowl and scatter the toasted pine nuts on top.

Serve with pita chips, crackers, or crudités.

Make-ahead: *The dip can be made 1 day ahead. Top with the pine nuts just before serving.*

makes two cups

Green Olive Tapenade

ingredients

1/4 cup blanched almonds

One 10-ounce jar green olives, pitted

1/4 cup fresh basil

1 teaspoon minced fresh thyme

2 tablespoons capers, drained and rinsed

1/2 cup extra-virgin olive oil

Crackers, toasted rustic bread, or sliced Granny Smith apples, for serving

Tapenade is a spread originating in Provence made of olives, anchovies, garlic, and olive oil. This highly flavorful version keeps in the refrigerator for 2 weeks, making it an on-the-spot, ready-when-you-are appetizer for friends and family who have just "popped in."

Dump the almonds into the bowl of a food processor and process until finely ground.

Add the olives, basil, thyme, and capers and process until a fine paste forms. Add the oil through the feed tube while pulsing to emulsify the tapenade.

Serve with crackers, toasted rustic country breads, or sliced Granny Smith apples.

Make-ahead: *Tapenade can be made up to 2 weeks ahead and kept, covered, in the refrigerator.*

makes about 1½ cups

Spicy Tomatillo Salsa

ingredients

- *12 ounces tomatillos, husked and rinsed*
- *2 serrano chiles*
- *½ cup chopped fresh cilantro*
- *½ cup finely chopped white onion*
- *4 cloves garlic, chopped*
- *2 tablespoons fresh lime juice*
- *2 tablespoons cider vinegar*
- *¼ teaspoon salt*
- *1 teaspoon sugar*
- *¼ cup water*
- *2 tablespoons vegetable oil*

Meredith's husband, David, is famous for this spicy, sweet-tart salsa. Whenever he makes it, the wonderful aroma of roasted tomatillos and chiles fills the house. In the past, he's not wanted to give away his secret recipe for this green salsa, but for this book, he relented.

Preheat the broiler. Place the tomatillos and chiles on a baking sheet and broil until darkly roasted, even blackened in spots. Let cool, and then transfer to a blender, including all the juices that have run out onto the baking sheet. Add the cilantro, onion, garlic, lime juice, cider vinegar, salt, sugar, and water. Blend to a purée.

Heat the oil in a medium skillet over medium heat. Add the tomatillo purée and bring to a boil. Cook until the salsa has thickened slightly, about 5 minutes. Remove from the heat and taste for seasoning. Transfer to a serving bowl. Serve at room temperature or chilled.

Make-ahead: *This salsa can be made ahead and kept, covered, in the refrigerator for up to a week or frozen for up to 2 months.*

makes about two cups

Pico de Gallo

ingredients

- *1 pound ripe tomatoes, seeded and chopped*
- *1/2 cup chopped red onion*
- *1/4 cup chopped fresh cilantro*
- *1/4 cup fresh lime juice*
- *2 small cloves garlic, minced*
- *1 tablespoon plus 1 teaspoon minced jalapeño or serrano chile*
- *Salt to taste*

When most people think of salsa, this fresh, uncooked version is what they're envisioning. Although it's tempting to throw all the ingredients into a food processor, this salsa is much better when they are chopped by hand. The food processor tends to pulverize everything together into one indiscernible pink mass. When the ingredients are chopped with a knife, they are much more colorful and attractive.

Combine the tomatoes, onion, cilantro, lime juice, garlic, and chile in a medium bowl; toss to blend well. Season to taste with salt. Let stand at room temperature for at least 30 minutes to allow the flavors to develop.

Make-ahead: *This salsa can be made up to 1 hour ahead.*

makes about 2½ cups

Guacamole

ingredients

- *3 ripe Hass avocados, quartered, pitted, and peeled*
- *½ cup chopped fresh cilantro*
- *½ cup minced white onion*
- *1 serrano chile, including seeds, minced*
- *1 tablespoon fresh lime juice, or to taste*
- *1 teaspoon salt, or to taste*

For the best guacamole, try to find dark pebble-skinned Hass avocados that give slightly when pressed. They are much creamier and more flavorful than the light, smooth-skinned variety.

Mash the avocados in a medium bowl with a fork until creamy, but with some lumps remaining. Add the cilantro, onion, chile, lime juice, and salt and stir to combine.

Make-ahead: *Guacamole can be made 1 hour ahead and chilled, its surface covered with plastic wrap.*

makes about 2½ cups

Easy Tomato and Chipotle Salsa

ingredients

- *One 28-ounce can fire-roasted tomatoes*
- *1 tablespoon fresh lime juice, plus more to taste*
- *2 canned chipotle chiles in adobo*
- *½ cup diced white onion*
- *½ cup chopped fresh cilantro*
- *Salt to taste*

When ripe red tomatoes are not in season, fresh salsa is just not worth doing. That doesn't mean you have to forgo salsa altogether, though. This quick and easy version is one of our favorites, and it tastes just as good in January as it does in August.

In a blender, combine the tomatoes, lime juice, and chiles. Purée until smooth. Pour into a bowl. Rinse the onion under cold running water in a colander. Add the onion and cilantro to the salsa and season with salt and more lime juice, if desired. If necessary, thin with a little water.

Make-ahead: *The salsa, without the onion and cilantro, can be made 1 week ahead of time and kept, covered, in the refrigerator. Add the onion and cilantro just before serving.*

makes about $3\frac{1}{2}$ cups

Warm Chipotle, Chorizo, and Cheddar Dip

ingredients

12 ounces fully cooked chorizo sausage, cut into chunks

1 pound cheddar cheese, grated

1 tablespoon cornstarch

1 cup lager-type beer

1 tablespoon fresh lemon juice

1 tablespoon finely chopped canned chipotle chile in adobo

Tortilla chips, for serving

This warm dip is essentially a spicy fondue. We recommend serving it in a fondue pot with a very low flame. Set a small ladle in the pot and allow your guests to make their own "nachos" by drizzling it over a pile of tortilla chips.

Place the sausage in the bowl of a food processor and process until it is finely chopped. In a medium bowl, mix the cheese, cornstarch, and sausage together. Set aside.

In a heavy-bottomed saucepan, combine the beer, lemon juice, and chipotle and bring to a simmer over medium heat. Add the cheese and sausage mixture, a handful at a time, stirring until melted and incorporated with the beer before adding the next handful. This may take a few minutes. If necessary, use a whisk to make sure the cheese is well blended. Transfer to a fondue pot and keep warm over a low flame. Serve with tortilla chips on the side.

Tips: *The chorizo sausage used here is the precooked type that is sold in links. If you would like to use fresh chorizo, skip the food processor step and just sauté it, breaking it up with the back of a spoon, until completely cooked. Allow it to cool before adding it to the cheese.*

If the cheese binds up and won't incorporate with the liquid, add another tablespoon of lemon juice. The extra acid will help the cheese blend with the other ingredients.

makes about three cups

Chile con Queso with Poblano Chiles

ingredients

- 4 poblano chiles
- 1 tablespoon olive oil
- 1 serrano chile, minced
- ½ cup finely chopped onion
- 2 cloves garlic, chopped
- 2 teaspoons ground cumin
- 2 cups grated Monterey Jack cheese
- ½ cup half-and-half
- Salt to taste

- Tortilla chips, for serving

This dip is a familiar sight on many Southwestern restaurant menus. Often it's made with melted American cheese and canned chiles, which don't make for an inspiring dish. When made properly, though, with a flavorful melting cheese and freshly roasted poblano chiles, it can be a wonderful, robust dip.

Roast the poblano chiles over a gas flame or on a tray under the broiler. Keep turning so the skin is evenly charred without burning and drying out the flesh. Transfer the charred chiles to a plastic bag, tie the top closed, and let steam for 5 minutes. Remove from the bag and peel off the skin. Once peeled, cut away the stems, seeds, and veins and dice the flesh.

In a heavy-bottomed saucepan, heat the oil over medium heat. Add the serrano chile and onion and sauté until lightly golden, about 10 minutes. Add the garlic, roasted poblano chiles, and the cumin. Cook for another minute. Reduce the heat to low. Add the cheese and half-and-half and cook, stirring constantly, just until the cheese is melted. Be sure not to bring the mixture to a boil or the dip will curdle.

Transfer the dip to a lit and warm fondue pot or small chafing dish. Serve immediately with tortilla chips.

makes about one cup

Sour Cream, Lime, and Cilantro Dipping Sauce

ingredients

- 1 cup sour cream
- Grated zest of 1 lime
- 1/4 cup chopped fresh cilantro
- 1 tablespoon fresh lime juice
- Salt to taste

Sour cream makes the perfect foil for spicy foods because the protein in dairy products helps to break the bond that hot chiles form with your taste buds. That's why we like to pair this dip with our hottest fare, like Corn and Jalapeño Fritters (page 201) or Smoke and Fire Beef Kebabs (page 156).

In a medium bowl, mix together the sour cream, zest, cilantro, and lime juice. Season with salt. Refrigerate for at least an hour to allow the flavors to blend.

Make-ahead: *This dip can be made 8 hours ahead and kept, covered, in the refrigerator.*

serves six to eight

Porcini Fonduta with Truffle Oil and Polenta Cubes

polenta cubes

4 cups water

1 teaspoon salt

1 cup polenta (coarse cornmeal) or yellow cornmeal

1/4 cup grated Parmesan cheese

2 tablespoons unsalted butter

2 tablespoons olive oil

fondue

1 ounce dried porcini mushrooms

2 tablespoons unsalted butter

2 tablespoons finely chopped shallot

1 cup dry white wine (such as sauvignon blanc or pinot grigio)

1 tablespoon white wine vinegar

1 pound fontina cheese, cut into small cubes

1 tablespoon cornstarch

1 tablespoon truffle oil

Dried porcini mushrooms are the essence of fall, and their deep, robust mushroom flavor is the basis for this Italian fondue. Fondues, by their nature, are fun, but they're even more so when the dippers go beyond the standard bread cubes. Here we use polenta that has set to a firm texture. We cut it up into cubes and then bake it until crispy on the outside and ready to dip into flavorful mushroom cheese fondue.

To make the polenta cubes: Bring the water and salt to a boil in a large, heavy saucepan. Gradually add the polenta, whisking until boiling and smooth. Reduce the heat to low. Cook until very thick, whisking often, about 25 minutes (about 15 minutes for yellow cornmeal). Whisk in the cheese and butter. Spread in an oiled 8-by-8-by-2-inch glass baking dish. Let cool slightly. Cover and chill until firm, at least 6 hours.

Preheat the oven to 425°F. Cut the polenta into 1-inch cubes and place on a baking sheet. Drizzle the olive oil over the polenta cubes and gently toss to coat. Bake until golden brown, about 25 minutes. Serve with the fondue.

To make the fondue: In a small bowl, combine the dried mushrooms with 1 cup of boiling water. Let stand until the mushrooms are completely softened, about 30 minutes. Carefully remove the mushrooms from the soaking water. (The water will contain grit, so don't just drain the mushrooms into a sieve, as you will also get the grit along with the mushrooms). Finely chop the mushrooms. Strain the soaking water through a coffee filter and set both mushrooms and water aside.

In a medium, heavy-bottomed saucepan, heat the butter over medium-high heat. Add the shallot and sauté for 2 minutes. Add the mushrooms and the soaking water and bring to a boil over high heat. Continue cooking until the liquid has evaporated.

Reduce the heat to medium and add the wine and vinegar. Bring to a simmer. Toss the cheese and cornstarch together and add to the pan, a handful at a time. Stir each addition until incorporated and melted. Allow the fondue to come to a light simmer, but don't let it boil. Transfer to a fondue pot and drizzle the truffle oil over the top. Keep warm over a low flame. Serve with the polenta cubes for dipping.

makes about one-half cup

Spicy Thai Dipping Sauce

ingredients

- 4 hot red chiles (about 2 inches long), finely chopped
- 1 clove garlic, finely minced
- 2 tablespoons sugar
- 2 tablespoons Asian fish sauce
- 1/4 cup fresh lime juice

We try to keep a little of this dipping sauce in our refrigerators at all times. Not only is it great as an accompaniment to most Asian appetizers, it's also wonderful the day after the party, dabbed on a simple meal of poached chicken, rice, and veggies.

In a small bowl, whisk together all the ingredients until the sugar has dissolved. Let the dipping sauce sit for 30 minutes before serving to allow the flavors to blend.

Make-ahead: *This sauce can be made up to a week ahead and kept, covered and refrigerated.*

makes two cups

Thai Peanut Dip or Sauce

ingredients

- *One 13½-ounce can unsweetened coconut milk*
- *1 tablespoon light brown sugar*
- *1 tablespoon Thai red curry paste*
- *1 tablespoon Asian fish sauce*
- *½ cup chunky peanut butter*

We love this dip because it's so versatile. It can be used as a dip for spring or summer rolls, vegetables, or even cut-up apples. Any leftover dip can be thinned with chicken or vegetable stock and tossed with cooked noodles for a delicious cold noodle salad. Whenever we can get two meals out of one dip, we're happy.

In a small saucepan, combine the milk, sugar, curry paste, and fish sauce over medium heat. Bring to a gentle boil and cook for 3 minutes, stirring occasionally. Reduce the heat to low and add the peanut butter. Continue to cook until the peanut butter is well blended, about 1 minute more. Serve warm.

Make-ahead: *This dip can be made 2 days ahead and kept, covered, in the refrigerator. It may become thicker while standing in the refrigerator. Just add a tablespoon of water or stock to thin it to the desired consistency.*

makes about two-thirds cup

Sesame-Soy Dipping Sauce

ingredients

- *¼ cup seasoned rice vinegar*
- *⅓ cup light soy sauce*
- *1 clove garlic, minced*
- *2 teaspoons peeled and minced fresh ginger*
- *2 teaspoons Asian (dark) sesame oil*

Try this sauce with pot stickers or summer rolls. Its salty, nutty flavor complements most Asian dishes, and it can stand in for Spicy Thai Dipping Sauce, (page 271) when you want a less spicy alternative.

Mix all the ingredients together in a small bowl.

Make-ahead: *The sauce can be made up to 5 days ahead and kept, covered, in the refrigerator.*

makes about 1½ cups

White Bean, Rosemary, and Pancetta Spread

ingredients

- *2 tablespoons olive oil*
- *3 ounces pancetta, finely chopped*
- *2 cloves garlic, minced*
- *2 tablespoons minced fresh rosemary*
- *One 19-ounce can cannellini beans, drained, reserving the liquid*
- *Salt and freshly ground black pepper to taste*
- *Extra-virgin olive oil, for drizzling*
- *Rosemary sprigs, for garnish*

Sometimes a trip to Tuscany is just not in the cards, but a virtual culinary tour can be accomplished quickly with this rosemary- and garlic-scented white bean spread. Just serve it with toasted bread slices and a glass of Chianti, and no matter where you are it will feel like Siena.

In a medium-size saucepan, heat the olive oil over medium heat and add the pancetta. Sauté for about 3 minutes, or until golden. Add the garlic and rosemary and continue to cook for another 2 minutes. Add the beans and, with a fork or potato masher, mash the beans, leaving some whole. The mixture should be creamy but slightly thick and lumpy. Add some of the reserved bean liquid if too dry. Season to taste with salt and pepper.

Transfer the mixture to a serving bowl. Drizzle a little olive oil on top of the spread and garnish with rosemary sprigs.

Make-ahead: *The spread can be made 1 day ahead and kept, covered, in the refrigerator.*

Tip: *Pancetta is a cured Italian pork product made from the same cut of meat as bacon. Although pancetta is not smoked, you can substitute bacon if you wish.*

makes two cups

Hummus

ingredients

Two 16-ounce cans garbanzo beans, drained

1 clove garlic, chopped

1/4 teaspoon salt

2 1/2 tablespoons fresh lemon juice, plus more to taste

2 tablespoons tahini

1/3 cup water

1/4 cup extra-virgin olive oil, plus more for drizzling

Pita Wedges (page 96) or crudités, for serving

Over the last decade, this Mediterranean spread has become increasingly popular. That's easy to understand, because now that a food processor can be found in almost every kitchen, hummus has to be one of the fastest "out of the pantry" appetizers we know.

In a food processor, purée the beans with the garlic, salt, lemon juice, tahini, water, and 1/4 cup olive oil until smooth. Taste for seasoning and add more salt or lemon juice if necessary. If it is too thick, add water, a tablespoon at a time, until the hummus is the desired consistency. Transfer to a serving bowl and drizzle with additional olive oil. Serve with pita wedges or crudités.

Make-ahead: *The hummus can be made 2 days ahead and kept, covered, in the refrigerator.*

makes two cups

Roasted Garlic Hummus with Toasted Pine Nuts and Garlic Oil

ingredients

1 head garlic

1 teaspoon olive oil

½ cup extra-virgin olive oil, divided

3 cloves garlic, chopped

Two 16-ounce cans garbanzo beans, drained

¼ teaspoon salt

2½ tablespoons fresh lemon juice, plus more to taste

2 tablespoons tahini

⅓ cup water

3 tablespoons pine nuts, toasted

1 tablespoon chopped fresh Italian parsley

Pita Wedges (page 96) or crudités, for serving

The pine nuts and garlic oil makes this hummus dish festive. The roasted garlic gives it depth and a slight sweetness. It's perfect for occasions when plain hummus just won't do.

Preheat the oven to 350°F.

Cut ½ inch off the top of the head of garlic. Place the garlic in a large square of foil, drizzle with 1 teaspoon olive oil, and enclose in the foil. Place the garlic "packet" in the oven and roast until the garlic is soft and golden brown, 45 minutes. When the garlic is cool enough to handle, squeeze out the soft cloves into a small bowl and smash with the back of a fork. Set aside.

In a small saucepan, heat ¼ cup extra-virgin olive oil and the chopped garlic cloves over low heat for 3 minutes. Watch to make sure the garlic does not burn. Remove from the heat and set aside.

In a food processor, purée the beans with the roasted garlic, salt, lemon juice, tahini, water, and remaining ¼ cup olive oil until the hummus is smooth. Taste for seasoning, adding more salt or lemon juice if necessary. If it is too thick, add water, a tablespoon at a time, until the hummus is the desired consistency. Transfer to a serving bowl, drizzle with the garlic oil, and scatter the pine nuts and parsley on top. Serve with pita wedges or crudités.

Make-ahead: *The hummus can be made and kept, covered, in the refrigerator for 2 days. Garnish with the garlic oil, pine nuts, and parsley right before serving.*

makes about 1½ cups

Kalamata and Fig Tapenade

ingredients

1 cup black kalamata olives, pitted

⅓ cup dried Mission figs, stems removed

Grated zest of 1 lemon

1½ tablespoons fresh lemon juice

1 clove garlic, minced

1 tablespoon capers, rinsed and drained

¼ teaspoon crushed red pepper flakes

2 teaspoons fresh thyme

½ teaspoon freshly ground black pepper

¼ cup coarsely chopped fresh Italian parsley

3 tablespoons olive oil

½ cup toasted walnuts

Tapenade is a Provençal olive paste that we like to refer to as one of our "gold in the fridge" items because it can add depth and interest to any number of dishes. Just a few spoonfuls can change everyday mashed potatoes, vinaigrettes, or omelets into something really special. This recipe is a great introduction to tapenade, because it doesn't contain the traditional anchovies, and the figs add a sweetness that mellows the strong, briny flavor of the olives.

Place the olives, figs, lemon zest and juice, garlic, capers, red pepper flakes, thyme, pepper, and parsley in the work bowl of a food processor. Pulse a few times to blend, but do not purée. Add the oil and pulse a few more times to form a cohesive but still coarse paste. Add the walnuts and pulse until they are chopped but small pieces are still visible.

Make-ahead: *Tapenade can be made up to 1 week ahead and kept, covered, in the refrigerator.*

makes about 1¼ cups

Buttermilk Ranch Dipping Sauce

ingredients

- ½ cup mayonnaise, homemade (page 334) or store-bought
- ½ cup buttermilk
- 1 clove garlic, minced
- 2 tablespoons minced fresh Italian parsley
- 2 tablespoons minced fresh chives
- 1 teaspoon white wine vinegar
- ¼ teaspoon salt
- Freshly ground black pepper to taste

Although it may be easy to find ranch salad dressing on the aisles of your local grocery store, you'll find this lively, fresh-tasting version well worth the few moments it takes to put together.

In a medium bowl, whisk together the mayonnaise, buttermilk, garlic, parsley, chives, vinegar, salt, and pepper to taste.

Make-ahead: *The sauce can be kept, covered, in the refrigerator for up to 3 days.*

serves six to eight

Hot Spinach and Bacon Dip

ingredients

5 slices bacon, chopped

1 medium red onion, diced

3 cloves garlic, minced

½ cup milk

8 ounces cream cheese

One 10-ounce package frozen chopped spinach, thawed and liquid squeezed out

One 8-ounce can water chestnuts, chopped

Pinch of ground nutmeg

3 dashes hot sauce, such as Tabasco

¾ cup grated Parmesan cheese, divided

Coarse salt and freshly ground black pepper to taste

Baguette slices, breadsticks, or crackers, for serving

Nothing warms up a party like a hot dip. Bacon and spinach have been paired for eons and go so well together because, hey . . . everything's better with bacon.

Preheat the oven to 425°F.

Heat a medium saucepan over medium heat. Add the bacon and cook, stirring occasionally, until crispy. Remove with a slotted spoon and drain on paper towels. Pour off all but 1 tablespoon of the fat. Return the pan to medium heat and add the onion and garlic; cook until lightly browned, 5 to 8 minutes.

In the same pot, add the milk to the cooked onions and warm the milk over medium heat. Whisk in the cream cheese until melted. Add the spinach, water chestnuts, nutmeg, hot sauce, and ¼ cup of the Parmesan; stir to combine. Season with salt and pepper. Pour into a lightly oiled 1½-quart shallow baking dish; sprinkle with the remaining ½ cup Parmesan.

Bake until bubbly and golden brown, 20 to 25 minutes. Serve hot with accompaniments, as desired.

Make-ahead: *The unbaked dip can be made 1 day ahead and kept, covered, in the refrigerator. Add 5 minutes to the baking time.*

Tip: *For a change, instead of a baking dish, try baking this in a hollowed-out loaf of sourdough bread. You can use the insides for dipping.*

Chapter 1

nd Cauliflower Soup *with* Dill

284 Parsnip *and* Apple Soup *with* Thyme

Thyme (Soupe Bonne Femme)

Tomato Gazpacho *with* Avocado Relish

Soup Shots

Roasted Tomato Soup *with* Pesto

Basil Crème Fraîche

Vichyssoise *with* Tarragon Pesto

makes two cups, or sixteen 2-ounce shots

Chilled Carrot and Cauliflower Soup with Dill

ingredients

- 1½ teaspoons cardamom seeds
- 2 medium leeks
- 4 tablespoons unsalted butter
- 1 pound carrots, peeled trimmed, and thinly sliced
- ⅓ cup dry white wine
- 2 teaspoons peeled and chopped fresh ginger
- 2 cups carrot juice
- ½ teaspoon salt
- ⅛ teaspoon freshly ground black pepper
- 1½ cups light chicken stock
- 1 cup small cauliflower florets
- 2 teaspoons fresh lemon juice
- 1 large bunch dill, snipped, for garnish

Cooking carrots in carrot juice results in such big carrot flavor that we were tempted to name this "What's Up Doc? Soup." Accents of ginger and dill make this a winner whether served chilled or hot.

Toast the cardamom seeds in a small, dry skillet over medium heat. Shake the pan until the seeds begin to smell fragrant, about 3 minutes. Transfer them to a spice mill and grind very fine, or crush them with a mortar and pestle.

Cut off and discard the tops of the leeks at the point where they turn medium green. Cut off the roots and split them in half lengthwise. Rinse them under running water to remove any sand that might be lodged between the layers. Slice thinly. You should have about 2 cups.

Melt the butter in a medium, heavy-bottomed saucepan over medium heat. Add the leeks and cook for 5 minutes, stirring. Add the carrots, cardamom, wine, and ginger. Cook, uncovered, until all of the liquid has evaporated, about 5 minutes. Add the carrot juice, salt, and pepper. Bring to a boil, cover, and simmer gently over low heat until the carrots are tender, about 20 minutes.

Heat the chicken stock over medium heat until it simmers. Blanch the cauliflower in the hot stock for about 3 minutes. Remove the cauliflower with a slotted spoon and refrigerate to use later as a garnish. Transfer the hot stock to a measuring cup with a pouring spout.

Transfer half the soup to a blender. Hold down the lid with a towel to make sure the soup doesn't splash up. Start at low speed and move up to high. Remove the center tab from the lid and add half the hot stock; blend until smooth. Pour the soup into a bowl and repeat with the remaining soup and stock. Add the lemon juice and chill.

When ready to serve, taste the soup and adjust the seasoning as desired with salt and pepper. Ladle the soup into 2-ounce cups and garnish with the cauliflower and dill.

Make-ahead: *This soup can be made 2 days ahead and kept, covered, in the refrigerator. Garnish right before serving.*

makes twenty-four 2-ounce shots, plus extra

Chilled Corn Soup with Shrimp

ingredients

- *3 tablespoons olive oil*
- *1 1/2 cups chopped onion*
- *1/2 cup peeled and diced potatoes*
- *2 teaspoons minced garlic*
- *1 teaspoon ancho chile powder*
- *1/2 teaspoon salt*
- *1/8 teaspoon ground nutmeg*
- *Dash of cayenne pepper*
- *3 cups chicken or shellfish stock, plus more if needed*
- *1 1/2 cups raw corn kernels, or frozen white corn, thawed*
- *2/3 cup heavy cream*
- *1/4 cup sour cream*
- *3 tablespoons fresh lime juice, divided*
- *1/4 cup chopped fresh cilantro*
- *Salt and freshly ground black pepper to taste*
- *1 teaspoon hot pepper sauce, or to taste*
- *8 ounces cooked bay shrimp, rinsed*
- *1/4 cup minced fresh chives, for garnish*

The natural sweetness of corn and shrimp complement each other in this chilled chowder. Although for a large party we recommend serving this soup in small shots, you'll like it so much you'll be tempted to serve it in mugs.

In a large saucepan, heat the olive oil. Add the onions, potatoes, garlic, ancho chile powder, salt, nutmeg, and cayenne. Sauté over medium heat until the onion is soft, about 3 minutes. Add the stock and corn and bring to a boil. Reduce the heat and simmer until the vegetables are very tender, about 10 minutes.

Remove from the heat and let cool. Transfer to a blender and purée, adding more stock to the soup to thin it if needed. Add the heavy cream and sour cream and chill for at least 4 hours or overnight.

Combine the chilled soup base, 2 tablespoons of the lime juice, and cilantro. Season to taste with salt and pepper and drops of hot pepper sauce. If the soup is thick, thin it as necessary with more chicken stock.

Toss the rinsed shrimp with the remaining tablespoon of lime juice and season the shrimp to taste with salt and pepper.

Ladle the soup into 2-ounce glasses and top each with a teaspoon of the shrimp. Garnish each shot with a sprinkling of chives. Serve chilled.

Make-ahead: *The soup can be made without the shrimp garnish 2 days ahead and kept, covered, in the refrigerator. It will thicken and need to be thinned with some of the extra stock. Add the shrimp right before serving.*

makes twenty-four 2-ounce shots, plus extra

Parsnip and Apple Soup with Thyme

ingredients

- 2 tablespoons unsalted butter
- ½ cup diced onion
- ½ teaspoon salt, plus more to taste
- 1 pound parsnips, peeled and sliced
- 1 pound sweet-tart apples such as Braeburn, Mutsu, or Crispin, peeled, cored, and diced
- 1 medium russet potato, peeled and diced
- 2 cups apple cider or apple juice
- 2 cups chicken stock
- 2 teaspoons cider vinegar
- ½ cup heavy cream
- 1 teaspoon minced fresh thyme
- Freshly ground black pepper to taste
- Sprigs of fresh thyme, for garnish (optional)

The sweetness of parsnips and apples is a pleasant surprise in this creamy fresh soup. We've cooked them in a mixture of apple cider and chicken stock for a light vegetable soup with just a hint of apples and thyme.

Heat a large saucepan over medium heat and melt the butter. When it is hot, add the onion and cook until it becomes translucent, about 2 minutes. Add the salt and cook for another minute or so. Add the parsnips and apples and cook, stirring, for about 3 minutes to warm them up. Add the potato, apple cider, and chicken stock to the pan. Bring to a simmer and cover, turning the heat down to low. Simmer until the parsnips and potatoes are tender, about 20 minutes.

Purée the soup in batches in a food processor or blender. Return the soup to the saucepan and add the cider vinegar, heavy cream, and fresh thyme. Adjust the seasoning with more salt and freshly ground black pepper to taste. Pour the soup into 2-ounce cups and garnish with fresh thyme if desired. Serve hot or chilled.

Make-ahead: *This soup can be made 2 days ahead and kept, covered, in the refrigerator. Garnish right before serving.*

Tip: *If serving the soup chilled, it may be necessary to thin it with a little extra chicken stock to achieve the desired texture.*

makes six cups, or forty-eight 2-ounce shots

Potato and Leek Soup with Lemon Thyme (Soupe Bonne Femme)

ingredients

- 2 tablespoons olive oil
- 3 leeks (white part only), washed and thinly sliced
- 1 pound Yukon Gold potatoes, peeled and thinly sliced
- 4 cups chicken stock
- 1 teaspoon minced fresh lemon thyme, or ½ teaspoon dried thyme
- ½ cup heavy cream
- Salt and freshly ground black pepper to taste
- 1 tablespoon finely minced fresh chives

Soupe bonne femme is French for "good woman soup." It has been said that a good housewife can make a meal from anything lying around the house, even water and a potato. This soup is certainly more intriguing than potatoes and water, but it is a distant cousin to that unassuming classic.

Heat the olive oil in a large pot over medium heat and add the leeks. Cook the leeks until they soften, about 2 minutes, and add the potatoes, chicken stock, and thyme. Bring to a simmer and turn the heat to low. Simmer the potato-leek mixture until the potatoes are tender, about 25 minutes.

Using an immersion blender, a blender, or a food processor, blend the soup so that it is creamy and thick. Add the cream and taste for seasoning, adding salt and freshly ground black pepper to taste. Serve the soup hot or chilled in 2-ounce cups, garnished with a sprinkling of fresh chives.

Make-ahead: *This soup can be made 2 days ahead and kept, covered, in the refrigerator. Garnish right before serving.*

Tip: *If serving the soup chilled, it may be necessary to thin it with a little extra chicken stock to achieve the desired texture.*

makes twenty-four 2-ounce shots, plus extra

Yellow Tomato Gazpacho with Avocado Relish

soup

- 1½ pounds yellow tomatoes, chopped
- ½ English cucumber, peeled, seeded, and chopped
- ½ cup sweet onion (like Vidalia), chopped
- 1 yellow bell pepper, chopped (reserve one fourth of the pepper for the relish)
- 1 clove garlic, minced
- 1 jalapeño chile, chopped
- 2 tablespoons sherry vinegar
- Salt and freshly ground black pepper to taste

relish

- ½ cup diced avocado
- ½ red bell pepper, finely diced
- 2 teaspoons fresh lime juice
- 2 tablespoons chopped fresh cilantro
- Salt and freshly ground black pepper to taste

This soup is summer on a spoon, and that's the best time to make it, because late summer is when tomatoes are at their peak. The food processor makes this recipe easy to prepare, but it needs to be made in advance to allow the flavors to blend and the soup to chill properly.

To make the soup: Toss the tomatoes, cucumber, onion, three fourths of the yellow bell pepper, the garlic, and chile into a food processor (you may have to do this step in two batches). Process to a slightly chunky consistency. Pour the soup into a bowl, add the vinegar, and season to taste with salt and pepper. Chill for at least 2 hours.

To make the relish: Gently toss the avocado, red bell pepper, remaining yellow bell pepper, lime juice, and cilantro in a small bowl. Season to taste with salt and pepper. Keep chilled. The relish should be made about ½ hour before the soup will be served.

Before serving, taste both the soup and the relish again to correct the seasonings. Divide the soup among 24 small cups or shot glasses. Pile a small spoonful of relish in a little mound on top of the soup. Serve cold.

Make-ahead: *This soup can be made 2 days ahead and kept, covered, in the refrigerator. Garnish right before serving.*

makes twenty-four 2-ounce shots, plus extra

Chilled Roasted Tomato Soup with Pesto

ingredients

3 pounds plum tomatoes, halved lengthwise

Salt and freshly ground black pepper to taste

5 tablespoons olive oil, divided

2 tablespoons minced garlic

1 tablespoon finely chopped fresh rosemary

1 tablespoon finely chopped fresh thyme

1/4 teaspoon crushed red pepper flakes, or more to taste

4 cups chicken stock or canned low-salt broth

1/4 cup pesto, homemade (page 337) or store-bought

Think of this soup as a slightly sweeter, more intense version of a gazpacho, which is made with uncooked tomatoes. The roasted tomatoes, along with the garlic, rosemary, and thyme, give this soup a big, bold flavor that holds up well when chilled.

Preheat the oven to 425°F.

Place the tomatoes, cut side up, on a large baking sheet. Sprinkle with salt and pepper. Drizzle with 2 tablespoons of the olive oil. Roast until the tomatoes are brown and tender, about 1 hour. Cool slightly.

Transfer the tomatoes and any accumulated juices to a food processor. Pulse until slightly chunky.

Heat the remaining 3 tablespoons oil in a large pot over medium-high heat. Add the garlic and sauté until fragrant, about 2 minutes. Stir in the tomatoes, rosemary, thyme, and red pepper flakes. Add the chicken stock; bring to a boil. Reduce the heat and simmer, uncovered, until the soup thickens slightly, about 25 minutes. Season with salt and pepper. Remove from the heat and let cool for 30 minutes. Cover and refrigerate for at least 4 hours. Taste again and adjust the seasoning if necessary.

Divide the soup among 24 small cups or shot glasses. Drizzle a small spoonful of pesto on top of each. Serve cold.

Make-ahead: *This soup can be made 2 days ahead and kept, covered, in the refrigerator. Garnish right before serving.*

makes twenty-four 2-ounce shots, plus extra

Roasted Red Pepper Soup with Basil Crème Fraîche

soup

1 tablespoon extra-virgin oil

1 small onion, chopped

1 tablespoon chopped garlic

1 cup white wine

6 red bell peppers, roasted, peeled, seeded, and diced

2½ cups rich chicken stock or vegetable stock, plus more as needed

Salt and freshly ground black pepper to taste

basil crème fraîche

⅓ cup packed fresh basil leaves

½ cup crème fraîche

This simple soup takes advantage of the deep, smoky flavor of roasted red peppers. It has very few ingredients and can be made well ahead. The pale green of the basil crème fraîche garnish contrasts beautifully with the deep red of this soup.

To make the soup: Heat the oil in a large saucepan over high heat until very hot. Add the onion and garlic and sauté for about 2 minutes. Add the white wine and reduce until about ½ cup remains, about 4 minutes. Add the peppers and stock, turn the heat down to medium, and simmer for about 20 minutes. Season with salt and pepper.

Carefully purée the soup in a blender or food processor. Transfer to a large bowl, cover, and refrigerate until well chilled, about 2 hours. (If the soup is too thick after chilling, thin it down with a bit more stock.)

To make the basil crème fraîche: In a food processor, pulse the crème fraîche with the basil leaves just until the basil is finely chopped. Do not overprocess.

Divide the soup among 24 small cups or shot glasses. Spoon a small dollop of crème fraîche on top of each. Serve warm or at room temperature.

Make-ahead: *This soup can be made 2 days ahead and kept, covered, in the refrigerator. Garnish right before serving.*

Tips: *In late summer, when red peppers are in abundance, we take advantage of the low prices and buy a ton. We roast them, peel them, and freeze them in a single layer on a baking sheet. Once they're frozen stiff, we transfer them to a freezer bag and keep them on hand for soups, sauces, pizzas—anything that needs a little brightening up.*

Sour cream is a good substitute if crème fraîche is not available. If using crème fraîche, be careful not to overprocess, as the crème will become curdled.

makes twenty-four 2-ounce shots, plus extra

Zucchini Vichyssoise with Tarragon Pesto

vichyssoise

2 tablespoons unsalted butter

1 medium onion, chopped

1 pound boiling potatoes, peeled and cut into 1/2-inch cubes

2 cloves garlic, chopped

4 sprigs fresh tarragon

6 cups chicken stock

2 pounds small (5-inch-long) zucchini, cut into 1/2-inch cubes

1/2 cup heavy cream, chilled

2 tablespoons fresh lemon juice

Salt and freshly ground black pepper to taste

tarragon pesto

3/4 cup fresh tarragon leaves

2/3 cup fresh Italian parsley leaves

1 clove garlic, minced

2 tablespoons sliced almonds

2 tablespoons grated Asiago cheese

3/4 cup extra-virgin olive oil

Salt and freshly ground black pepper to taste

The anise flavor of tarragon is subtle in this beautiful pale green soup. But a small spoonful of the not-so-subtle tarragon pesto really pulls out the flavor and gives this soup unforgettable character.

To make the soup: Melt the butter in a 5-quart, heavy pot over medium heat, add the onion, and cook, stirring occasionally, until softened, about 10 minutes. Add the potatoes, garlic, and tarragon sprigs and cook, stirring, for 1 minute. Add the stock and simmer, uncovered, until the potatoes are tender, about 20 minutes. Add the zucchini and simmer, uncovered, until it is very tender, about 15 minutes.

Remove the tarragon sprigs and purée the soup in batches in a blender or food processor until very smooth. (Use caution when blending hot liquids. It's best to cover the top of blender with a towel in case any hot soup should splatter out). Pour into a bowl. Stir in the cream, lemon juice, salt, and pepper. Cool to room temperature, uncovered. Chill the soup, covered, until cold, at least 4 hours and up to 2 days. Taste and reseason if necessary.

To make the pesto: Place the tarragon, parsley, and garlic in the bowl of a food processor and pulse until finely chopped. Add the almonds and cheese and pulse again several times. With the motor running, pour in the oil. Season with salt and pepper.

Divide the soup among 24 small cups or shot glasses. Spoon a small dollop of tarragon pesto on top of each. Serve cold.

Make-ahead: *This soup can be made 2 days ahead and kept, covered, in the refrigerator. Garnish right before serving.*

Chapter 12 Cooking

Horseradish Aïoli

quares *with* Saga Blue *and* Figs

rittata **295** Ham *and* Gruyère Strudel

ar **297** Phyllo Pizza *with* Four Cheeses

or a Crowd

enderloin *with* Apricot Marmalade

ruyère Quiche

nd Chutney

Chicken Salad *in* Phyllo Cups

makes about thirty-six slices

Beef Loin with Horseradish Aïoli

beef loin

1 tablespoon olive oil

1 trimmed and tied center-cut beef tenderloin roast, 3½ pounds, at room temperature

1 tablespoon salt

3 tablespoons coarsely ground black pepper

horseradish aïoli

¼ cup prepared horseradish

Mayonnaise (page 334)

Salt and freshly ground black pepper to taste

Fresh Italian parsley sprigs, for garnish

Few dishes are as elegant as beef tenderloin. The price may alarm you, but keep in mind that the beef is sliced thinly, allowing you to serve 15 to 20 people as part of a large buffet offering. We like to serve this with rolls so that people can create their own little sandwiches, making it easier to eat for a stand-up occasion.

Put a rack in the middle of the oven and preheat to 500°F.

Rub 1 tablespoon olive oil into the beef, and then rub in the salt and pepper. Place the beef on a rack on a small rimmed baking sheet. Roast for 10 minutes. Reduce the heat to 425°F and roast until a thermometer inserted into the thickest part of the meat registers 125°F for medium-rare, about 15 to 20 minutes longer. (It will continue to cook, reaching 130°F.) Remove from the oven and allow to cool to room temperature. (The tenderloin can be refrigerated at this point.)

To make the aïoli: Mix the horseradish with the mayonnaise and season to taste with salt and pepper. Cover and refrigerate until ready to serve.

Remove the string from the tenderloin and discard. Slice the tenderloin into ⅓-inch-thick slices. Arrange on a platter and garnish with parsley. Serve at room temperature with the horseradish aïoli.

Make-ahead: *The tenderloin and aïoli can be made 24 hours ahead and kept, covered and refrigerated. The tenderloin can be sliced cold ½ hour before you serve it.*

makes forty-eight pieces

Polenta Squares with Saga Blue and Figs

ingredients

- 7 cups water
- 2 teaspoons salt, plus more to taste
- 1/4 teaspoon freshly ground black pepper, plus more to taste
- 2 cups coarse polenta
- 4 tablespoons unsalted butter
- 8 ounces Saga blue cheese, at room temperature
- 4 ounces goat cheese, at room temperature
- 12 dried Calimyrna figs, stemmed and quartered
- 1/2 cup grated Parmesan cheese

Salty cheese and sweet figs turn polenta, a familiar, homey comfort food, into an elegant appetizer.

Preheat the oven to 425°F.

Butter a 9-by-13-inch pan and set it aside.

Bring the water to a boil in a large saucepan over medium-high heat. Add the salt and pepper and sprinkle in the polenta, whisking constantly. Turn the heat to low and stir with a wooden spoon or heatproof spatula. The polenta should be simmering. Continue to stir until the spoon can stand up in the center of the pan, about 20 minutes. Remove the polenta from the heat and add the butter. Correct the seasoning with more salt and pepper if desired.

In a small bowl, combine the blue cheese and goat cheese until mixed.

In another bowl, combine the figs and 1 cup of hot water. Let the figs soften for 5 minutes, then drain the water from them.

Spread half of the hot polenta into the buttered pan and top with dollops of the cheese mixture. Lay the sliced figs over the cheese, and top them with the remaining polenta. Sprinkle the Parmesan over the top.

Bake in the center of the oven until hot and golden, 25 to 30 minutes. Remove from the oven and let cool for 10 minutes. Slice the polenta into 2-inch squares and arrange on a decorative platter. Serve hot.

Make-ahead: *The unbaked dish can be kept, covered, in the refrigerator for up to 24 hours. Allow it to come to room temperature before baking.*

Tip: *For a knife-and-fork version, you can make this dish in 12 individual buttered ramekins. Start with a layer of polenta no more than 1 inch deep. Top with the cheese and figs and finish with another layer of polenta. Top with the Parmesan and bake the ramekins for 15 minutes. Let them sit for 5 minutes, then unmold onto individual plates and serve hot.*

makes fifty-two squares

Roasted Vegetable and Fontina Frittata

ingredients

5 tablespoons extra-virgin olive oil

1 eggplant, cut into ½-inch cubes

2 zucchini, cut into ½-inch cubes

8 ounces mushrooms, sliced

1 pint cherry tomatoes, halved

1½ teaspoons salt, divided

½ teaspoon freshly ground black pepper, divided

12 eggs

⅓ cup sour cream

8 ounces fontina cheese, diced

Rich fontina cheese oozes from every bite of this egg-based appetizer. The roasted vegetables give an intense flavor and color to this frittata.

Preheat the oven to 400°F.

Drizzle the olive oil in equal amounts onto 2 large rimmed baking sheets. Divide the vegetables between the 2 pans, sprinkle with ½ teaspoon of the salt and ¼ teaspoon of the pepper, and toss to coat with the oil. Place the pans in the oven and roast until very tender and browned, 20 to 25 minutes.

Transfer the roasted vegetables to an oiled 9-by-13-inch baking pan. In a large bowl, mix together the eggs, sour cream, remaining 1 teaspoon salt, and remaining ¼ teaspoon pepper until well combined. Sprinkle the cheese over the roasted vegetables and pour the egg mixture evenly on top.

Place in the oven and cook until the eggs are just set, about 20 minutes. Set the oven to broil and broil until golden on top, about another minute. Remove from the oven and let cool for 15 minutes. Cut into 1½-inch squares. Transfer the frittata squares to a serving platter and serve warm or at room temperature.

Make-ahead: *The vegetables can be roasted 2 days ahead. Allow them to come to room temperature before proceeding with the recipe.*

makes twenty-six pieces

Ham and Gruyère Strudel

ingredients

6 sheets phyllo pastry

½ cup (1 stick) unsalted butter, melted

2 tablespoons Dijon mustard

8 ounces Black Forest ham, thinly sliced

8 ounces Gruyère cheese, thinly sliced

Your guests will rave over this elegant version of a ham and Swiss cheese sandwich. This recipe is so easy to put together that doubling or tripling it for a large crowd is a breeze.

Preheat the oven to 400°F.

Remove the phyllo from its package. Cut each phyllo sheet in half, making two 7 ½-by-13-inch rectangles. Cover the phyllo with a large sheet of plastic and a damp paper towel to keep the pastry from drying out.

Working as quickly as possible, place one piece of phyllo on a work surface and brush it lightly with butter. Lay another piece on top and again brush lightly with butter. Repeat with 4 more layers. There should be 6 layers in all. Brush 1 tablespoon of Dijon lengthwise down the middle of the phyllo. Lay half of the ham down the middle lengthwise and then half the cheese. Starting at one of the long ends, roll the phyllo up into a log.

Place the strudel on a parchment-lined baking sheet and brush the top with butter. Using a serrated knife, score the dough crosswise at 1-inch intervals. This will make it easier to slice once baked.

Repeat with the remaining ingredients so that you have 2 strudels on the baking sheet.

Bake until the strudels are golden brown on top, about 20 minutes. Remove from the oven and allow to cool for 10 minutes before slicing. Carefully slice along the scored lines. Transfer the slices to a serving platter. Serve warm or at room temperature.

Make-ahead: *The unbaked strudels can be frozen on the baking sheet, covered with plastic and foil. Bake without thawing, adding 5 minutes to the baking time.*

makes 120 pieces

Baked New Potatoes with Topping Bar

potatoes

60 small new red potatoes, no more than 2 or 3 inches in diameter, washed and cut in half

¼ cup olive oil

Salt and freshly ground black pepper to taste

toppings

1 cup sour cream mixed with ¼ cup minced fresh chives

1 pound bacon, cooked until crisp, crumbled

1 cup finely grated cheddar cheese

Guacamole (page 265)

Yogurt Green Onion Dip (page 260)

Hot Spinach and Bacon Dip (page 279)

Buttermilk Ranch Dipping Sauce (page 278)

New potatoes are now available year round, but this appetizer is especially toothsome in the spring when farmers' markets are awash with the new crop. Almost everyone loves potatoes, and with a variety of toppings, you'll have created a sinfully delicious smorgasbord sure to please a variety of palates.

Preheat the oven to 400°F.

Using a melon baller, scoop the center out of each potato half, leaving a ¼-inch border. Brush the cut side of the potatoes with the olive oil and sprinkle with salt and pepper. Arrange the potatoes cut side down in a parchment-lined baking pan and bake until the potatoes are tender when pierced with a sharp knife, about 25 minutes.

Remove the potatoes from the parchment and arrange them on a decorative platter. Sprinkle with salt and pepper. Arrange the toppings in bowls around the platter of potatoes and let guests top their own potatoes.

Make-ahead: *The potatoes can be baked up to 1 day ahead, stored on the baking sheet covered with plastic, and refrigerated. Reheat in a 350°F oven for 10 minutes.*

makes thirty-six pieces

Phyllo Pizza with Four Cheeses

Four different kinds of cheese give this phyllo-based pizza great flavor, and the buttery pastry is to die for. We fell in love with this recipe years ago when Joanne Weir, a West Coast chef and cookbook author, taught a version of it at the Western Reserve School of Cooking in Hudson, Ohio.

ingredients

- *1/3 cup crumbled feta cheese*
- *1/3 cup grated mozzarella cheese*
- *1/3 cup grated Parmesan cheese*
- *1/3 cup grated Asiago cheese*
- *20 sheets phyllo pastry*
- *1/2 cup (1 stick) unsalted butter, melted*
- *3 large tomatoes, thinly sliced*
- *4 green onions, white and green parts, trimmed and thinly sliced*
- *Salt and freshly ground black pepper to taste*

Preheat the oven to 400°F.

Combine the feta, mozzarella, Parmesan, and Asiago cheeses in a medium bowl.

Remove the phyllo from its package and cover it with a large sheet of plastic wrap topped with a damp dish towel to weigh it down and keep the pastry from drying out.

Working as quickly as possible, lay 2 sheets of phyllo side by side on a baking sheet to cover it, and brush liberally with butter. Make sure to get the edges covered with the butter or they will become brittle and crack off. Lay another 2 sheets of phyllo on top of the first 2 and brush with butter again. Top the phyllo with about 1/4 cup of the cheese mixture. (It doesn't look like much, but there will be many layers.) Top the cheese with 4 more sheets of pastry, buttering each sheet. Continue to build 2 layers of phyllo with 1 layer of cheese for a total of 5 layers, using all the phyllo. Top the last layer with a thin layer of tomato and a sprinkling of green onion. Salt and pepper the tomatoes and top with the rest of the cheese.

Bake the phyllo pizza in the oven until the bottom is browned and crispy, about 20 minutes. Remove the pizza from the oven and let cool for 5 minutes. Slide the pizza from the pan onto a cutting board, and cut it into 36 pieces.

Make-ahead: *The unbaked pizzas freeze beautifully, wrapped in plastic and then foil, for up to 4 weeks. There's no need to thaw them—just bake them frozen, giving them a few more minutes in the oven.*

makes about eighty slices

Provençal Herbed Pork Tenderloin with Apricot Marmalade

dry rub

- ½ teaspoon crushed red pepper flakes
- 2 teaspoons salt
- 2 teaspoons cracked black pepper
- 2 teaspoons dried fennel seed
- 1 teaspoon dried rosemary
- 1 teaspoon dried thyme
- 1 teaspoon summer savory
- 1 teaspoon dried basil

- 4 tablespoons olive oil
- 4 pork tenderloins, trimmed and silver skin removed

The term "appetizer party" is a misnomer, as most of your guests will consider it dinner. That makes substantial dishes like this juicy pork tenderloin an even more important part of your buffet table. Here we've given it the French treatment in the form of a Provençal dry rub and topped it with a savory apricot marmalade just sweet enough to flatter the natural sweetness of the pork.

In a spice grinder or coffee mill reserved for that purpose, or in a mortar and pestle, grind the dry rub ingredients.

Rub the olive oil over the pork tenderloins, and then rub in the spice mixture. Allow them to rest in the refrigerator for at least 1 hour and up to 24 hours.

To make the marmalade: In a medium saucepan, combine the apricots, currants, onion, bell pepper, wine, orange juice, garlic, salt, and pepper. Bring to a simmer and cook until the fruit has absorbed most of the liquid in the pan and the mixture is thick, about 5 minutes. Remove the pan from the heat and add the parsley and thyme. Stir to combine and let the marmalade sit at room temperature until ready to assemble the tenderloin sandwiches.

To cook the pork: Prepare a grill or preheat the oven to 425°F. Remove the tenderloins from the refrigerator and let sit for about 30 minutes to take the chill off of them up before cooking. (They will cook faster, and as a result they will be juicier after cooking.) Grill the tenderloins, turning them after about 7 minutes for 3 turns, or roast them in the oven for 20 to 25 minutes. Use an instant-read thermometer to check for doneness. Remove the tenderloins from the heat when the meat registers 145°F, and tent them to keep them hot. Allow the meat to rest and redistribute the juices for at least 10 minutes (the temperature of the meat will climb to at least 152°F during this time).

apricot marmalade

1 1/2 cups dried apricots, snipped with kitchen shears into thirds

1/2 cup dried currants

1/3 cup minced onion

1/3 cup finely diced red bell pepper

1/4 cup dry white wine

1/4 cup orange juice

1 clove garlic, minced

1/4 teaspoon salt

1/8 teaspoon freshly ground black pepper

1/4 cup chopped Italian parsley

1 teaspoon chopped fresh thyme

Sprigs of rosemary and basil, for garnish

Slice the meat thinly on the diagonal and place a teaspoon of the marmalade in the center of each slice. Roll each slice up to enclose the marmalade and stick a short (4-inch) skewer through it to hold it closed. Serve arranged on a platter garnished with herb sprigs.

Make-ahead: *The marmalade can be made a few days ahead and kept, covered, in the refrigerator. Let it come to room temperature before using. The pork can be cooked 24 hours ahead of time and kept, wrapped in plastic and refrigerated. Slice the meat cold and let it come to room temperature before serving.*

makes sixty pieces

Spinach and Gruyère Quiche

ingredients

- 2 recipes Flaky Pastry (page 335)
- 1 pound lean bacon
- 2 cups thinly sliced onion
- 2 pounds spinach, washed and tough stems removed
- Salt and freshly ground black pepper to taste
- 8 large eggs, beaten
- 1 cup half-and-half
- 1 teaspoon salt
- 1/2 teaspoon freshly ground black pepper
- 1/4 teaspoon ground nutmeg
- 1/4 teaspoon cayenne pepper
- 2 cups grated Gruyère cheese

We don't know what it is about appetizers containing bacon, but they are always a favorite on the buffet table. The familiar smoky aroma seems to make everyone hungry. Making this quiche on a baking sheet gives you lots of leeway in terms of serving size. Cut them small for a large bash, or slice them more generously for a smaller event with fewer appetizer choices.

On a floured work surface, roll out each batch of pastry and fit them into a large baking sheet with sides, or a jelly roll pan (15 by 10 inches). The dough should fit up the sides of the pan. Seal the seams, trim the sides, and patch any holes with extra dough. Prick the bottom with a fork. Refrigerate for 30 minutes.

Preheat the oven to 375°F.

Line the chilled pastry with a sheet of parchment paper, leaving a 4-inch overhang around the edges. Cover the bottom with dried beans, rice, or pie weights. Bake in the lower half of the oven until the bottom of the shell is set, about 40 minutes. Remove from the oven and, using the edges of the parchment paper, remove the pie weights from the shell. Place them on a heatproof plate or baking sheet to cool. Cool the shell for 20 minutes before filling.

Meanwhile, heat a skillet over medium heat and fry the bacon in batches until it is crisp and brown. Pour off the bacon fat between batches. Remove the bacon to a plate and blot with paper towels.

Pour off all but 3 tablespoons of bacon fat. Add the onion to the bacon fat in the skillet and sauté over medium heat until tender and translucent, about 5 minutes. Set aside.

In a large, hot skillet over medium heat, toss a handful of the wet spinach until it wilts, about 30 seconds. Sprinkle with a little salt and pepper. Add more spinach as there is room for it in the pan and sauté until it is all wilted. Place the spinach in a colander and press on it to remove some of the water and dry it. Lightly chop the spinach and reserve.

In a medium bowl, whisk together the eggs, half-and-half, salt, black pepper, nutmeg, and cayenne.

Crumble the bacon in the bottom of the pastry shell. Lay the onions and spinach evenly over the top and sprinkle evenly with the cheese. Pour the egg mixture evenly over the entire surface of the quiche. Bake in the oven until the center is set, about 35 minutes. Remove from the oven and let cool for 10 minutes before cutting. For small pieces, make 6 long cuts and 10 short ones, to yield 60 pieces.

Make-ahead: *The quiche can be made up to 24 hours in advance and kept, covered and refrigerated. Crisp the pastry in a 350°F oven for 20 minutes before cutting. Serve hot or at room temperature.*

each batch makes twenty-two biscuits; you'll have enough ham for sixty biscuits

Spiral Sliced Ham with Biscuits and Chutney

biscuit dough (makes 1 batch)

- 3 cups unbleached all-purpose flour
- 4 teaspoons baking powder
- 1 tablespoon sugar
- 1½ teaspoons sea salt
- 1 teaspoon baking soda
- ¾ cup (1½ sticks) cold unsalted butter, cut into small pieces
- 1 cup buttermilk
- ⅓ cup heavy cream

- 3 bottles mango chutney (such as Major Grey)
- One 4-pound spiral-sliced ham, warmed in a 350°F oven for 30 minutes

It is just so easy to buy a good spiral-sliced ham, and serving it with homemade biscuits and condiments makes any occasion seem special. This recipe for biscuits makes 22, which is all we can make successfully in one batch. Because this is not enough to serve the entire ham, we recommend that you make three separate batches.

To make the biscuits: Preheat the oven to 425°F.

Place the flour, baking powder, sugar, salt, and baking soda in the work bowl of a food processor. Pulse until combined, about 5 pulses. Add the butter and process in short pulses until the mixture resembles coarse meal, about 16 pulses. Add the buttermilk and cream and pulse just until evenly moistened, about 6 pulses. Make 2 more batches of biscuit dough.

Using a small ice cream scoop or a 2-tablespoon measure, scoop the dough onto a parchment-lined baking sheet, spacing the scoops 2 inches apart. Flatten the biscuits lightly with your fingers. Bake in the oven until golden brown on top, 18 to 20 minutes. Remove from the baking sheet and continue to bake the biscuits. Let cool slightly and serve warm, split, with the chutney and ham slices.

Make-ahead: *Biscuits don't keep very well and are best made and eaten within 2 hours. If you must make them ahead, portion them onto the baking sheets and refrigerate the unbaked biscuits for up to 4 hours. Bake them cold from the refrigerator, and serve hot.*

makes about fifty pieces

Waldorf Chicken Salad in Phyllo Cups

ingredients

- *8 boneless, skinless chicken breast halves*
- *6 cups chicken stock*
- *½ cup white wine*
- *1 bay leaf*
- *1 teaspoon dried thyme*
- *2 cups red seedless grapes*
- *1 cup diced celery*
- *3 sweet-tart apples, such as Braeburn, Mutsu, or Golden Delicious, peeled, cored, and diced*
- *1 cup chopped toasted walnuts*
- *Grated zest of 2 lemons*
- *Juice of 1 lemon*
- *2 cups mayonnaise, homemade (page 334) or store-bought*
- *2 teaspoons ground cumin*
- *2 teaspoons salt, plus more to taste*
- *¼ teaspoon freshly ground black pepper, plus more to taste*
- *50 phyllo cups (see Tip)*

Fruity chicken salad can be made a day ahead and used to fill ready-made phyllo cups for a hearty, on-the-spot appetizer. We've taken red grapes, celery, apples, toasted walnuts, and tender chicken and tossed them with a mixture of creamy mayo, turmeric, and cumin for a colorful and spicy take on that tried and true favorite of our childhood.

In a large saucepan, combine the chicken, stock, white wine, bay leaf, and thyme and heat over medium heat until the liquid simmers. Cover the pan and turn the heat to low. Simmer the chicken, covered, until it is cooked through, about 20 minutes. Let the chicken cool in the liquid, remove it from the pan, and cut the chicken into small dice. Chill until ready to use.

Combine the grapes, celery, apple, walnuts, zest, and lemon juice in a large bowl. Add the chicken, mayonnaise, cumin, salt, and pepper. Toss to coat. Taste for seasoning and adjust with salt and pepper. Refrigerate until cold, about 2 hours.

Fill the phyllo cups with cold chicken salad and serve immediately.

Make-ahead: *The chicken salad can be made 1 day in advance, covered, and refrigerated.*

Tip: *Phyllo cups can be found in the freezer case at your grocery store. They are already baked and need only to be thawed before using.*

Chapter 13

Libations

serves six

Appletini

ingredients

- *12 ounces apple vodka*
- *3 ounces Sour Apple Pucker schnapps*
- *1 ounce Midori melon liqueur*
- *8 ounces sweet and sour mix*
- *6 slices Granny Smith apple, for garnish (optional)*

Flavored martinis have been the rage for quite a while now. Just when you think they are going out of fashion, a new genre is born. We find women to be the most ardent Appletini fans, so make up a batch of these along with the Dirty Martini (page 309) and the party will definitely be jumping.

Mix the vodka, liqueurs, and sweet and sour mix in a pitcher and freeze for 1 hour. Shake up 4 ounces per drink in a shaker with ice and strain into chilled martini glasses, or serve over ice in short glasses. Garnish each drink with an apple slice, if desired.

Make-ahead: *The mix can be made up to 8 hours ahead and kept in the refrigerator.*

serves six

Basil Lemonade

ingredients

- *3 cups water*
- *1 vanilla bean, split*
- *1 cup fresh basil leaves, lightly torn*
- *3/4 cup sugar*
- *1 cup fresh lemon juice*
- *Lemon wedges, for garnish (optional)*
- *Basil sprigs, for garnish (optional)*

Nothing says summer like fresh basil and lemonade. This unique spin on classic lemonade combines the flavor of basil and vanilla to a surprisingly refreshing effect. If you are lucky enough to have a purple basil plant in your herb garden, by all means use it. The purple leaves will make your lemonade pink.

Heat the water, vanilla bean, basil leaves, and sugar in a large saucepan over medium heat. When the water comes to a simmer, remove the pan from the heat and cover it with a lid. Let the mixture steep for about 15 minutes. Strain the mixture. (Don't scrape the vanilla bean. Just lay it out to dry and you can use it again the next time you make basil lemonade.) Add the lemon juice. Chill.

Divide the lemonade among 6 tall, ice-filled glasses and garnish with lemon wedges and basil sprigs, if desired.

Make-ahead: *The mix can be made up to 8 hours ahead and kept in the refrigerator.*

serves six

Cosmopolitan

ingredients

- *15 ounces vodka*
- *3 ounces Cointreau*
- *3 ounces fresh lime juice*
- *3 ounces cranberry juice*
- *6 lemon twists (twisted strips of lemon zest), for garnish (optional)*

Cosmos were made famous by a certain TV program about four women from New York City. This drink is all about attitude, so pick up one of those gadgets that make beautiful citrus peels and garnish this drink like a pro.

Mix the vodka, Cointreau, lime juice, and cranberry juice in a pitcher and freeze for 1 hour. Shake up 4 ounces per drink in a shaker with ice and strain into chilled martini glasses, or serve over ice in short glasses. Garnish each drink with a lemon twist, if desired.

Make-ahead: *The mix can be made up to 8 hours ahead and kept in the refrigerator.*

serves six

Dirty Martini

ingredients

- *22 ounces premium vodka, such as Belvedere or Grey Goose*
- *½ ounce dry vermouth*
- *1½ ounces brine from a jar of brine-cured green olives*
- *18 large green olives, stuffed with your choice of fillings (such as blue cheese, jalapeño, garlic, or pimiento)*

There is something about a martini glass that brings out the vamp in us. It's the perfect accessory, especially when filled with a Dirty Martini and at least 3 large olives. Whether you like the olives filled with blue cheese or the usual pimiento, who can disagree that a drink that comes with its own hors d'oeuvres is a brilliant idea?

Combine the vodka, vermouth, and brine in a pitcher and place it in the freezer for 2 hours. Chill 6 martini glasses in the freezer for 30 minutes. Using cocktail picks, skewer 3 green olives per pick.

Just before serving, remove the martini glasses from the freezer and add a skewer of olives to each glass. Shake 4 ounces of the chilled vodka mix per drink in a shaker with ice and strain into the glasses. Serve immediately.

Make-ahead: *The mix can be made up to 8 hours ahead and kept in the refrigerator.*

Tip: *Although we love the flavor of the blue cheese- or feta-stuffed olives, you should be aware that when you garnish with them a small oil slick develops on the top of the drink. This won't hurt the flavor, but some may find it distasteful.*

makes eight cups

Holiday Spiced Cider

ingredients

2 large oranges

8 cups apple cider

1 vanilla bean, split

2 tablespoons peeled and chopped fresh ginger

3 cinnamon sticks

5 whole cloves

1/4 cup brown sugar

2 tablespoons fresh lemon juice

Strips of orange zest and cinnamon sticks, for garnish

Warm cider makes your house smell so good, and no holiday party would be complete without it. Serving a nonalcoholic drink gives those that don't imbibe an option and the children a special drink that makes them feel a part of the grown-up action.

Peel the orange part of the skin from the oranges, using a vegetable peeler. Reserve for use as a garnish. Cut the oranges in half and squeeze them. Discard the oranges and, in a large pot, combine the juice with the cider, vanilla bean, ginger, cinnamon sticks, cloves, brown sugar, and lemon juice. Bring the mixture to a simmer over medium heat and cook for 5 minutes. Remove from the heat and strain the cider into a heat-proof pitcher, or serve the strained cider from another large pot kept over low heat. (The vanilla bean can be rinsed and dried and used again.) Serve warm in mugs, garnished with the orange zest and cinnamon sticks.

Make-ahead: *The cider can be made up to 2 days ahead and refrigerated. Rewarm it before serving.*

Variation: *For a sturdier version, add up to 1 ounce of apple brandy or Calvados to each mug of cider.*

serves four

Mango Daiquiri

ingredients

- *3 cups chopped mango (about 2 mangoes)*
- *6 ounces mango-flavored rum*
- *1/3 cup Coco Lopez sweetened coconut cream*
- *1/4 cup fresh lime juice*
- *2 cups ice*
- *1 lime*
- *1/3 cup sugar*

Welcome to paradise! This is the kind of drink that cruise ships hand out as soon as you walk on board. With a festive golden color and limey, fruity brightness, this retro drink is terrific at a summer barbecue or even to liven up a gray, chilly day. For the best flavor, buy ripe mangoes that yield to pressure when you squeeze them lightly.

Add the mango, rum, coconut cream, lime juice, and ice to a blender jar and blend until smooth.

Grate the zest from the lime, and cut the lime into quarters. Combine the lime zest with the sugar in a shallow dish. Run a quartered lime around the edge of each of 4 stemmed daiquiri glasses and dip the rim of the glass into the lime-sugar mixture. Carefully pour the daiquiri mixture into the center of each glass. Enjoy!

serves six

Melon Ball

ingredients

- *10 ounces Midori melon liqueur*
- *6 ounces Malibu coconut-flavored rum*
- *14 ounces pineapple juice*
- *6 maraschino cherries, for garnish*

Melon Balls are strikingly green, perfect for outdoor summer entertaining.

Combine the Midori, Malibu, and pineapple juice in a pitcher and freeze for 1 hour. Chill 6 martini glasses in the freezer for 30 minutes. For each drink, shake 5 ounces of the mixture in a shaker with ice and strain into the chilled martini glasses, or serve over ice in short glasses. Garnish with cherries.

Make-ahead: *The mix can be made up to 8 hours ahead and kept in the refrigerator.*

serves one

Mint Julep

ingredients

3/4 cup sugar

3/4 cup water

1 cup chopped fresh mint

1 1/2 ounces bourbon or whiskey

1 teaspoon fresh lemon juice

2 ounces club soda

Mint sprigs, for garnish

Don't wait for Derby day to make this refreshing version of a mint julep. The classic rendition can be a little hard on those who don't enjoy Kentucky bourbon, so we've added a touch of lemon and a little club soda to stretch out that strong bourbon taste. The mint is probably growing someplace in your backyard, so make up lots of the mint syrup and keep it on hand.

In a saucepan over medium-high heat, combine the sugar and water and bring the mixture to a boil. Remove the pan from the heat, add the mint, cover, and let the mixture steep for about 30 minutes. Strain the mint from the sugar syrup, pushing hard on the solids. You now have enough sugar syrup for about 10 mint juleps.

To make one mint julep, fill a 10-ounce silver julep cup or tall glass with crushed ice. Add 2 tablespoons of the mint syrup and the bourbon, lemon juice, and club soda. Stir the drink and garnish with a sprig of mint.

serves six

Nutty Godiva

ingredients

9 ounces Godiva chocolate liqueur

9 ounces crème de cacao

3 ounces vanilla vodka or plain vodka

3 ounces amaretto

12 ounces half-and-half

This drink is so delectable that you could serve it in place of dessert.

Mix all of the ingredients in a pitcher and freeze for 1 hour. Chill 6 martini glasses in the freezer for 30 minutes. For each drink, shake 6 ounces of the mixture in a shaker with ice and strain into a chilled martini glass, or serve over ice in a short glass.

serves six

Orange Mulled Wine

ingredients

One 750-ml bottle dry white wine

½ cup water

½ cup sugar

2 oranges, cut into slices

¼ cup Cointreau

¼ cup honey

3 cinnamon sticks

3 whole cloves

5 black peppercorns

Orange slices and cinnamon sticks, for garnish

It wouldn't be the holidays without mulled wine. Don't bother to use a wine costing more than $10 for this drink. The flavors from the oranges, cinnamon, and cloves dominate, while the peppercorns add spice.

In a large saucepan, combine the wine, water, sugar, oranges, Cointreau, honey, cinnamon sticks, and cloves and bring to a simmer over medium heat. Turn the heat to low and simmer for 10 minutes. Remove from the heat and let sit, covered, for 30 minutes. (It is important not to let it sit for too long, as the pith of the oranges can make the wine bitter.) Strain and serve warm in mugs, garnished with orange slices and cinnamon sticks.

Make-ahead: *You can make the mulled wine up to 2 days ahead, strain it, and keep it in the refrigerator. Reheat just before serving.*

serves six

Fresh Lime Margarita

ingredients

About 1/4 cup kosher or coarse salt

3 limes, quartered lengthwise and sliced

2 cups premium tequila, such as 1800 Silver

1/2 cup Cointreau, Grand Marnier, or Triple Sec

1/2 cup fresh lime juice

We prefer a shaken margarita to the frozen, slushy kind (less chance of brain freeze when drinking them fast). Your choice of tequila will really make a difference in the smoothness of this drink. We used 1800 Silver and Cointreau and thought they were the best margaritas we ever tasted. These can be dangerous, however, as they are so delicious that you will drink them faster than you probably should.

Pour the salt on a plate.

Run a lime wedge around the rim of each glass, then lightly dip the wet rim into the salt to coat it. Place the glasses in the freezer for at least 15 minutes and up to 30 minutes to chill them.

Combine the tequila, Cointreau, and lime juice in a pitcher. For each drink, measure 8 ounces of this mixture into a shaker with about 1/2 cup crushed ice. Shake until the shaker is frosty and cold. Pour the mixture, including the ice, into a prepared glass and add more of the crushed ice to the glass. Make the remaining drinks in the same manner. Garnish with some of the remaining lime quarters and serve immediately.

Make-ahead: *The mix can be made up to 8 hours ahead and kept in the refrigerator.*

serves six

Southern Comfort Manhattan

ingredients

- 16 ounces Southern Comfort, 100 proof
- ½ ounce sweet vermouth
- ½ ounce dry white vermouth
- 1 ounce water
- 6 maraschino cherries, for garnish

Carla claims to be an expert on the SCM, as she and husband, Rick, along with friends Tim and Jan, have been shamelessly putting this potion away over the twenty years of vacations they've had in Hilton Head. Use the high-test Southern Comfort and make the drinks in big glasses so you can sip them slowly as the ice melts.

Fill six 6-ounce glasses with ice.

In a pitcher, combine the Southern Comfort, vermouths, and water. Stir and pour over the ice in the glasses. Allow the drinks to sit for 2 or 3 minutes so the ice can melt and thin the drink somewhat. Garnish each glass with a cherry.

Make-ahead: *The mix can be made up to 8 hours ahead and kept in the refrigerator.*

serves six

Tequila Sunrise

ingredients

- *3 cups fresh orange juice*
- *12 ounces premium tequila*
- *2 ounces fresh lime juice*
- *2 ounces Cointreau*
- *2 tablespoons grenadine syrup*
- *6 lime slices, for garnish*

We've found that the secret to really spectacular fruit drinks lies in the quality of the fruit juice. Squeezing oranges really pays off when serving these classic fruit-based drinks, so get out that juicer and start squeezing. It is so worth it.

Fill 6 tall glasses with ice. In a pitcher, mix the orange juice, tequila, lime juice, and Cointreau. Stir to combine and pour over the ice in the glasses. Drizzle some of the grenadine syrup into each glass, but do not stir. Garnish each drink with a lime slice.

Make-ahead: The mix can be made up to 8 hours ahead and kept in the refrigerator.

serves six

Thin Mint

ingredients

- *3 ounces crème de menthe*
- *6 ounces crème de cacao*
- *6 ounces Bailey's Irish cream*
- *6 ounces vanilla vodka or plain vodka*
- *12 ounces half-and-half*
- *Semisweet chocolate shavings, for garnish (optional)*

The adult version of the Girl Scout cookie of the same name, this rich drink is a great way to end the night.

Mix the crème de menthe, crème de cacao, Irish cream, vodka, and half-and-half in a pitcher and freeze for 1 hour. Chill 6 martini glasses in the freezer for 30 minutes. For each drink, shake a little more than 5 ounces of the mixture in a shaker with ice and strain into the chilled glasses or serve over ice in short glasses. Garnish with chocolate shavings, if desired.

Make-ahead: *The mix can be made up to 8 hours ahead and kept in the refrigerator.*

serves six

Watermelon Cosmo

ingredients

12 ounces premium vodka

12 ounces cranberry juice

2 ounces Watermelon Pucker schnapps

2 ounces fresh lime juice

1 ounce Cointreau

3 ounces Midori melon liqueur

6 lime twists (twisted strips of lime zest), for garnish

We've added a touch of Midori to the usual cosmo ingredients to great effect. It creates a green layer on the bottom of the glass and is spectacular combined with the pink watermelon color on top.

Combine the vodka, cranberry juice, Watermelon Pucker, lime juice, and Cointreau in a pitcher and stir to mix. Place the pitcher in the freezer for 4 hours. Chill 6 martini glasses in the freezer for 30 minutes.

Just before serving, remove the pitcher and glasses from the freezer. Divide the pink vodka mixture among the 6 glasses, about 5 ounces per glass. Pour 1/2 ounce of Midori down the edge of each glass so that the green liquid sits on the bottom. Do not mix. Garnish each with a lime twist.

Make-ahead: *The mix can be made up to 8 hours ahead and kept in the refrigerator.*

makes eight cups

Connor's Fruit Punch

ingredients

- *2 cups cranberry juice*
- *1 cup pineapple juice*
- *1 cup orange juice*
- *1/4 cup grenadine syrup*
- *1/4 cup fresh lime juice*
- *1 lemon, cut into thin slices*
- *1 lime, cut into thin slices*
- *3 1/2 cups club soda, chilled*

Meredith's son Connor helped her create this tangy, sweet concoction on a warm, sunny day as the perfect party punch suitable for the entire family.

Mix everything but the club soda together in a large pitcher. Chill for at least 1 hour to allow the flavors to blend. Right before serving, add the club soda and serve in cups over ice.

Make-ahead: *The mix can be made up to 8 hours ahead and kept in the refrigerator. Add club soda just before serving.*

Tip: *For a lovely service, try arranging additional fruit slices on the bottom of a tube cake pan. Cover with about 1 1/2 inches of water and freeze solid. When ready to serve, pour your punch into a punch bowl. Place the pan in hot water for about 30 seconds and carefully unmold the ice ring. Gently slide the ring into the punch bowl.*

serves six

Mango Bellini

ingredients

One 750-ml bottle prosecco, chilled

12 ounces mango nectar

Lime wedges

The Bellini originated in Harry's Bar in Venice, Italy, in the 1940s. It's traditionally made with white peach purée and sparkling white wine. Here we've added a twist by using mango nectar, which gives the drink a sexy edge, made edgier with a splash of lime.

Place 6 champagne flutes in the freezer for 30 minutes. Open the prosecco and let it stand at room temperature for 5 minutes. Pour 2 ounces of mango nectar into each flute. Squeeze a lime wedge into each flute and drop it into the nectar. Fill the flutes with prosecco to within ½ inch of the top, and serve.

serves six

Peach Ginger Iced Tea

ingredients

6 cups cold water

1½-inch piece fresh ginger, peeled and thinly sliced

6 high-quality black tea bags

2 cups peach nectar

½ cup sugar

1 peach, thinly sliced, for garnish

Mint sprigs, for garnish

All you need to make this drink complete is a large, floppy hat, a rocking chair, and a veranda with a cool breeze.

Place the water and ginger in a large saucepan. Bring the water to a boil. Turn off the heat, add the tea bags, and steep for 3 minutes. Remove the tea bags and add the peach nectar and sugar. Stir until the sugar is dissolved. Strain the tea into a pitcher and chill. Pour into tall, ice-filled glasses, and garnish with peach slices and mint sprigs.

Make-ahead: *The tea can be made 1 day ahead and kept chilled.*

serves six

Bloody Mary

ingredients

4 cups tomato juice, chilled

9 ounces vodka (1 cup plus 2 tablespoons)

½ cup fresh lemon juice

2 tablespoons drained bottled horseradish

2 tablespoons Worcestershire sauce

½ teaspoon celery salt (optional)

¾ teaspoon Tabasco sauce

¾ teaspoon freshly ground black pepper

Lemon slices and/or inner celery stalks, for garnish

In our opinion, horseradish and Tabasco sauce are what makes a Bloody Mary sing. Always serve these with an extra bottle of Tabasco sauce on hand for those who like their Marys to sing a little louder.

Stir together the tomato juice, vodka, lemon juice, horseradish, Worcestershire sauce, celery salt, if desired, Tabasco sauce, and pepper in a pitcher and pour into ice-filled glasses. Garnish with lemon slices and celery sticks.

Make-ahead: The mix can be made up to 8 hours ahead and kept in the refrigerator.

serves six

Sea Breeze

ingredients

12 ounces vodka

12 ounces grapefruit juice

18 ounces cranberry juice

6 lime slices, for garnish

This drink's as refreshing as its name. Set up an umbrella and a lounge chair on your deck and mix up a pitcher. You'll feel as though you're sitting on a sandy beach, even if you're on the roof of an apartment building.

Pour the vodka, grapefruit, and cranberry juices into a pitcher and refrigerate until serving time. When ready to serve, divide the mixture among 6 highball glasses almost filled with ice. Stir well. Garnish each with a lime slice.

Make-ahead: *The mix can be made up to 8 hours ahead and kept in the refrigerator.*

serves eight

Cuba Libre

ingredients

- *2 cups white or dark rum*
- *½ cup fresh lime juice*
- *8 cups Coca-Cola, chilled*
- *8 lime wedges, for garnish*

This drink originated during the Spanish-American War, when American soldiers first mixed rum, cola, and lime juice together to toast to Cuba's independence. We drink it today because it's a refreshing drink that goes down easy and makes us all feel just a little bit freer.

Mix the rum, lime juice, and cola together in a pitcher. Pour into tall, ice-filled glasses and garnish each with a lime wedge.

serves four

Mojito

ingredients

- *6 ounces light rum*
- *14 fresh mint leaves, torn into pieces*
- *6 tablespoons fresh lime juice*
- *1/4 cup sugar*
- *Club soda, chilled*
- *4 lime slices, for garnish*
- *4 mint sprigs, for garnish*

Rum, mint, and lime juice are such a refreshing combination that when we tested this recipe we made them three nights in a row. No need to labor over smashing the mint leaves—use a martini shaker and let the ice do the job.

Place ice in a cocktail shaker and add the rum, torn-up mint leaves, lime juice, and sugar. Shake well and strain into 4 ice-filled highball glasses. Top off each glass with a splash of club soda. Garnish each with a slice of lime and a sprig of mint.

serves eight

Red Sangría

ingredients

- 2 bottles dry red wine, such as Beaujolais, chilled
- 1 cup brandy
- ½ cup orange liqueur
- ½ cup fresh orange juice
- ¼ cup superfine granulated sugar
- 2 oranges, cut into thin rounds
- 1 lemon, cut into thin rounds
- 1 lime, cut into thin rounds
- 2 cups club soda, chilled

Using a dry red wine and only a little bit of sugar makes this a refreshing party drink, rather than the cloyingly sweet beverage that sangría is often thought to be. Serve it at your next barbecue, whatever you're grilling.

In a large pot or bowl, combine the wine, brandy, orange liqueur, orange juice, and sugar and stir until the sugar dissolves.

Add the orange, lemon, and lime slices and refrigerate until well chilled, about 1 hour.

Remove from the refrigerator and add the club soda. Serve in glasses over ice.

Make-ahead: *The mix can be made up to 8 hours ahead and kept in the refrigerator. Add the club soda just before serving.*

serves ten to twelve

White Sangría

ingredients

- *3 bottles pinot grigio wine*
- *1 cup brandy*
- *½ cup orange liqueur*
- *½ cup sugar*
- *2 ripe mangoes, peeled, pitted, and cut into 1-inch cubes*
- *3 ripe Gala apples, peeled, cored, and cut into wedges*
- *1 lime, thinly sliced*

It may be revealing too much to say this, but we could sit outside with a pitcher of this delightful drink on a hot day with a big straw and a good book and experience about as much contentment as life has to offer.

In a large pitcher, combine the wine, brandy, and orange liqueur. Pour in the sugar, and stir or shake the pitcher to mix thoroughly. Add all the fruit at once. Allow the mixture to sit, refrigerated, for 1 hour before serving, to allow the flavors to properly blend. Serve in glasses over ice.

Make-ahead: *The sangría can be made up to 8 hours ahead and refrigerated.*

Chapter 14

Basic Recipes

333 Basic Crêpes

naise **335** Flaky Pastry

337 Pesto

makes one 10-by-25-inch sheet

Quick Puff Pastry

ingredients

- 1 1/2 cups unbleached all-purpose flour
- 1/2 cup cake flour
- 1/2 teaspoon salt
- 1 cup (2 sticks) unsalted butter, each stick quartered lengthwise and cut into 10 slices
- 1/2 cup ice water, plus more if needed

A great substitute for store-bought puff pastry, which can taste flat and definitely not buttery, this recipe is faster than classic puff pastry, which can take a great deal more time to pull together. Although it does take some time to roll out, fold, and chill the dough, this recipe is simple and delicious.

Place the flours, salt, and butter in a medium bowl, cover with plastic wrap without mixing, and freeze for 30 minutes.

Remove the ingredients from the freezer, dump them into the work bowl of a food processor, and pulse about 10 times. Add the ice water in a steady stream through the feed tube while pulsing, and continue to pulse until the dough comes together in 2 or 3 clumps. Do not overmix. (If the dough seems dry, add a tablespoon of water and pulse once or twice to mix until the dough sticks together when pressed.) There should be lots of chunks of butter visible in the dough.

Turn the pastry out onto a lightly floured work surface and press the dough with a floured rolling pin until you can shape it into a rectangle approximately 4 by 8 inches. (It might still be crumbly at this point. Don't worry; it will come together as you fold and will hydrate evenly as it sits in the refrigerator.) Using a metal spatula for support, fold the dough as you would a letter, folding the top third down and the bottom third up over the top to make 3 layers. This is called a turn. Rotate the dough so the open end is toward you. Using a rolling pin, press the lightly floured dough again into a 4-by-8-inch rectangle. Give the dough another turn, folding as before. Rotate the dough again so that the open end is facing you, and roll the pastry out to about 4 by 12 inches. Roll up the pastry, starting at the short end, to form a tight cylinder. Flatten it somewhat, wrap it in plastic, and refrigerate for at least 1 hour.

Make-ahead: *The pastry can be kept in the refrigerator, tightly wrapped in plastic, for up to 2 days. It can also be rolled out, wrapped, and frozen for up to 2 months.*

Tip: *Try not to use any more flour than necessary when rolling out the dough, as excess flour can make the pastry tough.*

serves six

Basic Crêpes

ingredients

- *1¼ cups milk*
- *3 large eggs*
- *1¼ cups unbleached all-purpose flour*
- *1 teaspoon salt*
- *3 tablespoons unsalted butter, melted and cooled*
- *2 tablespoons vegetable oil*

Few things are as impressive and easy to make as crêpes. It is nice to have a well-seasoned crêpe pan, but a nonstick 7-inch skillet works just fine.

Combine the milk, eggs, flour, salt, and melted butter in the jar of a blender. Blend at high speed for about 10 seconds. Turn the machine off and scrape down the inside of the jar with a rubber spatula and blend again for about 30 seconds. The batter should be the consistency of heavy cream. Transfer the batter to a bowl and let it sit, covered, at room temperature for an hour before using it.

Heat a 7-inch crêpe pan or nonstick skillet over medium-high heat. Sprinkle a drop of water into the pan. It should evaporate instantly. Fold a sheet of paper towel 2 or 3 times, and dip one corner of it into the vegetable oil. Rub the oil-soaked paper towel around the inside of the hot pan. Ladle 2 tablespoons of the crêpe batter into the pan and immediately swirl the pan so that the batter covers the bottom. The crepe should be paper-thin. When the top of the crepe looks dry and leathery, about 1 minute, turn the crêpe with a metal spatula to cook the other side. Cook the second side for 30 seconds, then slide it onto a plate. Rub the crêpe pan with the oil-soaked paper towel again and proceed with the rest of the crêpes.

Make-ahead: *You can freeze the crêpes for up to 1 month or hold them in the refrigerator for up to 2 days. To do so, place a layer of parchment or wax paper between the crêpes to make peeling them apart easier, cover with plastic, and, if freezing, cover with a layer of aluminum foil.*

makes 1⅓ cups

Mayonnaise

ingredients

2 large egg yolks
2 tablespoons fresh lemon juice
2 tablespoons water
½ teaspoon sugar
1 teaspoon dry mustard
1 teaspoon salt
Dash of cayenne pepper
1 cup safflower oil

For some dips and sauces where mayonnaise is the star performer, homemade mayo can make all the difference. It is so easy to make your own mayonnaise in a blender or food processor that there is no reason to suffer the taste of the store-bought jars.

Add the yolks, lemon juice, water, sugar, dry mustard, salt, and cayenne to the work bowl of a food processor or the jar of a blender. Process or blend for a few seconds to mix. Make sure the oil is in a container with a good pouring spout. Turn on the food processor or set the blender to blend. Pour the oil very slowly into the yolk mixture through the feed tube or the opening in the lid of the blender in a thin, steady stream. The mixture will become thicker as the oil is emulsified into the sauce. It should take 2 or 3 minutes to pour all the oil in. Remove the lid and taste the mayonnaise; adjust for seasoning.

Red Bell Pepper Aïoli: In a small saucepan, simmer 5 cloves of peeled whole garlic in the safflower oil until tender, about 20 minutes. Let cool. Make the mayonnaise using the cooled oil and, when thick, add the garlic and ⅓ cup diced roasted red bell pepper. Process until the aïoli looks smooth and rusty colored. Season to taste with salt and pepper.

Make-ahead: *The mayonnaise keeps, covered and refrigerated, for up to 4 days.*

Tips: *Sometimes we like to make mayonnaise with olive oil (not extra-virgin, as it will sometimes break the emulsion, and the flavor is too strong). Experiment with different oils to find the one that best suits you or its accompaniment .*

Mayonnaise can be flavored with all sorts of herbs, spices, peppers, or fruits. Try adding a few tablespoons of sun-dried tomato, chipotle pepper, pesto, chutney, green onion, curry powder, or other flavorful ingredient.

A bacterium known as Salmonella enteritidis *can infect perfectly normal appearing eggs. Though the risk is small, the elderly, infants, and those with impaired immune systems can be affected more severely. To be safe, use pasteurized whole eggs when consuming raw eggs.*

makes one 14-inch pastry round

Flaky Pastry

ingredients

- *1½ cups unbleached all-purpose flour, chilled in the freezer for 1 hour*
- *9 tablespoons (1 stick plus 1 tablespoon) unsalted butter, cut into ½-inch pieces and chilled in the freezer for 1 hour*
- *¼ teaspoon salt*
- *⅓ cup ice water*

It is so easy to make your own pastry. We like to make four or five at a time, roll them out, and then freeze them on baking pans, with parchment paper between the layers and the pans wrapped in plastic. When you need a pie or tart shell, remove a layer from the freezer on its piece of parchment, let it thaw on a work surface for about 30 minutes, and use it as directed in your recipe.

Place the flour, butter, and salt in the bowl of a food processor and pulse 7 or 8 times, until the butter is reduced to pea-sized pieces. Add the cold water in a steady stream through the feed tube while pulsing 4 to 6 times to incorporate the water into the flour and butter. As soon as the water has been poured, stop processing and turn the pastry mixture out onto a cool work surface. The mixture will not have come together yet and will look shaggy and dry. (Stopping the processing at this point yields flaky, tender pastry. If you continue to process until the dough forms a ball, the pastry will be tough.)

Using the heel of your hand, smear the pastry mixture against the counter, bit by bit, until it comes together and forms a rough dough. Gather the dough together, shape it into a disk, and wrap it in plastic. Refrigerate for at least 1 hour. Roll out and use as directed in your recipe.

Make-ahead: *The pastry dough can be made up to 2 days ahead, wrapped in plastic, and refrigerated. It can also be frozen, as described in the headnote.*

makes about eight cups

Basic Sushi Rice

ingredients

1/3 cup rice wine vinegar

3 tablespoons sugar

1 1/2 teaspoons salt

3 cups short-grain white rice

3 cups water

If you're going to make sushi, properly made sushi rice is critical. The short-grain rice necessary for this recipe can now be found in the Asian section of almost any grocery store. Do not substitute long-grain rice. It isn't sticky enough to hold the sushi together.

In a small saucepan over low heat, combine the vinegar, sugar, and salt. Stir gently to dissolve the salt and sugar. Let cool to room temperature.

Place the rice in a large pot, or the inner pot of an electric rice cooker, and rinse with cold water. Each time, let the rice settle and carefully pour the cloudy water off. Repeat this process 3 or 4 times, or until the water runs clear. After you've drained the water from the final rinse, add the 3 cups water and allow the rice to soak for 30 minutes. Cook on the stovetop or in a rice cooker according to the package directions.

While the rice is still warm, transfer it to a large, nonreactive bowl. Using a rice paddle or wooden spoon, gently break up and spread out the rice. Gradually drizzle the vinegar mixture over the rice. Fold it gently without mashing the grains, fanning the rice as you go. Continue to fold and fan until you can no longer see steam rising from the bowl. This will help to keep the rice from becoming overcooked and mushy. Keep the rice covered with a damp cloth at room temperature until ready to make sushi. Do not refrigerate.

Make-ahead: *Sushi rice cannot be refrigerated. It becomes hard and the grains separate. You can make it 4 hours ahead of time and keep it, covered, at room temperature.*

makes about one cup

Pesto

ingredients

- *3 cloves garlic, peeled*
- *½ cup fresh basil leaves, stemmed*
- *⅓ cup grated Parmesan cheese*
- *⅓ cup extra-virgin olive oil*
- *1 teaspoon salt, plus more to taste*
- *Grated zest of 1 lemon*
- *3 tablespoons fresh lemon juice*
- *⅛ teaspoon freshly ground black pepper, plus more to taste*

Everybody needs to know how to make pesto. It's easy to do, and the store-bought versions leave a lot to be desired.

Turn on a food processor and add the garlic through the feed tube. Process until finely chopped, about 5 seconds. Remove the lid and add the basil and process again for about 5 seconds. Remove the lid and add the cheese, olive oil, 1 teaspoon salt, zest, lemon juice, and ⅛ teaspoon pepper to the work bowl and process again until a green sauce is achieved. Taste the pesto for seasoning and adjust with salt and pepper if necessary.

Make-ahead: *The pesto can be made 3 days ahead. Keep it in a jar or plastic container. Smooth the surface of the pesto and cover it with a layer of olive oil to help prevent darkening. The top may still darken slightly, but it will not affect the taste of the pesto.*

Acknowledgments

It truly takes a village to create a cookbook of this size. Our families, friends, colleagues, and students have all been instrumental in bringing our ideas to the page. We've been fortunate to be surrounded by countless inspired cooks throughout our lives. We would especially like to thank long-time culinary mentors Pat Weckerly and Zona Spray for their years of encouragement. We'd also like to thank our dear friend Toni Allegra, without whose guidance this book wouldn't have been possible.

Thanks to recipe testers Barbara Tatum, Ann Norvell, Julie Neri, Alicia Ravens, and students too many to name who gave their time and resources to help in fine-tuning our recipes.

Special thanks to our intrepid agent, Lisa Ekus, for finding this book a home at Chronicle Books. We'd like to thank Bill LeBlond and Amy Treadwell for helping us to bring this book to life. Also many thanks to our copyeditor, Rebecca Pepper, for crossing our t's and dotting our i's.

We'd like to thank our husbands, Rick and David, as well as our kids for embracing the concept of appetizers for lunch and dinner (and sometimes breakfast too).

And lastly, we would like to thank the diners of the world who take the time to enjoy that first bite, that small dish, that priceless opportunity to linger at the table just a little longer and savor the moment.

Index

d

Table of Equivalents

The exact equivalents in the following tables have been rounded for convenience.

Liquid/Dry Measures

u.s.	***metric***
1/4 teaspoon	1.25 milliliters
1/2 teaspoon	2.5 milliliters
1 teaspoon	5 milliliters
1 tablespoon (*3 teaspoons*)	15 milliliters
1 fluid ounce (*2 tablespoons*)	30 milliliters
1/4 cup	60 milliliters
1/3 cup	80 milliliters
1/2 cup	120 milliliters
1 cup	240 milliliters
1 pint (2 cups)	480 milliliters
1 quart (*4 cups, 32 ounces*)	960 milliliters
1 gallon (*4 quarts*)	3.84 liters
1 ounce (*by weight*)	28 grams
1 pound	454 grams
2.2 pounds	1 kilogram

Length

u.s.	***metric***
1/8 inch	3 millimeters
1/4 inch	6 millimeters
1/2 inch	12 millimeters
1 inch	2.5 centimeters

Oven Temperature

fahrenheit	***celcius***	***gas***
250	120	1/2
275	140	1
300	150	2
325	160	3
350	180	4
375	190	5
400	200	6
425	220	7
450	230	8
475	240	9
500	260	10

Liquid Measurements

- Bar spoon = 1/2 ounce
- 1 teaspoon = 1/6 ounce
- 1 tablespoon = 1/2 ounce
- 2 tablespoons (pony) = 1 ounce
- 3 tablespoons (jigger) = 1 1/2 ounces
- 1/4 cup = 2 ounces
- 1/3 cup = 3 ounces
- 1/2 cup = 4 ounces
- 2/3 cup = 5 ounces
- 3/4 cup = 6 ounces
- 1 cup = 8 ounces
- 1 pint = 16 ounces
- 1 quart = 32 ounces
- 750 ml bottle = 25.4 ounces
- 1 liter bottle = 33.8 ounces

- 1 medium lemon = 3 tablespoons juice
- 1 medium lime = 2 tablespoons juice
- 1 medium orange = 1/3 cup juice

Check out these other titles in the *Big Book* series:

The Big Book of Casseroles
By Maryana Vollstedt

The Big Book of Soups & Stews
By Maryana Vollstedt

The Big Book of Breakfast
By Maryana Vollstedt

The Big Book of Backyard Cooking
By Betty Rosbottom

The Big Book of Potluck
By Maryana Vollstedt

The Big Book of Vegetarian
By Kathy Farrell-Kingsley

The Big Book of Easy Suppers
By Maryana Vollstedt

The Big Book of Low Carb
By Kitty Broihier and Kimberly Mayone

The Big Book of Fish & Shellfish
By Fred Thompson